T0207288

Communications
in Computer and Information Science   1809

Rationale

The CCIS series is devoted to the publication of proceedings of computer science conferences. Its aim is to efficiently disseminate original research results in informatics in printed and electronic form. While the focus is on publication of peer-reviewed full papers presenting mature work, inclusion of reviewed short papers reporting on work in progress is welcome, too. Besides globally relevant meetings with internationally representative program committees guaranteeing a strict peer-reviewing and paper selection process, conferences run by societies or of high regional or national relevance are also considered for publication.

Topics

The topical scope of CCIS spans the entire spectrum of informatics ranging from foundational topics in the theory of computing to information and communications science and technology and a broad variety of interdisciplinary application fields.

Information for Volume Editors and Authors

Publication in CCIS is free of charge. No royalties are paid, however, we offer registered conference participants temporary free access to the online version of the conference proceedings on SpringerLink (http://link.springer.com) by means of an http referrer from the conference website and/or a number of complimentary printed copies, as specified in the official acceptance email of the event.

CCIS proceedings can be published in time for distribution at conferences or as postproceedings, and delivered in the form of printed books and/or electronically as USBs and/or e-content licenses for accessing proceedings at SpringerLink. Furthermore, CCIS proceedings are included in the CCIS electronic book series hosted in the SpringerLink digital library at http://link.springer.com/bookseries/7899. Conferences publishing in CCIS are allowed to use Online Conference Service (OCS) for managing the whole proceedings lifecycle (from submission and reviewing to preparing for publication) free of charge.

Publication process

The language of publication is exclusively English. Authors publishing in CCIS have to sign the Springer CCIS copyright transfer form, however, they are free to use their material published in CCIS for substantially changed, more elaborate subsequent publications elsewhere. For the preparation of the camera-ready papers/files, authors have to strictly adhere to the Springer CCIS Authors' Instructions and are strongly encouraged to use the CCIS LaTeX style files or templates.

Abstracting/Indexing

CCIS is abstracted/indexed in DBLP, Google Scholar, EI-Compendex, Mathematical Reviews, SCImago, Scopus. CCIS volumes are also submitted for the inclusion in ISI Proceedings.

How to start

To start the evaluation of your proposal for inclusion in the CCIS series, please send an e-mail to ccis@springer.com.

Abolfazl Mirzazadeh · Babek Erdebilli ·
Erfan Babaee Tirkolaee ·
Gerhard-Wilhelm Weber · Arpan Kumar Kar
Editors

Science, Engineering Management and Information Technology

First International Conference, SEMIT 2022
Ankara, Turkey, September 8–9, 2022
Revised Selected Papers, Part II

Editors
Abolfazl Mirzazadeh (iD)
Kharazmi University
Tehran, Iran

Erfan Babaee Tirkolaee (iD)
Istinye University
Istanbul, Türkiye

Arpan Kumar Kar (iD)
Indian Institute of Technology Delhi
New Delhi, India

Babek Erdebilli (iD)
Ankara Yıldırım Beyazıt University
Ankara, Türkiye

Gerhard-Wilhelm Weber (iD)
Poznań University of Technology
Poznań, Poland

ISSN 1865-0929   ISSN 1865-0937 (electronic)
Communications in Computer and Information Science
ISBN 978-3-031-40397-2   ISBN 978-3-031-40398-9 (eBook)
https://doi.org/10.1007/978-3-031-40398-9

This Springer imprint is published by the registered company Springer Nature Switzerland AG
The registered company address is: Gewerbestrasse 11, 6330 Cham, Switzerland

Preface

International Conference on Science, Engineering Management and Information Technology (SEMIT 2022) was held virtually in Ankara, Turkey. The 2022 event was executed in two sections with different structures and programs meanwhile the same subjects and approaches. The first section was held on 2–3 February 2022 and the second was held on 8–9 September 2022, both online. The following is the book for the latter event (SEMIT 2022-Sep.)

It provided an energetic knowledge-transferring atmosphere for participants (as several feedbacks revealed).

SEMIT 2022 attracted the attention of students and professionals internationally. The covering subjects included, but not limited to "IT and EM based case studies of manufacturing/service industries (including automotive, food, tourism, petroleum, healthcare, insurance and banking, energy, etc.)", "E-government, E-commerce, E-learning", "Marketing and E-marketing for resources management", "Data science, big data, data mining and knowledge management in EM", "Decision making and support systems in an uncertain environment and risk management", "Industry 4.0, supply chain 4.0, and logistics 4.0", "Supply chain management (green SCM, sustainable SCM, agile SCM, JIT SCM, global SCM, etc.)", "Optimization and decision making: methods and algorithms", "Applied soft computing in engineering management", "Metaheuristic algorithms and applications", "Project management", "Blockchain in engineering management", "Artificial intelligence and expert systems", "Digital city", "Internet of things (IoT)", "Other fields of study related to EM and IT".

SEMIT 2022-Sep. was honored to be enriched by outstanding keynote speakers from Macau, Malaysia, Germany, Portugal, Oman and USA. In this event, eleven universities from UK, France, Czech Republic, USA, India, Morocco and Turkey in addition to a society from Tunisia were present as scientific sponsors.

The conference included participation of 46 countries. The geographical diversity of international scientific committee members was from 22 countries.

The conference team received 123 English and Turkish papers, which were reviewed by at least three international reviewers (single blind reviews). Considering the reviewers' comments in the first round of review, the papers have been reviewed once more with stricter criteria to select the most appropriate ones for Springer's Publication. Finally, the two-round review process resulted in the selection of 11 papers (around 9%).

The review criteria in this step were: content; originality; relevance; contribution to the professional literature; significance and potential impact of the paper; language accuracy; study validity; accuracy of methodology and analysis; paper organization, required relevant data, citations and references; adequate referring of the background information; consistency of references, symbols and units throughout the paper; quality and clarity of tables and figures.

The papers in SEMIT 2022-Sep. were presented in 13 panel sessions: "artificial intelligence applications in engineering", "economic, social and technology factors affecting business and social sciences aspects in era of industry 4.0", "sustainable logistics and transportation under uncertain environments", "recent trends and applications in networks communications", "recent advances of circular economy and sustainable development in supply chain management", "cyber security and cyber resilience in next-generation connected supply chain networks", "analytical decision making", "emerging topics in operations research and game theory", "recent trends and practices of machine learning in marketing and operations management", "sustainability", "reliability and safety engineering, system engineering and system safety, safety in industry 4.0", "quality and productivity improvement", "other fields related to em and it".

SEMIT 2022-Sep. included five applied workshops by outstanding lecturers with a good number of audiences. The workshop subjects were very well received by the participants which were entitled: "Approximation methods under uncertain environments"; "Machine learning: select and implement"; "Metaheuristic for combinatorial optimization problems: from design to implementation"; "Assessing the impact of information and communication technology implementation on regional economic development and growth"; "Revamping low carbon performance in the green practices for a sustainable society: an empirical analysis".

December 2022

Abolfazl Mirzazadeh
Babek Erdebilli
Erfan Babaee Tirkolaee
Gerhard-Wilhelm Weber
Arpan Kumar Kar

Organization

Conference Chairs

Abolfazl Mirzazadeh   Kharazmi University, Iran
Ibrahim Yilmaz   Yildirim Beyazit University, Turkey

Conference Coordinator

Leyla Chehrghani   Kharazmi University, Iran

Ankara Yildirim Beyazit University Authorities

Ibrahim Aydinli (Rector)
Hasan Okuyucu   Dean of Faculty of Engineering and Natural
         Sciences
Mete Gundogan   Head of IE Department

Technical and Editorial Chairs

Abolfazl Mirzazadeh   Kharazmi University, Iran
Babek Erdebilli   Yildirim Beyazit University, Turkey
Erfan Babaee Tirkolaee   Istinye University, Turkey
Gerhard-Wilhelm Weber   Poznan University of Technology, Poland
Arpan Kumar Kar   Indian Institute of Technology Delhi, India

Programming Committee Members

Sırma Zeynep Alparslan Gök   Suleyman Demirel University, Turkey
Marilisa Botte   University of Naples, Italy
Eloisa Macedo   University of Aveiro, Portugal
Aybike Özyüksel Çiftçioğlu   Manisa Celal Bayar University, Turkey
Esra Sipahi Dongul   Aksaray University, Turkey
Dinh Tran Ngoc Huy   International University of Japan, Japan
Chefi Triki   University of Kent, UK

Scientific Committee Members

Maher Agi	Rennes School of Business, France
Ali Allahverdi	Kuwait University, Kuwait
Bernardo Almada-Lobo	Porto University, Portugal
Fayçal Belkaid	Abou Bekr Belkaid University of Tlemcen, Algeria
Jaouad Boukachour	University of Le Havre-Normandy, France
Alexandre Dolgui	IMT Atlantique (former Ecole des Mines de Nantes), France
Elif Kilic Delice	Ataturk University, Turkey
Leopoldo Eduardo Cárdenas-Barrón	Tecnológico de Monterrey, Mexico
Ergun Eraslan	Yildirim Beyazit University, Turkey
Serap Ergun	Isparta University of Applied Sciences, Turkey
Michael G. Kay	North Carolina State University, USA
Paulina Golinska	Poznan University of technology, Poland
Maria Grazia Speranza	University of Brescia, Italy
Josef Jablonsky	University of Economics and Business, Czech Republic
Mehmet Kabak	Gazi University, Turkey
AllaEldin H. Kassam	University of Technology, Iraq
Reza Kiani Mavi	Edith Cowan University, Australia
Sachin Kumar	University of Plymouth, UK
Vijai Kumar Gahlawat	National Institute of Food Technology, India
Nasr Hamood Mohamed Al-Hinai	Sultan Qaboos University, Oman
Rahul S. Mor	NIFTEM, Deemed to be University, India
Beata Mrugalska	Poznan University of Technology, Poland
Mustapha Oudani	International University of Rabat, Morocco
Michael Pecht	University of Maryland, USA
Sujan Piya	Sultan Qaboos University, Oman
Svetlana Rastvortseva	National Research University, Russia
Ruben Ruiz Garcia	University of Polytechnics, Spain
Sadia Samar Ali	King Abdul Aziz University, Saudi Arabia
Yavuz Selim Özdemir	Ankara Science University, Turkey
Kathryn Stecke	University of Texas at Dallas, USA
Tatiana Tchemisova	University of Aveiro, Portugal
Stefan Wolfgang Pickl	Bundeswehr University, Germany
Abdullah Yildizbasi	Yildirim Beyazit University, Turkey

Opening and Closing Sessions Speakers

Gerhard-Wilhelm Weber	Poznan University of Technology, Poland
Josef Jablonsky	University of Economics and Business, Czech Republic

Keynote Speakers

Bernardo Almada-Lobo	University of Porto, Portugal
Michael G. Kay	North Carolina State University, USA
Hakan Gultekin	Sultan Qaboos University, Oman
Kok Lay Teo	Sunway University, Malaysia
Janny M. Y. Leung	The University of Macau, Macau
Stefan Wolfgang Pickl	University of Bundeswehr München, Germany

Reviewers

Otman Abdoun	University of Abdelmalek Essaadi, Morocco
Mohamed Abedelgadir	University of Technology, Malaysia
Mohamed Nezar Abourraja	Normandy University, France
Negar Afzali Behbahani	Islamic Azad University, Iran
Maher Agi	Rennes School of Business, France
Hadi Ahmed	Cairo University, Egypt
Sara Ahmed	Concordia University, Canada
Ghada Alhudhud	King Saud University, Saudi Arabia
Tarak Ali Hossein	University of Benghazi, Libya
Aylin Alkaya	Nevsehir Haci Bektas Veli University, Turkey
Ali Allahverdi	Kuwait University, Kuwait
Richard Allmendinger	University of Manchester, UK
Bernardo Almada Lobo	Porto University, Portugal
Sırma Zcynep Alparslan Gok	Suleyman Demirel University, Turkey
Shabnam Amirnezhad Barough	Yıldırım Beyazit University, Turkey
El-Saed Ammar	Tanta University, Egypt
Le Thi Diep Anh	National Economics University, Vietnam
Hichem Aouag	Batna University, Algeria
Mst. Anjuman Ara	Bangladesh Army University of Science and Technology, Bangladesh
Selcen Aslan Ozsahin	TOBB University, Turkey
Nadi Serhan Aydin	Istinye University, Turkey
Erfan Babaee Tirkolaee	Istinye University, Turkey

Rahmi Baki	Aksaray University, Turkey
Srinivasan Balan	North Carolina State University, USA
Igor Barahona	Institute of Mathematics, Mexico
Faycal Belkaid	University of Lorraine, France
Abderaouf Benghalia	Algiers I University, Algeria
Jamal Benhra	National School of Computer Science and Systems Analysis, Morocco
Mohamed amine Ben Rabia	National School of Computer Science and Systems Analysis, Morocco
Abdelaziz Berrado	Mohammed V University, Morocco
Subir Bhattacharya	National Institute of Technology, India
Satyajit Bhunia	Midnapore City College, India
Papatya Sevgin Bicakci	Başkent University, Turkey
Shazia Bilal	Comsats Institute of Information Technology, Pakistan
Sanjib Biswas	Calcutta Business School, India
Bonaventure Boniface	Sabah University, Malaysia
Eleonora Bottani	University of Parma, Italy
Marilisa Botte	University of Naples, Italy
Jaouad Boukachour	Normandy University, France
Gercek Budak	Yıldırım Beyazıt University, Turkey
Victor Camargo	Federal University of Sao Carlos, Brazil
Leopoldo Eduardo Cardenas-Barron	Monterrey University of Technology, Mexico
Patricia Cano-Olivos	Logistics and Supply Chain Management Postgraduate, Mexico
Ying-Hua Chang	Tamkang University, Taiwan
Leyla Chehrghani	Kharazmi University, Iran
Kevin Cullinane	University of Gothenburg, Sweden
Duong Cuong	Hanoi University of Science and Technology, Vietnam
Soumen Kumar Das	Vidyasagar University, India
Manoranjan De	Vidyasagar University, India
Bikash Koli Dey	Hongik University, Korea, Republic of
Oshmita Dey	Techno India University, India
Oleksandr Dluhopolskyi	West Ukrainian National University, Ukraine
Alexandre Dolgui	IMT Atlantique University, France
Aman Dua	NIFTEM University, India
Mustafa Ekici	Çanakkale Onsekiz Mart University, Turkey
Karim El Bouyahyiouy	Mohammed V University, Morocco
Adiba El Bouzekri El Idrissi	Doukkali University, Morocco
Nizar El Hachemi	Mohammed VI Polytechnic University, Morocco

Mohamed El Merouani	Abdelmalek Essaâdi University, Morocco
Moulay Driss El Ouadghiri	Moulay Ismail University, Morocco
Ali Emrouznejad	Surrey Business School, UK
Ergun Eraslan	Yildirim Beyazit University, Turkey
Serap Ergun	Isparta University of Applied Sciences, Turkey
Oliveria Fabiana	University of State Amazonas, Brazil
Goncalo Figueira	INESC TEC, FEUP, Portugal
Vijay Gahlawat	National Institute of Food Technology Entrepreneurship and Management, India
Rakesh Garg	Amity University Uttar Pradesh, India
Mitsuo Gen	Tokyo University of Science, Japan
Michel Gendreau	University of Montreal, Canada
Peiman Ghasemi	University of Calgary, Canada
Bibhas C. Giri	Jadavpur University, India
Beata Glinkowska-Krauze	University of Lodz, Poland
Alireza Goli	University of Isfahan, Iran
Paulina Golinska	Poznan University of Technology, Poland
Mete Gundogan	Ankara Yildirim Beyazit University, Turkey
Shunsheng Guo	Wuhan University of Technology, China
Achraf Haibi	Moulay Ismail University, Morocco
Sondes Hammami	University of Carthage, Tunisia
Nasr Hamood Mohamed Al-Hinai	Sultan Qaboos University, Oman
Amit V. Hans	Guru Gobind Singh Indraprastha University, India
Khandaker Hasan	United International University, Bangladesh
Gholamreza Haseli	Monterrey Institute of Technology, Mexico
AllaEldin H. Kassam	University of Technology, Iraq
Muhammad Hoque	Management College of Southern Africa, South Africa
Olena Hrechyshkina	Polessky State University, Belarus
Change-Ling Hsu	Ming Chuan University, Taiwan
Jianwen Huang	China Three Gorges University, China
Dinh Tran Ngoc Huy	National University of Japan, Japan
Dina M. Ibrahim	Qassim University, Saudi Arabia
Hamid Reza Irani	University of Tehran, Iran
M. Y. Jaber	Ryerson University, Canada
Josef Jablonsky	University of Economics and Business, Czech Republic
Madhu Jain	IIT Roorkee, India
Ajay Jain	GGSIP University, India
Suresh Jakhar	Indian Institute of Management Lucknow, India
Mehmet Kabak	Vidyasagar University, India

Deepshikha Kalra	Management Education and Research Institute, India
Burcin Kaplan	Aydin University, Turkey
Michael kay	North Carolina State University, USA
Sarika Keswani	Symbiosis International University, India
Mohd Khairol Anuar Ariffin	Putra University Malaysia
Marzieh Khakifirooz	Monterrey University, Mexico
Hamiden Khalifa	Cairo University, Egypt
Soheyl Khalilpourazari	Kharazmi University, Iran
Manjeet Kharub	National Institute of Technology, India
Mazdak Khodadadi Karimvand	University of Science and Culture, Iran
Reza Kiani Mavi	Edith Cowan University, Australia
Elif Kilic Delice	Ataturk University, Turkey
Iryna Kramarenko	National University of Shipbuilding, Ukraine
Aalok Kumar	Jaipuria Institute of Management, India
Manoj Kumar	Management Education & Research Institute, India
Sachin Kumar	University of Plymouth, UK
Pavan Kumar	VIT Bhopal University, India
Vijay Kumar Gahlawat	National Institute of Food Technology Entrepreneurship and Management (NIFTEM), India
Arpan Kumar Kar	Indian Institute of Technology, India
Martina Kuncova	Prague University of Economics and Business, Czech Republic
Tanmoy Kundu	National University of Singapore, Singapore
Emily Lee	California State University, USA
Viacheslav Liashenko	Academy of Economic Science of Ukraine, Ukraine
Sunil Luthra	SIET Jhajjar, India
Gour Mahata	Sidho Kanho Birsha University, India
S. Maheswaram	University of Peradeniya, Sri Lanka
Arunava Majumder	Lovely Professional University, India
Dragana Makajic-Nikolic	Belgrade University, Serbia
Fouad Maliki	University of Tlemcen, Tunisia
Paulo Manrique	National University of Mexico, Mexico
Malek Masmoudi	University of Lyon, France
Tafadzwa Matiza	North-West University, South Africa
Abu Md Mashud	Hajee Mohammad Danesh Science and Technology University, Bangladesh
Adeel Mehmood	COMSATS University, Pakistan
Fatima-Zahra Mhada	Mohammed V University, Morocco
Karima Mialed	University of Hassan II, Morocco

Sudipta Midya	Vidyasagar University, India
Shashi Mishra	Banaras Hindu University, India
Froilan Mobo	Philippine Merchant Marine Academy, Philippines
Chanicha Moryadee	Suan Sunandha Rajabhat University, Thailand
Regaieg Mouna	Sfax University, Tunisia
Beata Mrugalska	Poznan University of Technology, Poland
Aung Munn	Edinburgh Napier University, Myanmar
Mahabub Musa	Northwest University Kano, Nigeria
Mahantesh M. Nadakatti	KLS Gogte Institute of Technology, India
Peter Nadeem	The University of Derby, UK
Ahmed Nait Sidi Moh	University Jean Monnet, France
Mehdi Najib	International University of Rabat, Morocco
Behnam Nakhai	Millersville University of Pennsylvania, USA
Muhammad Irwan Padli Nasution	Universitas Islam Negeri Sumatera Utara, Indonesia
Luka Neralic	University of Zagreb, Croatia
Lewis Njualem	Texas Tech University, USA
Mohammed Nusari	Lincoln University College, Malaysia
Mehmet Onur Olgun	Suleyman Demirel University, Turkey
Khaoula Ouaddi	National school for Computer Science, Morocco
Rachid Oucheikh	Cyber-Physical Systems Lab, Norway
Mustapha Oudani	International University of Rabat, Morocco
Kenza Oufaska	International University of Rabat, Morocco
İsmail Ozcan	Suleyman Demirel University, Turkey
Eren Ozceylan	Gaziantep University, Turkey
Aybike Ozyuksel Ciftcioglu	Manisa Celal Bayar University, Turkey
Fatima Ouzayd	National School for Computer Science, Morocco
Ayse Ozmen	Committee Member on IFORS Web-based Re-sources on OR for Development
Manvinder Pahwa	Manipal University Jaipur, India
Brojeswar Pal	University of Burdwan, India
Osman Palanci	Suleyman Demirel University, Turkey
Iztok Palcic	University of Maribor, Slovenia
Anupama Panghal	National Institute of Food Technology Entrepreneurship and Management, India
Sarla Pareek	University of Science and Technology, Korea
Hiren patel	Ganpat University, India
Michael Pecht	University of Maryland, USA
Stefan Pickl	Bundeswehr University, Germany
Sujan Piya	Sultan Qaboos University, Muscat, Oman
Jaroslav Pushak	Lviv State University of Internal Affairs, Ukraine

V. Devika Pushparaj	Kalasalingam University
Juanjuan Qin	Tianjin University of Finance and Economics, China
Kumar Rahul	National Institute of Food Technology Entrepreneurship and Management (NIFTEM), India
Yanamandra Ramakrishna	United Arab School of Business, UAE
Shivani Rana	Hoshiarpur S.D. College, India
Shalendra Rao	Mohanlal Sukhadia University, India
Svetlana Rastvortseva	National Research University, Russian Federation
Naoufal Rouky	Le Havre University, France
Sankar Kumar Roy	Vidyasagar University, India
Ruben Ruiz	University of Polytechnics, Valencia, Spain
Darin Rungklin	Suratthani Rajabhat University, India
Sahara Sahara	Bogor Agricultural University, Indonesia
Tkatek Said	University Ibn Tofail, Morocco
Luis Salinas	New Jersey Institute of Technology, UK
Guruprasad Samanta	Institute of Engineering Science and Technology, India
Sadia Samar Ali	King Abdul Aziz University, Saudi Arabia
Sushant Samir	PEC University of Technology, India
Shib Sankar Sana	Kishore Bharati Bhagini Nivedita College, India
Fanny Saruchera	University of the Witwatersrand, South Africa
Yavuz Selim Ozdemir	Ankara Science University, Turkey
Marc Sevaux	University of South Brittany, France
Bhavin Shah	IIM Sirmaur, India
Nita Shah	Gujarat University, India
Asadullah Shaikh	Najran University, Saudi Arabia
Sita Ram Sharma	Chitkara University, India
Bindu Sharma	Merry College, India
Ali Akbar Sheikh	University of Burdwan, India
Arun Kumar Shettigar	National Institute of Technology, India
Om Ji Shukla	National Institute of Technology, India
L. P. Singh	NIT Jalandhar, India
Avanish Singh Chauhan	Manipal University, India
Gyanesh Sinha	Bennett University, India
Rahul S. Mor	NIFTEM, Deemed to be University, India
Roya Soltani	Khatam University, Iran
Maria Grazia Speranza	University of Brescia, Brescia, Italy
Aditi Srivastava	Noida International University, India
Kathryn Stecke	University of Texas at Dallas, USA
Karan Sukhija	Panjab University, India

Aneerav Sukhoo	Ministry of ITC and Operations, Mauritius
Faustino Taderera	National University of Science and Technology, Oman
Nezih Tayyar	Usak University, Turkey
Tatiana Tchmizova	University of Aveiro, Portugal
Vikas Thakur	University of Science and Technology, Norway
Sunil Tiwari	National University of Singapore, Singapore
Mehdi Toloo	Technical University of Ostrava, Czech Republic
Achraf Touil	Laboratory of Engineering, of Industrial Management and Innovation, Morocco
Chefi Triki	University of Kent, UK
Rakesh Tripathi	Dr. APJ Abul Kalam Technical University, India
Pinar Usta	Isparta University of Applied Science, Turkey
Anak Agung Gde SatiaUtama	University of Airlangga, Indonesia
Tatapudi Vasista	Srinivas University Mangalore, India
Agnes Nalini Vincent	University of Third Age, Mauritius
Gongming Wang	Tsinghua University, China
Gerhard-Wilhelm Weber	Poznan University of Technology, Poland
Wenqing Wu	Southwest University of Science and Technology, China
Liangping Wu	Sichuan Normal University, China
Abdullah Yildizbasi	Ankara Yıldırım Beyazıt University, Turkey
Ibrahim Yilmaz	Ankara Yıldırım Beyazıt University, Turkey
Nurullah Yılmaz	Suleyman Demirel University, Turkey
Ramadan Zenedean	Cairo University, Egypt
Haining Zheng	Massachusetts Institute of Technology, USA
Karim Zkik	School of Engineers, France
Shakib Zohrehvandi	Technical University of Kosice, Slovakia

Executive Committee

Melda Kevser	Yıldırım Beyazıt University, Turkey
Nurullah Güleç	Yıldırım Beyazıt University, Turkey
Emine Nur Nacar	Yıldırım Beyazıt University, Turkey
Leyla Chehrghani	Kharazmi University, Iran

Scientific Sponsors

Kent Business School

University of Maryland

International University of Rabat

Suleyman Demirel University

The University of Texas at Dallas

Prague University of Economics and Business

Ankara Science University

Tunisian Operational Research Society

Vidyasagar University

Ataturk University

Istinye University

Manisa Celal Bayar University

Contents – Part II

Contents – Part I

**Human Factors Management Systems Based on Information
Technology**

**Technology-Aided Decision-Making: Systems, Applications, and
Modern Solutions**

Application of Computer Science and Technology in Operations and Supply Chain Management

Predicting the Energy Demand for Micro-grids in an Industrial Entity Using EEMD-LSTM-AM Model

Chaymae Makri[1](✉), Said Guedira[2], Imad El Harraki[3], and Soumia El Hani[1]

[1] Energy Optimization, Diagnostics and Control Team, ENSAM, Mohammed V University, Rabat, Morocco
chaymae.makri@gmail.com, s.elhani@um5r.ac.ma

[2] Laboratory of Control, Piloting and Monitoring of Electrical Energy, National Higher School of Mines of Rabat, Rabat, Morocco
guedira@enim.ac.ma

[3] Laboratory of Applied Mathematics and Business Intelligence, National Higher School of Mines of Rabat, Rabat, Morocco
elharraki@enim.ac.ma

Abstract. Energy demand forecasting plays a crucial role in the analysis, estimation, management, and optimization of electricity consumption, specifically in micro-grid structures. Our objective is to propose a new, more efficient, and accurate method for forecasting energy demand. This method brings together two important techniques to meet our objective, signal analysis algorithm and artificial intelligence algorithms. The proposed method combines ensemble empirical mode decomposition (EEMD), long-term short-term memory (LSTM), and attention mechanism (AM) called EEMD-LSTM-AM. The model starts by applying the EEMD method on our input time series to decompose them into IMF components and a residual. Then, LSTM layers extract the characteristics of the input time series. Next, add a layer of AM to estimate the importance of input characteristics. LSTM and AM layers are applied for each IMF component and residual. Next, add a fully connected layer to generate the component predictions. Towards the end, the prediction of final consumption is determined by adding all the predictions of the series components. To prove the applicability of the proposed model, it is applied to data on electricity consumption in an industrial entity. The proposed approach is evaluated by comparing the performance of the prediction results with EEMD-LSTM and EEMD-MLP-AM, with MLP is a multi-layer perceptron. The experimental results show that the proposed method is more efficient in terms of precision and efficiency. Then, we can see the importance of the decomposition of the input signal to reduce the difficulty of prediction and the attention layer in improving the forecast fidelity.

Keywords: Energy consumption prediction · Micro-grids · Ensemble Empirical Mode Decomposition (EEMD) · Long Short-Term Memory (LSTM) · Attention Mechanism (MA)

A. Mirzazadeh et al. (Eds.): SEMIT 2022, CCIS 1809, pp. 3–22, 2023.
https://doi.org/10.1007/978-3-031-40398-9_1

1 Introduction

Predicting electricity consumption for a micro-grid allows us to: (1) analyze our consumption in order to estimate energy bills and also to make better decisions; and (2) good management of the consumption of our future consumption without affecting the productivity of the industrial entity [1, 2]. In addition, a better analysis of the consumption data collected can lead to a more accurate forecasting model. Therefore, an efficient forecast of electricity demand will ensure a stable power supply and an uninterruptible production process.

A micro-grid is a small-scale network with limited geography. This network can be connected to a large network or operate independently. The benefits of micro-grids are maximizing local resources and reducing economic and energy losses in the transmission of electricity. A micro-grid ensures power stability, shaves peak load demand, and reduces carbon emissions [3]. Predicting short-term power consumption in a micro-grid allows better planning of the electrical system's operations [4].

1.1 Literature Review

To solve prediction problem, many researchers have conducted studies with various methods to predict energy demand. These methods are partitioned into three categories, statistical analysis, machine learning, and deep learning [5]. Statistical methods such as the auto-regressive integrated moving average model (ARIMA) are employed to predict temporal data. In [6], the authors used this model for forecasting short-term energy consumption and greenhouse gas emission for a pig iron manufacturing organization in India and give positive forecasting performances. However, this method is not the right choice for predicting long-term time series because it relies only on historical data without taking into account the variability of the data [7, p. 2021119708].

Machine learning approaches, such as Support Vector Machine (SVR), k-Nearest Neighbors, and Artificial Neural Networks (ANN), have a great ability to learn nonlinear features between data from the input and output in order to build the relationship between these data from the history of changes [8]. The authors of [9] developed an SVR-based model for long-term electrical load prediction based on annual peak load and energy demand data. Particle Swarm Optimization (PSO) was used to establish the parameters of the proposed method. However, these exploiting techniques do not effectively explore the correlations between time series variables.

The deep learning methods are the technologies of neural networks (NN) developed by increasing the number of layers hidden in the network. These methods give very good results in the treatment of strongly nonlinear characteristics. Among the algorithms most used in the prediction of electrical energy consumption, there are the Back Propagation Neural Network (BPNN) and the Recurrent Neural Network (RNN). The disadvantage of the model obtained through BPNN is the difficulty guaranteeing optimal performance because of the serious problems of vanishing gradient [10, 11]. Unlike BPNN, RNN has the advantage of retaining temporal information using the recurring layer that gives the choice of whether to keep the information from previous moments [11]. However, in the long term and because of the problem of vanishing gradient, the RNN cannot properly maintain the dependence. Yahya and others developed a model for short-term electrical charge prediction, using the Recurrent Neural Network model with Lavenberg-Marquardt and the Bayesian regularization-training algorithm [12].

In 1997, after 7 years, an improved RNN called a long-term memory network (LSTM) was developed to address these issues [13]. The LSTM introduces the memory cell and the grid structures to maintain the temporal correlation and to solve the gradient disappearance problem respectively. Son and others proposed a forecasting model with social and weather-related variables by introducing the LSTM method. This model has the possibility of forecasting energy demand for a long period that can reach a month [14].

In addition, we find the hybrid method which is a mixture of two or more techniques. This method allows benefiting from the strengths of each technique to increase the efficiency of the final model and the prediction performance.

Marino and others compare two models based on LSTMs to forecast future demand. Both models, standard LSTM, and auto-encoder LSTM (AE-LSTM) integrated as input the hour, day of the month, and day of the week. The results obtained by these two models conclude that the auto-encoder is better [15]. In [16], Chandramitasari and others suggested a model of forecasting the demand for electric power for the short-term using a model based on NN technology. The model combines the LSTM which performs the time series forecasting with the historical data and the Feed-Forward Neural Network (FFNN) for the forecast with the additional information, the day, timescale, and season informational, to minimize the forecast losses. Kim and others proposed two different models for forecasts of the energy demand from the defined state. The first model consists of a projector, LSTM, which defines an appropriate state for a given situation, and a predictor, based on RNN [17]. The second model associates Conventional Neural Networks (CNN) and LSTM [18]. Both models give good results but require efficient and clear pre-processing, such as eliminating some variables and adding else variables, which gives better results. In [19], the authors developed a hybrid CNN with the AE-LSTM model for future energy prediction in residential and commercial buildings. The experimental results show that the proposed hybrid model works well. Le and others proposed a model that uses CNN and Bi-directional Long Short-Term Memory (Bi-LSTM) to predict electric energy consumption [20]. So, we can see that artificial intelligence methods have proven its effectiveness in forecasting compared to other methods.

To reduce the difficulty of prediction by analysis of the consumption data, there are methods of decomposition of data. Among these methods, we find the empirical mode decomposition (EMD) which allows decomposing of a signal into an intrinsic mode set (IMF) and a residue. Next, add a prediction model for each component of the signal, and towards the end, add all the predictions to build the final prediction. In[21], Aghmadi et al. propose a model that combines EMD and BPNN to predict short-term solar radiation. EMD is used to break down the solar radiation data set and BPNN to predict all components. Short-term price forecasting is done in [22] using the hybrid EMD-CNN-LSTM method. CNN layers to analyze data characteristics and LSTM layers to generate predictions. Chen et al. propose an enhanced EMD method called Empirical Ensemble Decomposition (EEMD) based on noise-assisted analysis and LSTM [23]. EEMD is used to break down the measured signal and LSTM layers are used to predict the missing measured data from structural sensors.

To allocate resources to important parts of the input signal, the Attention Mechanism (AM) module is used to improve the accuracy of the forecast model [24]. The authors of [25] develop a short-term load prediction model combining LSTM, MLP, and AM. First, a sequence architecture (seq2seq) has the role of extracting the characteristics of historical data as that of a single sequence to make predictions. Second, MLP is used for residual modification. AM layer is added to improve seq2seq performance. A short-term wind speed forecast model that combines CNN, AM, LSTM, and ECA (Effective Channel Attention) is proposed in [26]. The model is proposed to demonstrate its effectiveness and accuracy compared to other models.

1.2 Contributions of Proposed Method

The purpose of this study is to provide a model to accurately forecast the electricity demand of a micro-grid based on EEMD-LSTM-AM. The model is known as an advanced and powerful algorithm for analyzing time series data among deep learning approaches. In addition, we add data pretreatment and correlation analysis that improves model reliability. This article presents the following contributions:

- A novel combination for forecasting energy demand for micro-grids in an industrial entity,
- A correlation analysis of the data collected to keep the variables that affect the prediction,
- Add variables that represent the consumption profile,
- A decomposition with EEMD of the input series to reduce the difficulty of prediction,
- LSTM layers to extract input time series characteristics,
- An AM layer to estimate the importance of input characteristics,
- A comparison with different methods to show model capacity.

1.3 Paper Organization

The rest of this article is organized as follows: Sect. 2 gives the general framework of predictive modeling and the specific implementation techniques. Section 3 provides the data set, the proposed method, an analysis of the variables, internal architecture and discusses the experimental results. Finally, Sect. 4 contains the conclusions and recommendations.

2 Methodology

In general, forecasting electricity demand is one of the most difficult problems due to many uncertainties. This section details the proposed methodology used to solve such a regression problem, Fig. 1.

The specific steps for the universal process of time series prediction are as follows:

- **Step 1:** After collecting the data related to the prediction based on the forecast target, the next action is to replace the missing values with the average of each variable to obtain filtered data. These missing values are due to the sensor failure, the aberrant values with abrupt variation, and the noise.

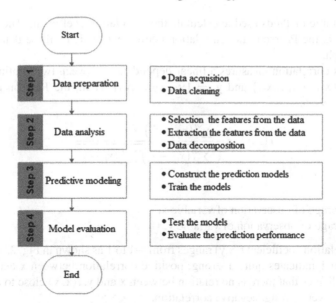

Fig. 1. Methodology.

- **Step 2:** In this step, we explore the filtered data. We use statistical methods that can help provide reference opinions for the subsequent selection of research variables. For example, calculate the correlation matrix between the variables to determine the correlation degree among these variables. Also, the Principal Components Analysis (PCA) is one of the most used linear dimensional reduction techniques. The next sub-step is feature extraction in aims to reduce the number of unnecessary features in our data by creating new features from the existing ones (and then discarding the original features). After extracting the new variables, decompose the input signal using the decomposition methods such as EEMD.
- **Step 3:** MLP, LSTM, and other approaches we can use to forecast the time series. In addition, adds AM layers to focus on the essential part of the series. After prepro-cessing the data, we are achieving the proposed models and adjusting the parameters until the highest prediction accuracy will be is obtained.
- **Step 4:** To evaluate the prediction performance and the generalization ability of the models, some indicators are used, for example, Root Mean Squared Error (RMSE), Mean Squared Error (MSE), and Mean Absolute Error (MAE).

2.1 Correlation

Normally, the variables on one system are related to each other. To extract the relationship between these variables, correlation analysis is used. The correlation analysis is the statistical tool used to calculate the correlation between the variables. The first step is to determine whether the relationship exists and then measure it (The measure of correlation is determined by the Coefficient of Correlation). The second step is to establish the cause-and-effect relation for this correlation if it exists. Pearson rank correlation coefficient [27], Kendall rank correlation coefficient [28], and Spearman rank correlation coefficient

[29], are the three methods used to calculate the correlation coefficient. The frequently used method is the Pearson rank correlation coefficient, which will be detailed in the next paragraph.

Pearson's correlation measures a linear dependence between two continuous variables $x_{ij} = \{x_{1j}, x_{2j},...,x_{nj}\}$ and $y_i = \{y_1, y_2,...,y_n\}$ Then, the Pearson correlation coefficient r(x,y) is:

$$r(x, y) = \frac{\sum_1^n (x_{ij} - \bar{x}_i) - (y_i - \bar{y})}{\sqrt{\sum_1^n (x_{ij} - \bar{x}_i) \sum_1^n (y_i - \bar{y})}} \tag{1}$$

With:

- $\bar{x}j$: the average of observation of variable x_j,
- $\bar{y}$: the average of observation of variable y.

The correlation coefficient r(x,y) ranges from -1 to 1 as shown in Fig. 2. r(x,y) close to or equal to 1 indicates quite a strong, positive correlation between x and y. r(x, y) equal to 0 indicates that there is no relation between x and y. r(x, y) close to or equal to -1 indicates a very strong, negative correlation.

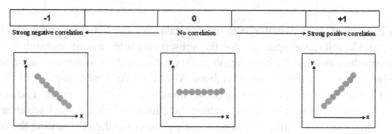

Fig. 2. The correlation coefficient.

2.2 Ensemble Empirical Mode Decomposition

Empirical mode decomposition (EMD) is a method of analysis of nonlinear and non-stationary signals proposed by Huang et al. in 1998 [30]. EMD is an iterative process that decomposes an original signal x(t) into intrinsic mode functions IMF(t) and a residue r(t). In addition, each component must verify the following criteria: 1) the difference between the number of extremes and the number of passes per zero in the data set must be zero or greater than 1; and 2) The average sum of the local maxima and minima for each moment must be zero. The EMD process for a time series is as follows:

Step 1:

- Insert signal x(t),
- Locate local minima and maxima for x(t) signal,
- Bind local minima by a cubic spline, also for local maxima.

Step 2: Build the average envelope $m_1(t)$ from the average of the upper and lower envelopes.

Step 3: Extract the first component $h_1(t)$ by the following relation:

$$h1(t) = x(t) - m1(t) \tag{2}$$

Step 4: check if $h_1(t)$ is an IMF:

- If yes, proceed to the next step,
- Otherwise, return to step 1 and use $h_1(t)$ as the initial signal:

$$h_2(t) = h_1(t) - m_2(t) \tag{3}$$

Steps 1 to 4 are repeated k times until h(t) meets the above criteria. With: $IMF_1(t) = h_k(t)$

- **Step 5:** Obtain the residue by:

$$r_2(t) = x_1(t) - IMF_1(t) \tag{4}$$

Step 6:

•Replace the initial signal x(t) with the residue r1(t),
•Repeat steps 1 to 5 to find another residual signal,
•Check if rn(t):

- If yes, the initial signal x(t) becomes:

$$x(t) = \sum_{i=1}^{n} IMF_1(t) + r_n(t) \tag{5}$$

- Otherwise, repeat steps 1 through 5.

With n is the number of repetitions of steps 1 to 5 so that $r_n(t)$ is a monotonous signal.

The ensemble empirical mode decomposition (EEMD) is an improved method of the EMD method. EEMD is based on noise-aided analysis [31]. It consists in introducing several times a white noise with an average zero value in the decomposition process. This noise allows you to hide the noise of the original signal to obtain more accurate upper and lower envelopes. The EEMD process is presented in Fig. 3.

1) Add random white noise $n_L(t)$ to the x(t) signal to form new $Y_i(t)$ signals, with $i = \{1, 2,...,L\}$,
2) Apply EMD decomposition on each $Y_i(t)$ to determine the IMF component $s_i(t)$,
3) The result of the EEMD method is determined by averaging the results of the EMD decomposition:

$$a_i = \frac{1}{N} \sum_{j=1}^{L} s_{ij}(t) \tag{6}$$

For $i = \{1, 2,...,E\}$, with E is the number of tests.

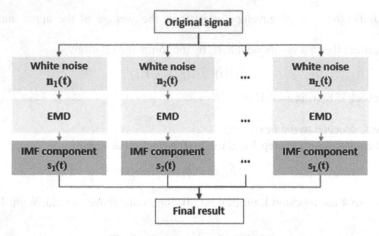

Fig. 3. The procedure for EEMD.

2.3 Long Short-Term Memory Network

LSTM was introducing by Hochreiter and Schmidhuber in 1997. LSTM is an advanced and deep architecture of recurrent neural network (RNN) able to handle the learning of long-term dependencies [13]. This method is intended to overcome the gradient disappearance problem that has occurred in RNN. Both methods, either LSTM or RNN, are generally using the Backpropagation Through Time (BPTT) [32].

The main idea of LSTM involves replacing the traditional neuron in an RNN with three gates, known as the input, output, and forget gates, and memory cell, as illustrated in Fig. 4.

In the relation of forecasting electricity demand, $p_{ij} = p_{1j},...,p_{nj}$ is the historical input data and $h = \{ h_1,...h_T]$ is the forecast data. The future electricity demand can be calculated as:

$$f_t = \sigma\left(w_f p_t + u_f h_{(t-1)} + b_t\right) \tag{7}$$

$$i_t = \sigma\left(w_t p_t + u_i h_{(t-1)} + b_t\right) \tag{8}$$

$$\overline{C}_t = \tanh\left(w_C x_t + u_c h_{(t-1)} + b_C\right) \tag{9}$$

$$C_t = f_t * C_{t-1} + i_t * \overline{C_t} \tag{10}$$

$$o_t = \sigma\left(w_o p_t + u_o h_{(t-1)} + b_o\right) \tag{11}$$

$$h_t = o_t * \tanh(C_t) \tag{12}$$

where:

- I_t, f_t, o_t: the input gate, forget gate, and output gate respectively,

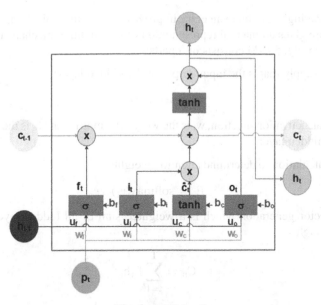

Fig. 4. LSTM cell.

- C_t: cell state,
- $\overline{C_t}$: candidate cell state,
- w_f, w_i, w_c, w_o: weight matrices of forgetting gate, the input gate, memory cell, and output gate respectively,
- u_f, u_i, u_c, u_o: the recurrent connections of forgetting gate, the input gate, memory cell, and output gate respectively,
- b_f, b_i, b_c, b_o: bias vectors of forgetting gate, the input gate, memory cell, and output gate respectively,
- p_t: the current input,
- h_t, $h_{(t-1)}$: the outputs at the current time t and the previous time t-1, respectively.

The activation function $\sigma(x')$ and $\tanh(x')$ used for the input, forget, and output gates, and memory cell, are written as:

$$\sigma(x') = \frac{1}{1 + e^{-x'}} \tag{13}$$

$$\tanh(x') = 1 - \frac{2}{e^{2x'} + 1} \tag{14}$$

2.4 Attention Mechanism

Attention Mechanism (AM) is a method inspired by the human vision treatment system. When a human being is reading a text, he concentrates on the word he reads and neglects the rest. So, AM can imitate the same behavior on deep learning models [24]. It assigns to each input/output of hidden layers a weight of attention that indicates the importance of this input. Paying attention to an entry improves the quality of the final forecast. The following figure gives an internal representation of the attention mechanism.

As shown in Fig. 5, AM consists of 3 parts:

- The power supply that is the input/output of the hidden layer:

$$e_t = \sigma(h_t w_t + b) \tag{15}$$

With, σ is an activation function, w_t is the weighting matrix, and h_t is the input/output vector of the hidden layer.

- Softmax calculation to determine attention weights:

$$E_t = \text{softmax}(e_t) \tag{16}$$

- Context vector generation which is a weighted sum of all hidden layers and their attention weights:

$$C_n = \sum_{t=1}^{T} E_t h_t \tag{17}$$

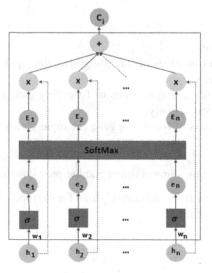

Fig. 5. AM layer.

2.5 The Performance Metrics

The performance metrics used for evaluating the models are MSE, RMSE, and MAE which can be computed using the following two formulas:

$$\text{MSE} = \frac{1}{M} \sum_{i=1}^{M} (y_i - \hat{y}_i) \tag{18}$$

$$\text{RMSE} = \sqrt{\frac{1}{M} \sum_{i=1}^{M}(y_i - \hat{y}_i)} \tag{19}$$

$$\text{MAE} = \frac{1}{M} \sum_{i=1}^{M}|y_i - \hat{y}_i| \tag{20}$$

where y_i is the true load value of a specific hour, $\hat{y}_i$ is the predicted load value, and M is the number of samples [33].

3 Experiments and Results

3.1 Data

To validate the proposed power consumption prediction architecture, several time series variables are used. This data set was collected over four months (October 12, 2020, to January 21, 2021) in an industrial entity placed in the industrial zone of Casablanca in Morocco. Table 5 shows the collected variables encompassing the time variables namely day, month, year, hour, and minute. The energy consumption variables include effective current and voltage for the three phases. Table 1 shows also the instantaneous global active and reactive power of the factory. The last variable is the frequency of the electrical signal.

Table 1. The variables of prediction entity.

Variables	Description	Index	Unit
Day	An integer value between 1 and 31	–	–
Month	An integer value between 1 and 12	–	–
Year	An integer value between 2020 and 2021	–	–
Hour	An integer value between 0 and 23	–	H
Minute	An integer value between 0 and 59	–	min
Intensity 1	Effective current for the 1st phase	I1	MA
Intensity 2	Effective current for the 2nd phase	I2	MA
Intensity 3	Effective current for the 3rd phase	I3	MA
Voltage 1	Effective voltage for the 1st phase	V1	MV
Voltage 2	Effective voltage for the 2nd phase	V2	MV
Voltage 3	Effective voltage for the 3rd phase	V3	MV
Global active power	Global minute-averaged active power	P	KW
Global reactive power	Global minute-averaged reactive power	R	KVAr
Frequency	The frequency of the electrical signal	f	Hz

3.2 Implementation

The Proposed Method. The overall architecture proposed for forecasting power consumption using the EEMD-LSTM-AM model is shown in Fig. 6. The model starts by applying the EEMD method on our input time series to decompose them into IMF components and residual. Then, LSTM layers extract the characteristics of the input time series. Next, add a layer of AM to estimate the importance of input characteristics. LSTM and AM layers are applied for each IMF component and residual. Next, add a fully connected layer to generate the component predictions. Towards the end, the prediction of final consumption is determined by adding all the predictions of the series components. So, the methodology of the proposed approach for electricity demand forecasting requires historical data of electricity consumption in order to forecast electricity demand.

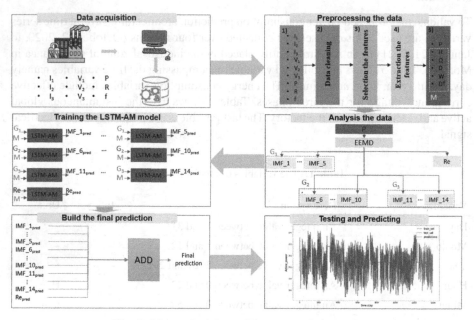

Fig. 6. The methodology of the proposed approach.

Analysis the Variables. Initially, the data must be preprocessed by replacing the missing values with the average of each variable and reassembled by 10 min to obtain filtered data. Subsequently, to reduce the number of features in our data, we calculate the correlation matrix between the variables. This matrix allows us to neglect the global currency variable and global reactive power. This elimination is due to the coefficients of correlation between the global currency, global reactive power, and global active power is almost equal to 1, shown in Fig. 7. In addition, we know that the current is the image of the active power multiplied by a ratio.

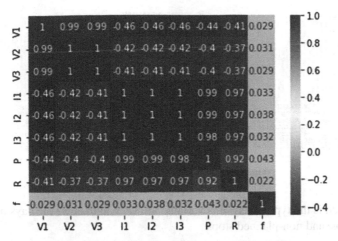

Fig. 7. The correlation matrix between the variables.

We can also neglect the voltage and frequency variables. If we plot their averages for each day for four months, we can see that their variations are almost zero, as shown in Figs. 8 and 9.

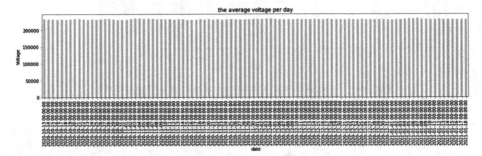

Fig. 8. The average voltage per day

After eliminating the variables that do not contain important information for the prediction, it is necessary to extract other significant variables from the remaining variables, namely the global active power and the time variables. If we plot the evolution of the electrical energy consumption of the company as a function of the four months, we can note that this consumption is affected by several variables, as shown in Fig. 10. This consumption almost is similar for each day except for the stop days of production where the consumption differs. From this observation, we can introduce those new variables. The first two variables are the hour and the quarter, which give information on the periodicity over a day. The third variable is the day of the week in order to give the information on the day of starting and stopping of the production. The fourth variable is the week of the year, which gives information on which season of the year. The last

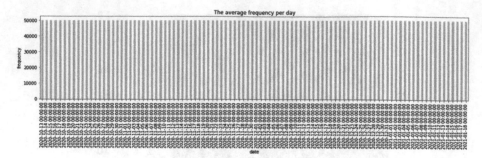

Fig. 9. The average frequency per day.

variable to add is the type of day, this variable allows you to enter the days of vacation, planned stops, and non-planned stops.

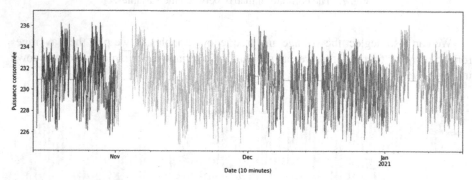

Fig. 10. The evolution of the electrical energy consumption.

Table 2. The variables of prediction after preprocessing.

Variables	Description	Index
Total active power	Global minute-averaged active power	P
Hour	A decimal value between 1 and 5.84	H
Quarter	An integer value between 0 and 3	Q
Day of week	An integer value between 0 and 6	D
Week of year	An integer value between 0 and 52	W
Day type	An integer value between 0 and 1	DT

After preprocessing the data, we decompose the active power variable by using the EEMD method, as shown in Fig. 11. In each graph of the Fig. 11, the x-axis represents the time steps of our historical data (10 min), and the y-axis represents the values of the EEMD decomposition (the IMFs plus a residue R). The 14 IMFs of our signal are classified in order of frequency decrease.

Then we grouped our IMFs into three groups. The first group G1 comprises the first five IMFS (IMF$_1$ to IMF$_5$), the second group G2 comprises the components of IMF-6 to IMF-10, and group G$_3$ comprises the components of IMF-11 to IMF-14. So, our model inputs are G$_1$, G$_2$, G$_3$, R, H, Q, D, W, and DT.

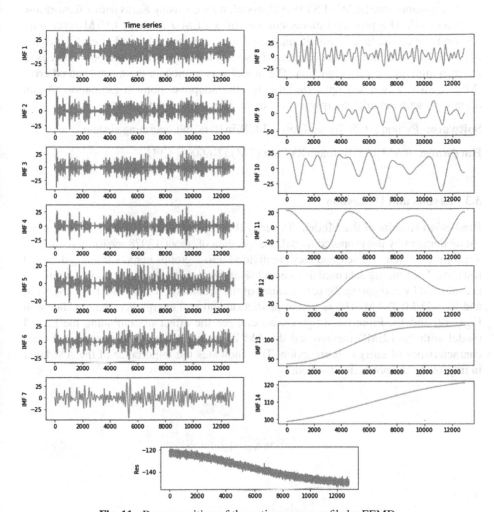

Fig. 11. Decomposition of the active power profile by EEMD.

Internal Architecture. The next step is to divide our data into two parts, train data and test data. To train the EEMD-LSTM-AM model on our data, the shape of this base requires a transformation of the two-dimensional format (tables) into a three-dimensional format (cube). This three-dimensional format makes it possible to build an entry that contains the measurements of the previous state. Then it allows the introduction of the variation of consumption as an input variable, which helps the model in improving the forecast quality. So, to forecast active power for 6 and 24 h, we use the total P, G_1, G_2, G_3, R, H, Q, D, W, and DT for the previous 6 and 14 h as inputs for our model.

For example, to predict the IMF1 component values for the next 6 h, we give as input for the model the values of G_1, R, H, Q, D, W, and DT from the previous 6 h.

To implement the EEMD-LSTM-AM model, we were using Keras with a TensorFlow backend [34]. The proposed model consists of a EEMD method, LSTM layer with 100 units, attention layers with 35 units, and fully connected layer. For each layer it's necessary to adjust the number of filters, the size of the core and the number of strides in order to minimize the loss function. The model was trained on the mean-squared error (MSE) loss function and optimized through the adaptive moment estimation (Adam optimizer) with default hyperparameters in the Keras library of python.

Software: Python 3.6.5, Tensor Flow 1.14, Win10 64-bit operating system.

Hardware: RAM 16 GB, Inter (R) Core (TM) i7-6600U CPU.

3.3 Results and Discussion

Prediction Results of the Model. To verify the capacity to predict 6 and 24 h of electricity demand by the proposed model, we use data of about 13978 measurements with a resolution of ten minutes, and they are divided into 2 groups namely training data and test data. The training data used takes up 90\% of the global data. The proposed approach is evaluated by comparing the performance of the prediction results with EEMD-LSTM and EEMD-MLP-AM. The results of prediction and real energy demand are shown in Figs. 12, and 13. From these figures, we can see the effect of combining the LSTM model with the EEMD method and the AM layer in predicting the overall and local characteristics of energy consumption. This indicates the importance of the AM layer in improving the prediction method.

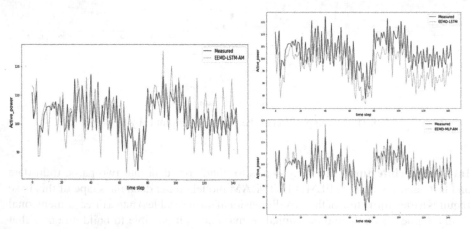

Fig. 12. The predicted and actual electric energy consumption demand for different methods for 6 h.

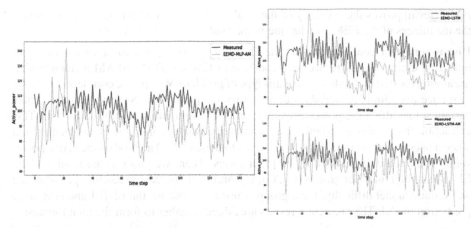

Fig. 13. The predicted and actual electric energy consumption demand for different methods for 24 h.

Prediction Performance Comparison. We performed measurements to validate the ability of the proposed method versus other learning methods for predicting energy consumption.

Table 3. Performances comparison.

	EEMD-LSTM	EEMD-MLP-AM	EEMD-LSTM-AM
6 h			
MAE	8.888	6.068	5.201
MSE	104.358	606.809	47.587
RMSE	10.215	7.793	6.898
24 h			
MAE	19.268	14.462	17.532
MSE	579.235	337.797	435.144
RMSE	24.067	18.379	20.860

Table 3 shows the performance of each model according to the time prediction. With each of the measurements considered in this study, we can agree that the prediction of the electric charge using the EEMD-LSTM-AM model with the correlation analysis has better accuracy. Model prediction error values introduce the attention mechanism indicating the importance of this layer. By adding this mechanism to a forecast model, it is possible to identify the important characteristics in the input series and therefore to assign it a significant weight. So, we can summarize that a prediction model with an

AM layer improves the accuracy of the final prediction. In addition, we cannot forget the usefulness of the EEMD technique in the analysis of the input series.

Discussion. Our goal is to predict the electricity consumption for a micro-grid in an industrial entity. Therefore, we have combined EEMD, LSTM and AM method, which are among the best methods, to solve this type of problem. We applied correlation analysis to reduce and eliminate variables unnecessary for prediction. Next, we extracted new variables that affect the power consumption of the remaining variables, Table 2. This extraction from a single variable is an economic advantage in terms of data acquisition since it uses a single sensor. After that, we applied the EEMD method on the active power signal to increase the quality of the input series. Then, we grouped the results of the EEMD method into four groups (G_1, G_2, G_3, and R) to increase prediction performance and reduce model difficulty. Each group is used as input for the LSTM and AM layer prediction model. The prediction results are added together to form the final forecast.

Afterward, we compared the performance of our model with EEMD-LSTM, and EEMD-MLP-AM which are competitive learning methods for predicting energy consumption, as shown in Figs. 12 and 13. We have found that the proposed model shows better accuracy performance compared to other methods as shown in Table 3. The experimental results show that the proposed method is more efficient in terms of precision and efficiency. Then, we can see the importance of the decomposition of the input signal to reduce the difficulty of prediction and the attention layer in improving the forecast fidelity. This novel combination has proven its effectiveness in predicting energy consumption. Also, the addition of variables helped to present the consumption profile well and therefore pushes the model to reduce its prediction error.

4 Conclusion

The forecasting of the consumption of electrical energy has become essential nowadays, especially in a micro-grid, which requires regular monitoring of consumption profiles. In this article, we propose an EEMD-LSTM-AM model for efficient and robust forecasting of energy consumption. We see that the consumption of electric charge is influenced by many variables, which complicates the forecasting problem. So that, we analyzed our data by EEMD method. Then, we tried to divide the IMF components into four parts. This division allowed us to reduce the complexity of the model and improve the prediction results. Moreover, to not make the proposed model more complex, we used in the prediction part a simple LSTM neural network (2 layers).

In the other hand, to improve the performance of the final model based on EEMD-LSTM-AM, we can add to our data other variables, such as Real electricity price or the time shift. In addition, we can replace the LSTM with other NN technology, because with the rapid development of deep learning methods, we can find a less complex and more efficient model in the future.

References

1. Arias, M.B., Bae, S.: Design models for power flow management of a grid-connected solar photovoltaic system with energy storage system. Energies **13**(9), 9 (2020). https://doi.org/10.3390/en13092137

2. Arkhangelski, J., Mahamadou, A.-T., Lefebvre, G.: Data forecasting for optimized urban microgrid energy management. In: 2019 IEEE International Conference on Environment and Electrical Engineering and 2019 IEEE Industrial and Commercial Power Systems Europe (EEEIC / I&CPS Europe), p. 1-6 (2019). https://doi.org/10.1109/EEEIC.2019.8783853

3. Slowik, M., Urban, W.: Machine learning short-term energy consumption forecasting for microgrids in a manufacturing plant. Energies **15**(9), 9 (2022). https://doi.org/10.3390/en1 5093382

4. Yaprakdal, F., Yılmaz, M.B., Baysal, M., Anvari-Moghaddam, A.: A deep neural network-assisted approach to enhance short-term optimal operational scheduling of a microgrid. Sustainability **12**(4), 4 (2020). https://doi.org/10.3390/su12041653

5. Kiefer, D., Grimm, F., Bauer, M., Dinther, C.V.: Demand forecasting intermittent and lumpy time series: comparing statistical, machine learning and deep learning methods. In: Hawaii International Conference System Science 2021, HICSS-54 (2021). https://aisel.aisnet.org/ hicss-54/da/decision_support_for_scm/4

6. Sen, P., Roy, M., Pal, P.: Application of ARIMA for forecasting energy consumption and GHG emission: a case study of an indian pig iron manufacturing organization. Energy **116**, 1031–1038 (2016). https://doi.org/10.1016/j.energy.2016.10.068

7. Fan, D., Sun, H., Yao, J., Zhang, K., Yan, X., Sun, Z.: Well production forecasting based on ARIMA-LSTM model considering manual operations. Energy **220**, 119708 (2021). https:// doi.org/10.1016/j.energy.2020.119708

8. Pano-Azucena, A.D., Tlelo-Cuautle, E., Tan, S.X.-D.: Prediction of CHAOTIC TIME SERIES BY using ANNs, ANFIS and SVMs. In: 2018 7th International Conference on Modern Circuits and Systems Technologies (MOCAST), p. 1-4 (2018). https://doi.org/10.1109/MOCAST. 2018.8376560

9. Kazemzadeh, M.-R., Amjadian, A., Amraee, T.: A hybrid data mining driven algorithm for long term electric peak load and energy demand forecasting. Energy **204**, 117948 (2020). https://doi.org/10.1016/j.energy.2020.117948

10. Wu, J.-Y.: Forecasting chaotic time series using an artificial immune system algorithm-based BPNN. In: 2010 International Conference on Technologies and Applications of Artificial Intelligence, pp. 524-531 (2010). https://doi.org/10.1109/TAAI.2010.88

11. Aishwarya, D.C., Babu, C.N.: Prediction of time series data using GA-BPNN based hybrid ANN model. In: 2017 IEEE 7th International Advance Computing Conference (IACC), pp. 848-853 (2017). https://doi.org/10.1109/IACC.2017.0174

12. Yahya, M.A., Hadi, S.P., Putranto, L.M.: Short-Term electric load forecasting using recurrent neural network (study case of load forecasting in Central Java and Special Region of Yogyakarta). In: 2018 4th International Conference on Science and Technology (ICST), pp. 1-6 (2018). https://doi.org/10.1109/ICSTC.2018.8528651

13. Hochreiter, S., Schmidhuber, J.: Long short-term memory. Neural Comput. **9**(8), 1735–1780 (1997). https://doi.org/10.1162/neco.1997.9.8.1735

14. Son, H., Kim, C.: A deep learning approach to forecasting monthly demand for residential–sector electricity. Sustainability **12**(8), 8 (2020). https://doi.org/10.3390/su12083103

15. Marino, D.L., Amarasinghe, K., Manic, M.: Building energy load forecasting using Deep Neural Networks. In: IECON 2016 - 42nd Annual Conference of the IEEE Industrial Electronics Society, pp. 7046-7051 (2016). https://doi.org/10.1109/IECON.2016.7793413

16. Chandramitasari, W., Kurniawan, B., Fujimura, S.: Building deep neural network model for short term electricity consumption forecasting. In: 2018 International Symposium on Advanced Intelligent Informatics (SAIN), pp. 43-48 (2018). https://doi.org/10.1109/SAIN. 2018.8673340

17. Kim, J.-Y., Cho, S.-B.: Electric energy consumption prediction by deep learning with state explainable autoencoder. Energies **12**(4), 4 (2019). https://doi.org/10.3390/en12040739

18. Kim, T.-Y., Cho, S.-B.: Predicting residential energy consumption using CNN-LSTM neural networks. Energy **182**, 72–81 (2019). https://doi.org/10.1016/j.energy.2019.05.230
19. Khan, Z., Hussain, T., Ullah, A., Rho, S., Lee, M., Baik, S.: Towards efficient electricity forecasting in residential and commercial buildings: a novel hybrid CNN with a LSTM-AE based framework. Sensors **20**(5), 1399 (2020). https://doi.org/10.3390/s20051399
20. Le, T., Vo, M.T., Vo, B., Hwang, E., Rho, S., Baik, S.W.: Improving electric energy consumption prediction using CNN and Bi-LSTM. Appl. Sci. **9**(20), 4237 (2019). https://doi.org/10.3390/app9204237
21. Aghmadi, A., El Hani, S., Mediouni, H., Naseri, N., El Issaoui, F.: Hybrid solar forecasting method based on empirical mode decomposition and back propagation neural network. E3S Web Conf. **231**, 02001 (2021). https://doi.org/10.1051/e3sconf/202123102001
22. Bao, G., Liu, Y., Xu, R.: Short-term electricity price forecasting based on empirical mode decomposition and deep neural network. Int. J. Artif. Intell. Tools **31**(06), 2240019 (2022). https://doi.org/10.1142/S021821302240019X
23. Chen, Z., et al.: An improved method based on EEMD-LSTM to predict missing measured data of structural sensors. Appl. Sci. **12**(18), 9027 (2022). https://doi.org/10.3390/app12189027
24. Vaswani, A., et al.: Attention is all you need. Adv. Neural Inf. Process. Syst. **30** (2017). Accessed 17 Octobre 2022. https://proceedings.neurips.cc/paper/2017/hash/3f5ee243547dee91fbd053c1c4a845aa-Abstract.html
25. Xie, Y., Ueda, Y., Sugiyama, M.: A two-stage short-term load forecasting method using long short-term memory and multilayer perceptron. Energies **14**(18), 5873 (2021). https://doi.org/10.3390/en14185873
26. Yu, E., Xu, G., Han, Y., Li, Y.: An efficient short-term wind speed prediction model based on cross-channel data integration and attention mechanisms. Energy **256**, 124569 (2022). https://doi.org/10.1016/j.energy.2022.124569
27. The Mantel Test versus Pearson's Correlation Analysis: Assessment of the Differences for Biological and Environmental Studies on JSTOR. https://www.jstor.org/stable/1400528. Accessed 30 Novembre 2022
28. Evaluation of Gene Association Methods for Coexpression Network Construction and Biological Knowledge Discovery | PLOS ONE. https://doi.org/10.1371/journal.pone.0050411. Accessed 30 Novembre 2022
29. Xiao, C., Ye, J., Esteves, R.M., Rong, C.: Using Spearman's correlation coefficients for exploratory data analysis on big dataset. Concurr. Comput. Pract. Exp. **28**(14), 3866–3878 (2016). https://doi.org/10.1002/cpe.3745
30. Huang, N.E., et al.: The empirical mode decomposition and the Hilbert spectrum for nonlinear and non-stationary time series analysis. Proc. R. Soc. Lond. Ser. A **454**, 903–998 (1998). https://doi.org/10.1098/rspa.1998.0193
31. Wu, Z., Huang, N.E.: Ensemble empirical mode decomposition: a noise-assisted data analysis method. Adv. Adapt. Data Anal. **01**(01), 1–41 (2009). https://doi.org/10.1142/S1793536909000047
32. Werbos, P.J.: Backpropagation through time: what it does and how to do it. Proc. IEEE **78**(10), 1550–1560 (1990). https://doi.org/10.1109/5.58337
33. Huang, L., Wang, J.: Global crude oil price prediction and synchronization based accuracy evaluation using random wavelet neural network. Energy **151**, 875–888 (2018). https://doi.org/10.1016/j.energy.2018.03.099
34. Keras: the Python deep learning API. https://keras.io/. Accessed 1 Décembre 2022

Modified Trigger Quantity Model in Digital Kanban System

Bhaskar Tambi[✉] and Anil Mashalkar[✉]

MIT WPU, Pune, India

tambibhaskar@gmail.com, anil.mashalkar@mitwpu.edu.in

Abstract. This paper describes the digitalization and implementation of two-bin Kanban frameworks for inventory management. The principal objectives of this paper are to give a foundation on productive stock administration which leads to the lean business, to introduce an outline of stock viability and the executives, and to present a move forward strategy that is utilized to add a few advantages to an organization's all-out costing which gauge customary Kanban technique yet with a couple of computerization and numerical methodology. Gemba and PFEP (Plan for every part) are two methods that have been utilized to distinguish the dark spots in stock administration. The focal point of the two-bin Kanban framework approach is to decrease cost, and unexpected deficiency end by killing non-esteem added exercises and redesigning the setting off instrument with mechanization by Python language. Applications spread over various areas including automobile, medical, education canter points, and so on. In this paper, a numerical methodology is formulated toward the Kanban trigger which assists in finding out several parts. The focus of the two-bin Kanban system approach is on cost reduction, and sudden shortage elimination by eliminating non-value-added activities. A mathematical model-based planning approach is applied here for part filling in the mechanical production system which is used to examine the wastage/holding regions. This approach can be utilized in inventory control. The results conclude cost saving in terms of inventory holding, labour reduction, and total production loss.

Keywords: Kanban system · Two Bin Kanban system · Inventory management · supply chain management · logistics and material management

1 Introduction

Kanban framework is created by Toyota as a subsystem of the Toyota production system which was made as a stock control component. A stock is the first and essential need of any industry to store unrefined components as well as the result [1]. Dealing with stock could be a difficult errand on the off chance that it is concerning a Multi-National Company or some other bigger industry. A cycle comprises requesting, putting away, utilizing, selling, and reordering. In profound, it's the administration of the natural substance, parts, and completed items. The stock should be overseen proficiently. Whenever there is a discussion of a large industry there are many unrefined components that need to store called in stock [1]. Stock administration attempts to smooth out inventories to stay away from both higher stock holding and deficiencies. By and large, stock administration has two sorts First is JIT - Just in time and the second is MRP - material Requirement planning [2]. There are many methods, that are used to rearrange and deal with stock, one of them is the two-bin Kanban framework. Two- bin Kanban framework is one of the broadly utilized conventional stock administration methods [3].

Kanban, which essential objective is to stop the aggregation of overabundance stock that will prompt better apportioning of accessible assets like people, apparatuses, and funds to build throughput and productivity and to eliminate squanders from various strategies by various techniques [3]. It lays out a strategy or procedure where the draw comes from the interest of the market and items are Just in Time made given interest. The main variable is that this strategy likewise stresses keeping the result at constant scope of limit.

Generally, a two-bin Kanban framework deals with designating two containers for each part/part then, at that point, as indicated by the vacancy of canisters a Kanban card is shared for them as reorder point [3]. While sending the way towards lean industry stock administration is the greatest undertaking since it is the central issue of efficiency of any plant and to effectively execute that need to figure out how to utilize a few administration methods and there comes two-receptacle Kanban framework in the image [4]. From the day Toyota fostered this framework in the late Nineteen, steps are being followed same to execute it yet while concentrating on this profoundly, thing observed that there are a ton of slacks and because of that there could be a disappointment in this cycle [4]. There is plenty of purposes behind the disappointment of this framework for instance off-base part feed on the mechanical production system, comparative part representation botch, part felt down, high utilization than it should be, and so on this multitude of reasons or disappointment at last influence creation speed and could be an explanation of creation or line stoppage. So to limit it to irrelevant, some points are thusly added and adjusted a portion of the means from the conventional two-bin Kanban to create it commendable for the present creation which can settle all the creation misfortune issues because of high stock or related. Aside from two-bin Kanban frameworks, there is an alternate technique too for dealing with the stock which is RFID [5]. RFID is a Radio Frequency Identification Device that is put on a specific rack or spot then, at that point, by filtering the weightage of a specific canister or space it computes the ongoing measure of part amount accessible in it however because of significant expense over the long haul of this framework, involving in enterprises at primary inventory isn't ideal [5]. So because of that high running expense Kanban is less expensive and more secure to utilize. Kanban could be the initial step then further this can be utilized with blockchain components and computerization.

2 Literature Review

Toyota fostered this Kanban framework there isn't anything changed. Every one of the enterprises utilizes this strategy correspondingly [6]. Large numbers of them attempted numerical methodologies toward the Kanban tree however they were for a mechanical production system as it were [7]. So, during the writing, get to be aware of adaptable Kanban and without a moment to spare framework which was initially intended for deterministic creation conditions, for example, consistent handling times and smooth and stable interest. Notwithstanding, once executed, JIT is full of various sorts of vulnerabilities that remembers varieties for handling time and request, arranged interferences, for example, recommended, support, and spontaneous interferences like abrupt hardware disappointment. This framework is associated with the back-and-forth framework [7]. These all cycles are straightforwardly associated with Lean Inventory, or it can express straightforwardly to the Lean Industry which makes the business creation higher. These all strategies can be involved in the change of an organization into a high-performing lean undertaking for which worth stream planning will be gainful use which can be involved fundamentally to recognize the open doors for different lean methods.

The fundamental focal point of this Literature study is to comprehend various kinds of methods accessible for stock administration. One of them was RFID which is a radio recurrence ID gadget for stock administration. The latest technique is far and wide in various regions. It has numerous impressive applications with nonstop benefits like stock amount clarity, process capacity, and diminishing confounded and brutal conditions however it likewise has a negative point which is its significant expense. Upkeep of RFID is too expensive that businesses don't involve this much as their savvy stock item. The Automobile business has A and B class parts which are somewhat large and significant in use so consequently, likewise, we can't involve RFID as our principal source [8].

Lean assembling (which comprises brilliant and robotized or digitalized/shrewd stock, less capacity as per the system, low labor supply cost, with low stock holding cost with less support) is the popular expression in the space of assembling and creation for the beyond a couple of years. The two-bin Kanban framework is one of the assembling systems for lean creation with insignificant stock and diminished costs it is a zero venture and hundred percent benefit methodology.

Here likewise performed an improvement of the numerical methodology so the situation can be found which is made. Here is a numerical improvement of the situation applied. X as a contribution for the request and y as a contribution for the trigger amount which is got from the recipe. As Optimization is a term otherwise called numerical programming which is an assortment of numerical standards and strategies utilized for tackling quantitative issues in many disciplines. Numerical programming incorporates the investigation of the numerical construction of improvement issues, the innovation of techniques for tackling these issues, and the investigation of the numerical properties of these strategies.

One of the most incredible procedures is by sending lean assembling rehearses that can be utilized to work on the functional exhibitions and efficiency of the plant. Lean assembling alludes to assembling processes without squandering it very well may be any sort of waste. Squander is something besides the base measure of gear, materials, parts, and working time, which are significant objects of loss of creation. Thus, Industries need to assess and evaluate the present status of activities in their assembling offices/mechanical production systems. Subsequently, one of the vital pushes in great assembling rehearses is setting up lean assembling with a powerful Kanban framework so for this here is the execution of digitalized Kanban framework which will lead towards objective likewise at a savvy stock framework. This is certainly not a conventional Kanban as said before, it is a redesigned rendition or can be called a digitalized Kanban framework [9].

As per one of the papers which manage the execution of the Kanban framework to tack the motivation behind that survey paper was to break down and carry out in Kanban framework in a notable assembling office to deal with its subcontract stock. The plant was having a ton of line stoppage issues because of an absence of stock and holding costs for wrong parts. This was a significant issue because of the shortfall of a legitimate model of stock administration and a framework to find the situation with close stock aside from SAP since there was a limited-scale industry that can't bear the cost of SAP. Following unrefined components was troublesome, as the range of models produced in the office was wide. The issue of natural substance non-accessibility was addressed by setting up a model of stock to decide the expected stock levels for every one of the models. The issue of following the situation with close-by stock was tended to by carrying out the two-receptacle Kanban framework0 however a conventional technique guaranteed natural substance accessibility and helped in laying out a force framework yet if we are getting some information about disappointment focuses on which we are working is far various what this industry is executing since it's a zero scale novice association which is as of now making the way towards the enhanced stock framework [10].

3 Objective and Scope

The Research zeroed in on decreasing creation misfortunes because of abrupt deficiencies, labor deficiencies, and tedious manual agendas or errors. As it went through many papers and concentrated on the administration of the stock frameworks, we found two-bin Kanban and stock administration processes [11, 12]. The objective was to utilize the conventional strategy yet with an impact of up-degree regarding steps and methods. This idea covers the foundation of the two-bin Kanban framework (customary) adding a numerical methodology with mechanization through python which can help the business concerning every issue (Related to stock and creation) on a pattern level.

4 Methodology and Step–Up Work

The methodology has been developed based on current literature review and technology to build a strong base of any industry even if it is a small scale. According to the current situation of the industries if it is a push type then it must have a large level of floating inventory to develop a large scale of orders to push the market. If the industry type is pull then organizers should have a control inhouse inventory so that they can be ready when order arrives. When we talks about the lean industry then the organizers should have a limited inventory because the production will be pull type and it meant to less storage and high production.

Current/Conventional Methodology depends more upon the container sizing and lot sizing but due to uncertain demand and wrong forecast system industries are facing a lot of miss communication and over inventory costing.

The customary technique continues in light of a straightforward methodology yet proposed an alternate methodology that is more proficient for the present shrewd industry for producing Kanban, overseeing stock, and robotized strategies so it can be lessened to a base level. The greatest errand is to continue this further to acquire brings about a brief time frame to feature before the administration of the business. As probably if an industry is giving their devices and information to any project, they also requesting a player bring about a brief time frame, due to that it needs to be grandstand to them the capability of the undertaking to concede the consent for pushing ahead because Business holds very nearly twelve thousand no of parts altogether and that is a tremendous, disappointment is precluded.

Our approach is a combination of four steps they are like:

1. Gemba & PFEP Process (Plan For Every Part)
2. VSM (value Steam Mapping), Motion study & Traditional Scheduling Method
3. Strategical Dividation for parts
4. Implementation, Trial Run & Check

4.1 Gemba and PFEP Process

So, this methodology begins from the principal cycle which is Gemba which will demonstrate the issue of the different underlying drivers. Gemba is a course of finding the main driver of the issue or defective focuses by just making a six-step work process that notices the flawed marks of creation, imparts for past outcomes or work, collaborate in tracking down another arrangement, stroll to the board for endorsement, tackle the issue, perceive the arrangement working appropriately or not. Gemba's importance is 'the real spot'. From this investigation of Gemba we figured out how to discover a portion of the significant issues connected with creation misfortune which are recorded here:

a. Unnecessary movement of workers for parts.
b. sudden shortages cause the production loss
c. inventory mismatch
d. consumption gap
e. similar part (wrong picking list)
f. part count/supplier is high
g. high lead time
h. complex Nonstandard Manufacturing process

Presently moving forward at PFEP- Plan for Every Part which is the plan for each part that likewise incorporates the plan do check act (PDCA). So for preliminary, it can be accepted any neighborhood provider as in Business, dealt with something similar to evaluate strategy approach then process went for another basic provider then it transformed into a standard technique. The process began first and foremost from information assortment of parts which incorporates part no, description, store area, utilization for month one and month two, kind of stockpiling, sort of parts, the rough amount in the canister, SAP supply of a part, Physical load of part, covering, No of the container. Here this can be seen in information in the record displayed beneath as a dummy file (Table 1).

Table 1. Dummy Excel File for data collection

Sr. No.	Part No	Description	Location	MAP	Consumption M1	Consumption M2	Type of storage	Type of part	Approx. Qty in	SAP stock	Physical Stock	Coating	No of Bins
1	P11/N11	Part ABC 1	Store -A13/B5	39.31	−40	−32	Small	Medium	100	70	73	Silver	2
2	P22/N22	Part ABC 2	Store -A19/B6	37.2	−32	−32	Medium	Medium	200	150	158	Silver	2
3	P11/N12	Part ABC 3	Store -A14/B7	84.89	−254	−200	Medium	Small	350	150	220	Golden	2
4	P22/N23	Part ABC 4	Store -A14/B8	24.29	−79	−82	Small	Medium	150	0	9	Alloy	2
5	P11/N13	Part ABC 5	Store -A15/B9	38	−8	0	Large	Small	300	42	46	Unpainted	1

4.2 VSM, Motion Study and Traditional Scheduling Method

VSM is value steam mapping. So, after Gemba, the process got the underlying driver of the issue which expresses the slack in the stock administration method through SAP and physical. SAP – System Application Product is programming that sudden spikes in demand for framework applications and items or it is system application and software. To tackle this issue, the Kanban framework in which the two-bin Kanban strategy is utilized. Presently after realizing, that strategy is tied in with distributing containers and requesting the part as per Kanban card, every one of them a manual cycle can be skipped erroneously so it very well may be a reason for the human blunder [13]. Presently while moving part from stock to sequential construction system due to comparable outwardly of two sections some another part can be fitted so it could again be a reason for human blunder. Presently here movement concentrate on what happens and concentrated on movement investigation of the part which is the development of a specific part from stock to store. By this was effectively ready to find the main driver of the human blunder and for that, the essential arrangement is the commonization of parts and stickers of AMD (average monthly demand) (normal month-to-month interest) on each canister for a superior comprehension of laborers to empty the receptacle. By this AMD stickering laborers are more mindful of binning parts for line likewise, we did an adjustment of bundling amount as indicated by the information gathered.

Here as in the motion study created a path from unloading to the assembly line as seen in the figure below (Fig. 1):

Here the part movement study is introduced. Any part which is coming from the provider will initially go to the dumping point. From that point, it will move towards their separate putting away offices. For Business providers, it relies upon the part development type. If it is sluggish (slow-moving) means, it is put away inside which is a compactor store. What's more, if it is medium or quick sort, it would be put away in Ext store or Heavy line Business unit store. So this was found that 77 parts were having twofold area, seven parts were not having area and nearly thirty parts were having incorrectly area actual versus SAP (system application product) so every one of these was shut down and made the ideal part at the perfect area just single at an ideal opportunity procedure.

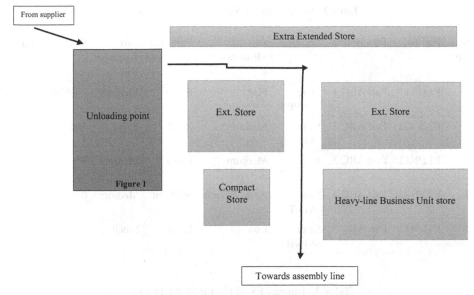

Fig. 1. Motion Study Path from supplier to assembly line

4.3 Strategical Dividation of Parts

Here three distribution theories have been applied for a clear picture of inventory. By these three distributions, inventory costs can be reduced by just changing the part storing size, bin, or movement according to need based on data. So these three distribution theories are (Table 2):

a. Part distribution is based on its size which could be small, medium, or large.
b. The second theory is Part storage type which is a small bin, medium bin, or large type bin.
c. Third, part distribution is based on the movement of parts which is Fast, Medium, Low & Non-moving and it is done manually.

After dividation, according to the strategy, the process can start involving suppliers because will need MOQ (minimum order quantity) and EOQ (economic order quantity) then based on that trigger quantity could be defined easily. For trigger quantity, the process went through a different mathematical approach which is going to discuss later in our experimental work (Table 3).

After this a master file will be developed which will hold the data of Part no, Description, MOQ (Minimum order quantity), Trigger quantity, Standard Packaging Size, Max bin Strength to hold Quantity, supplier name, Location of part in-store/inventory area, Commodity, AMD (Average Monthly Demand), Remarks (to be edited by planner according to data).

Now here is the main step of this whole process here is an MPO –Monthly Planning Oriented File which is used for monthly planning according to the production plan. MPO includes part no, Description, MAP, Vertical (models), Quantity per model to be used in

Table 2. Dummy Excel file for part distribution

Sr. No.	Part No	Description	Location	Part Movement	Part Size	Part Storing Bin	Consumption
1	P11/N11	Part ABC 1	Store -A13/B5	Fast	Small	Medium	−4890
2	P22/N22	Part ABC 2	Store -A19/B6	Medium	Small	Large	600
3	P11/N12	Part ABC 3	Store -A14/B7	Medium	Large	Medium	350
4	P22/N23	Part ABC 4	Store -A14/B8	Non-Moving	Medium	Medium	0
5	P11/N13	Part ABC 5	Store -A15/B9	Low	Large	Small	9

Table 3. Dummy Excel file for MOQ, EOQ

Sr. No.	Part No.	Description	MOQ	EOQ	Trigger Qty
1	P11/N11	Part ABC 1	50	100	50
2	P14/N45	Part ABC 2	50	50	50
3	P23/N44	Part ABC 3	100	200	100
4	P11/N15	Part ABC 4	125	100	125
5	P15/N16	Part ABC 5	10	50	10

a particular month, GRN (Gate receipt no) day-wise with qty, and opening stock of the month.

Here v-lookup is applied in MPO and associated with the Production report from another file. MPO is associated with the GRN report and SAP – System Application Product actual stock information for each part and with large-scale code. So when creation increments or diminishes, simply need to duplicate that report to our success sheet which is as of now associated with the MPO, so it will tell us the right no for deficiency (if any part) in the month with the amount. The process simply needs to duplicate the creation report and glue it to the principal success sheet and the remainder of the work it will consequently do.

4.4 Implementation, Trial Run and Check

Presently here comes the significant assignment of area arranging. As realize that all parts for every provider are not put away together, they are put away in light of their part class (A, B, C in which a class part is a Heavy line and fundamental gear of machines like motor, undercarriage, seat, and tire. B class parts comprise other significant hardware like hydrodynamics, ECU, and electronic unit while c class parts resemble limited scope parts like braces, latches, clamps, and so on.). So a Facility made for them that will store parts in light of their utilization obtainment technique which means parts that are in a one-month acquisition methodology will be put away together so in that column workers just need to go once every month to create a trigger. So that is the way the process adjusted the stock framework which leads toward Lean Inventory Management.

Now based on Procurement Strategy, parts that cover more than a month are contributed to the excess list (Physically checked). So neither schedule will generate for them nor will it be procured. After this step, this process was successfully able to remove a double location for a part, no location for the part, wrong location (Table 4).

Table 4. Dummy Excel file for procurement

Part Distribution	Procurement strategy
Below AMD 100	30 days stock
AMD 101 to 5000	15 days stock
AMD 5001 to 10000	10 days stock
Above AMD 10000	4 days stock

Now for reducing excess feeding on the assembly line workers pasted the AMD sticker according to the process generated on every part bin so only one week of material will go to the line because the packaging is also changed according to AMD and trigger quantity. After this, Process was successfully able to drop down inventory. So from September to January inventory dropped down around fifty lakhs.

5 Mathematical and Simulation Approach for Automation

5.1 Mathematical Approach

Presently once the process completely mechanized the trigger record, success is associated with SCAN - TO - IT - OFFICE programming which is associated with respected versatile and checks standardized tag once the receptacle is unfilled. Then, at that point, the trigger consequently comes in success which is further sudden spikes in demand for Python code. Presently here is the numerical methodology which characterized the trigger amount for this Lean methodology. This assists with saving time as well as playing the protected side on deficiencies.

In Kanban traditional system uses a Kanban card to reorder parts. So according to that, there is a standardized Kanban formula which we traditionally used to find the exact Kanban no for any part to reorder them or it can be said that there is a reorder point from which calculate the Kanban no could be calculated, which is:

$$N = \left[DT \frac{1+x}{c} \right]$$ (1)

Here N = the number of Kanban cards needed before we replenish inventory.
D = demand of the part (measured days or months as according to need)
T = Lead time (length of production from beginning to end)
C = Capacity of container
X = Safety factor (quantity of part or safety stock)

It can be stated that according to the traditional formula if C is lower than D then automatically (in many cases) N will be higher than D which is a kind of formula failure. So basically this standard formula only works when C is higher than D whereas if it happens then N will be as per need or actual Kanban card limit.

$$[C > D] - \text{Condition 1}$$

$$[D > N] - \text{Condition 2}$$

The two circumstances are associated if condition 1 is valid, just condition 2 will succeed. So till now, we have gone through the customary technique for two-container Kanban framework, Kanban card no age. Presently process will anticipate our proposed and numerical methodology for another recipe age for the Kanban trigger.

The main step in the approach is procurement strategy which is divided into four parts, for standardization we can divide this into three steps too as it is shown in the table (Table 5):

Table 5. Table for in-house stock availability

Strategical Distribution	In-House stock available
Below 100 – slow-moving	1-month stock
100 to 5000 – medium moving	15 days stock
5000 to 10000 – fast-moving	10 days stock
10000 above – v. fast-moving	4 days stock

Average Monthly Demand: suppose process have a part ABCD which average monthly demand is X and X = (M1 + M2 + M3)/3 (where M is month)
Let M1 demand ↑, M2 demand ↓, M3 demand ↓
So X = ↓
But there is a high possibility for part ABCD to reach the monthly demand of the M1 limit.

Reason – Production is high in M1

– Particular part demand is high due to particular model making high qty.

So for this process, the high limit of part demand will be for a safety (2X) Because Demand + safety stock (here safety stock is 25% of demand sometimes causes sudden shortage)

Let trigger qty = Tg

Trigger qty is called Kanban qty which is denoted from N (according to standard denotation)

Let suppose AMD = x

$$So\ x/30\ =\ per\ day\ demand$$

$$\left[\frac{x}{30} = Dd\right]$$

[Note – Lead time is for 1 day as constant. Business got a high backup supplier who used to hold their inventories for 45 days stock for every part in their warehouse].

So for Strategy 1:

$$Tg = \frac{AMD}{1} - \text{Condition 3}$$

Or

[Tg = Dd * 30] – Condition 3 is a special case that is used to get once at one time for a month because this is a slow movement of parts. – Special Case.

For rest

Strategy 2:

$$[Tg = Dd * (Ps/2)]$$
$$[Tg = Dd * 7.5]$$

– Condition 4

Strategy 3:

$$[Tg = Dd * (Ps/2)]$$
$$[Tg = Dd * 5]$$

– Condition 5

Strategy 4:

$$[Tg = Dd * (Ps/2)]$$
$$[Tg = Dd * 2]$$

– Condition 6

From conditions 4, 5, and 6 we can say that.

$$[MOQ \leq Tg]$$

– Condition 7.

So finally we have our new formula:

$$Tg = \left[Dd * Lt * \left(\frac{Ps}{2} \right) \right] \qquad (2)$$

(Here Tg can be represented from N too).

Example 1:
Let part A's Monthly demand/Consumption is 1000. Find the Kanban trigger qty for
Firstly

Now firstly according to the part movement, it is a medium moving part so the procurement strategy will be 15 days stock.

$$\text{Now } D = 1000$$
$$\text{So } Dd = D/30$$
$$Dd = 33.33 \text{ nearly } 34$$

Now according to the procurement strategy $Ps = 15$
$Lt = 1$ as contestant so put all in the formula

$$Tg = [Dd * Lt * (Ps/2)]$$
$$Tg = [33.33 * 1 * (15/2)]$$
$$Tg = 33.33 * 7.5$$
$$Tg = 249.975 \text{ nearby } 250$$
$$\text{So } N = 250 \text{ (Kanban trigger qty)}$$

Now compare the standard approach vs our approach: Eq. 1 vs Eq. 2

$$N = DT[(1+X)/C] \qquad\qquad Tg = Dd * Lt * (Ps/2)$$

For the main formula, the process wants compartment limit and security stock, and afterward, likewise, it will get an opportunity of unexpected deficiency since, in such a case that creation limit increments then a lack will be there yet as per the second equation which is the methodology that process will have an obtainment system which will lead the system towards a safe Kanban trigger. Likewise, with this methodology, the process is driven by security stock entanglements because the forecast of part requests will assume a protected part.

Let's compare both formulae by putting values:
Let's take Eq. 1 first:
Let $D = 1000$/month
$T = 3$ days
$C = 800$
$X = 25\%$ of D

Put all in the formula

$$N = 1000 * 3[(1 + 250)/800]$$
$$N = 1000 * 3[251/800]$$
$$N = 941.25$$

Let's take another example

$D = 5000$
$T = 7$
$C = 6000$
$X = 25\%$ of D

Put all in the formula

$$N = 5000 * 7[(1 + 1250)/6000]$$
$$N = 7297.5$$

So as it seems in the first example container capacity was lower than the demand for the part so the value of the Kanban card came lower than the actual demand. In the second example, because container capacity was higher than demand, the Kanban card came with a higher value but as it seems that this value is too higher than the actual demand it should be almost 6250 or a maximum of 6500 but it came around 7300.

Now will see Eq. 2 and take different input values to plot the graph for optimization.

Example 2:
Let part B's Monthly Demand/Consumption = 2000
    Find the trigger quantity.
    Now this comes under the medium moving part and the procurement strategy will be for 15 days of stock so $Ps = 15$

$$Now\ D = 2000$$
$$And\ Dd = D/30$$
$$Dd = 2000/30$$
$$Dd = 66.66$$
$$Lt = 1\ as\ constant$$
$$Now\ put\ all\ in\ formula\ TgQ = [Dd * Lt * (Ps/2)]$$
$$TgQ = [66.66 * 1 * (15/2)]$$
$$TgQ = [66.66 * 7.5]$$
$$TgQ = 499.95\ neaby = 500$$

Similarly, Example 3:
Let Part C's Monthly demand/Consumption = 50
    Find trigger quantity.
    Now, this is a special type of case because the part is a slow-moving type. So this comes under 30 days or 1-month stock type. Because as per economic order quantity supplier won't agree on our demand quantity part but still for optimization process will

find the trigger quantity for this.

$$So\ Ps\ = 30\ days$$
$$Now\ D\ = 50$$
$$Dd\ =\ D/30$$
$$Dd\ =\ 50/30$$
$$Dd\ =\ 1.66$$
$$Lt\ =\ 1$$
$$Now\ put\ all\ in\ Formula$$
$$TgQ\ =\ [Dd\ *\ Lt\ *\ (Ps\ /2)]$$
$$TgQ\ =\ [1.66 * 1 * (30/2)]$$
$$TgQ\ = 24.9$$
$$TgQ\ = 25$$

So here process gets 25 as per our formula for a healthy Kanban trigger quantity but as per special case theory, it is under one-month slow-moving type stock part.

Example 4:

Let part D's Monthly Demand/Consumption = 500

   Find trigger quantity.

   Now this is a medium moving type part so it comes under procurement strategy = 15 days

$$So\ Ps\ = 15$$
$$D\ = 500D$$
$$d\ = 500/30$$
$$Dd\ = 16.66$$
$$Lt\ = 1$$
$$Now\ put\ all\ in\ formula$$
$$TgQ\ =\ [Dd\ *\ Lt\ *\ (Ps/2)]$$
$$TgQ\ =\ [16.66 * 1 * (15/2)]$$
$$TgQ\ = 124.95 = 125$$

Example 5:

Let part E's Monthly Demand/Consumption = 8500

Find trigger quantity.

Now this is a Fast-moving type part so it comes under procurement strategy = 10 days

$$So\ Ps = 10$$
$$D = 8500$$
$$Dd = 8500/30$$
$$Dd = 283.33$$
$$Lt = 1$$

Now put all in formula

$$TgQ = [Dd * Lt * (Ps/2)]$$
$$TgQ = [283.33 * 1 * (10/2)]$$
$$TgQ = 1420$$

Similarly Example 6:

Let part F's Monthly Demand/Consumption = 15000

Find trigger quantity

Now this is a Very Fast-moving type part so it comes under procurement strategy = 4 days

$$So\ Ps = 4$$
$$D = 1500$$
$$Dd = 15000/30$$
$$Dd = 500$$
$$Lt = 1$$

Now put all in formula

$$TgQ = [Dd * Lt * (Ps/2)]$$
$$TgQ = [500 * 1 * (4/2)]$$
$$TgQ = 1000$$

Put all the inputs and outputs in graphical form (Graph 1):

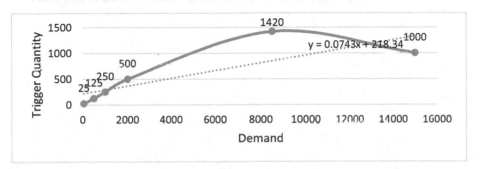

Graph 1. Graph between Demand & Trigger Quantity

Here, presented a graphical form representation of 6 different input values which is Demand, D = 50, 500, 1000, 2000, 8500, 15000 and TgQ = 25, 125, 250, 500, 1420, 1000. Here lead time was a constant as one. Here it can be seen that there is a downstream in the graph when talking about very fast-moving parts because their process is only asking for two days of stock every two days which equals four days of total stock two days in store and two days in transit.

Let's put the comparison table between Eq. 1 and Eq. 2 with the same input values (Table 6):

Table 6. Table for Comparison of Eq. 1 & 2

Equation 1 input and result	Equation 2 input and result
D = 1000 & T = 3 so N = 941.25	D = 1000 & T = 1 so TgQ = 250
D = 5000 & T = 7 so N = 7300	D = 5000 & T = 1 so TgQ = 1250

Here it can be seen a comparison of both the equation while putting the same values and it can be stated that our defined equation is much more helpful than the traditional one.

5.2 Simulation Approach

Here the main aim is: A Kanban-generated automated trigger file (excel) will be in the system which will receive daily Kanban triggers. File location and name will be the same, but data in it will be different according to trigger quantity. Code will read excel, sort excel according to the need of sorting, then an automated mail will be generated to the supplier with a pre-defined subject and mail body, mail will automatically attach the excel and send it to a particular supplier.

- It Reads the excel file which is created in the system which has six sheets in which one sheet is named as trigger sheet which is an exact dummy to the trigger sheet.

- Starting code is reading the excel file as in path form which is never going to change. Second-line is reading the particular named sheet. The third and fourth lines is showing the max row and column. For loop is showing the I as row and J as column max quantity and all the data.

Code A:

```
import openpyxl
wb=openpyxl.load_workbook("Paste path of file ")
sh1=wb['trigger']
row=sh1.max_row
column=sh1.max_column
for i in range (1,row+1):
    for j in range (1,column+1):
        print (sh1.cell(i,j).value)++
```

Output – Read the excel file and read the needed sheet in the file and print the maximum row and column by data. This code is performed in Pycharm. By this code, we will be checking our sheet for the read.

The next five lines are for inserting or adding something or writing the excel file without opening the file and saving it as a new file. The last line is to save the file as a new file in the same location. We can also change the save location by giving them a new path.

Code B:

```
sh1.cell(row=7,column=1,value='6')
sh1.cell(row=7,column=2,value='P45/N56')
sh1.cell(row=7,column=3,value='Part ABC 6')
sh1.cell(row=7,column=4,value='500')
sh1.cell(row=7,column=5,value='500')
wb.save ("projectpart1.xlsx")
```

Output – by this second code process will be rewriting or adding data in the file without opening the file and in addition, we can save the file as a new file without opening it with any name at any location.

Code is completed in a jupyter notebook with panda and python. Code is created to read and sort excel according to need then generated an automated mail and attached excel sheet data which we sorted with pre-defined credentials, subject, and msg body. Code run successfully.

```
Code C:
import openpyxl
import smtplib
import pandas as pd
import os
import email.mime.multipart
from email import encoders
from email.message import Message
from email.mime.base import MIMEBase
from email.mime.multipart import MIMEMultipart
from email.mime.text import MIMEText
import email.mime.text
from email.mime.application import MIMEApplication
from smtplib import SMTP
wb=openpyxl.load_workbook(r"paste path of file")
wb = pd.read_csv(r"Path of file")
wb.drop("Unnamed: 6", axis=1, inplace=True)
wb.drop("Unnamed: 7", axis=1, inplace=True)
wb.drop("Unnamed: 8", axis=1, inplace=True)
wb.drop("Unnamed: 9", axis=1, inplace=True)
wb1 = wb.dropna()
from_addr=' add from mail I'd '
to_addr='add to mail'
msg=MIMEMultipart()
msg['From']=from_addr
msg['To']=to_addr
msg['Subject']='Kanban Shortage Trigger'
body='Dear Team, Here is the shortage Trigger. Please share dispatch plan
immediately'
msg.attach(MIMEText(body,'Plain'))
# open the file to be sent
filename = "New Microsoft Excel Worksheet.xlsx"
attachment = open(r"paste the path of file", "rb")
# instance of MIMEBase and named as p which is described
p = MIMEBase('application', 'octet-stream')
# To change the payload into encoded form we apply attachment to read
p.set_payload((attachment).read())
# encode into base64
encoders.encode_base64(p)
p.add_header('Content-Disposition', "attachment; filename= %s" % filename)
# attach the instance 'p' to instance 'msg'
msg.attach(p)
email="Type your Mail id "
Password="Type your password"
mail=smtplib.SMTP('smtp.gmail.com',587)
mail.ehlo()
mail.starttls()
mail.login(email,Password)
text=msg.as_string()
mail.sendmail(from_addr,to_addr,text)
mail.quit()
```

Output – Received mail as per predefined credentials. Check seven times in the trial and run method and found no error as such. All the given credentials and code are checked seven times one by one and found no error which states that the code runs successfully.

6 Result and Conclusion

Paper is managed to contribute a major role towards the digitalized Kanban process through which we can resolve the time related issues, High inventory holding issues with the newly developed 4 step moving process formula and procurement strategy. We won't be finding any relevant formula creation other than this research because all other focused either on the assembly line Kanban or to the implementation of conventional Kanban process but due to the modern civilization and technologies conventional Kanban is no longer valid to Mega industries due to its loophole in process.

Intention of this Research was formed in 4 steps:

a. To gain Knowledge of the Lean Manufacturing and Different Kanban process.
b. To develop an updated formula depending upon the 4-step moving strategy.
c. To develop a Programming based automation script for Kanban Trigger Generation.
d. To minimal all the output and fill the loophole of the process.

Human mistakes cannot be minimized to zero but it can be minimal as possible, depending upon the technicality of the vendor or service provider. Due to this methodology what we have performed and implemented here all 4 groups we only need to check once in a month to slow moving parts weather quantity of parts increases or decreases, for medium moving parts we only need to check 1 time in every 15 days same as fast moving parts for 1 time in every 10 days and for very fast moving 1 time in every 4 days as a supervisor or maybe not because whole process is being automated, also same process list has been sent to the GRC team (Gate Receipt Check) for matching the quantity in every particular days wise so if any part ordered by mistake and it comes to GRC then it wouldn't permitted in inventory (it will be treated as rejected and it will sent back to the supplier itself).

Conventional Kanban process has ma drawbacks comparing to updated Automated Kanban what we have prepared and Invented. Each motion or moving strategy is a step wise process which describes the particular necessary step to follow to gain the required result. This Update Kanban formula have a base of conventional formula without disturbing them. Loophole have been found and filled with automation and formula upgradation. If we deeply compare both the formulas in Sect. 5 then we will find out that there are not major changes, we just replaced some of the elements with the live automated implemented one for a batter result gain. This procurement strategy have a base line behind the scene containing major 3 moving strategies which are pillar of this whole research and system. We cannot minimize the human mistake but we can automate the whole process for minimal the chances of human mistake.

So, we Developed a new move-forward framework for decreasing disappointment possibilities and high stock expense and stock as indicated by the need of the goal. This paper went through plenty of studies, and afterward, by a numerical and coding approach, the system can get done with jobs. Every one of the information was cross-checked with

SAP and endorsed by the more significant position. This framework Mechanism has been laid out with four simple cycles, two python code reproduction approach, a Mathematical methodology, and some manual data set. With this framework, we are therefore figured out how to lessen.

- Overall inventory cost at almost sixty-five lakhs.
- Almost twenty-seven lakhs of excess material have been analyzed and stopped for further procurement and unloading till further notice. No of the parts in the excess list were 127 which holds almost 27 lakhs costing. Then it reduced to 117 and then 115 according to the progress of the project (Fig. 2).

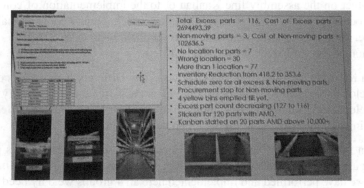

Fig. 2. Official mail communication and pictures of the project

- Manpower losses have been reduced.
- Sudden shortages reduced to zero.
- SAP stock, SAP location matched with Physical.
- Right Part at Right Location in Right Quantity.
- Time saved about one hour (shortage generation by macro code).
- Inventory Space Reduction.
- Similar Part Reduction, still Work in progress.
- Human error reduced.
- Chances of error/ Faults in generating reports/ Trigger reduced.
- The Whole system is reduced

In general, if seen, this methodology of the Kanban system is executed effectively with such a lot of data and subtleties it tackled a ton of issues and moved toward the Lean Manufacturing Industry. With this approach, this process is effectively ready to find broken focuses and we effectively can satisfy our prerequisites. The distinction is before and after carrying out two-bin Kanban frameworks with an updated rendition. The execution of a two-bin Kanban framework redesign form or it can be said that digitalized Kanban has guaranteed natural substance accessibility and thus forestalls creation line stoppages. The digitalized Kanban framework has likewise assisted in forestalling overproduction and unloading of stock or with canning say it decreased stock holding costs. This paper exhibits how digitalized Kanban can successfully be used to apply control on stock, which contributes considerably to expenses and make a way toward a lean and shrewd stock framework.

Appendix Reference

https://jupyter.org/ link for Jupyter notebook where we performed our Programming code. We used our Kanban trigger Microsoft excel file, E-mail id – password, Panda, Anaconda, and Pycharm for all of three codes.

References

1. Panneerselvam, R.: Research gate publication, Review of the Kanban system. Pondicherry university
2. Pull process: Just in time (JIT), University of California. Managemen science: A mathematical programming approach to a deterministic Kanban system (2018)
3. MDPI, the impact of the planning from the Kanban system on the company's operating benefits (2016)
4. Ramnath, B.V.: Technical journals online, application of Kanban system implementation lean manufacturing. Anna University, MIT campus, Chennai
5. Ghelichi, A.: Conference of central university, A study based RFID Kanban system in inventory management. School of engineering & technology, central Michigan university (2019)
6. Huang, Q., Chen, J.: A note on "modeling an industrial strategy for inventory management in supply chains: the 'consignment stock' case." Int. J. Prod. Res. **47**, 6469–6475 (2009)
7. Apan Industrial Management Association. Handbook of Industrial Engineering. Maruzen, Tokyo (1975). (in Japanese)
8. Sheng, D., Fan, T., He, W.: Analysis the impact of the RFID technology on reducing inventory shrinkage. In: 2010 International Conference on Optoelectronics and Image Processing (ICOIP), vol. 1 (2010)
9. Yoho, K.D., Rappold, J.A.: Beyond lean: production and inventory policy for the old economy. Prod. Invent. Manag. J. **47**, 56 (2011)
10. Murama'su, R.: Production Planning and Production Control (in Japanese), (Tokyo: Kigyo-Shindan-Tsushin-Gakuin), 1976, Production Control. Asakura-Shoten, Tokyo (1977) (in Japanese)
11. Gupta, S.M.: Int. J. Oper. Prod. Manag. Northeastern University, Boston, USA
12. Toyota motor co., ltd. Toyota Production System (1973). (in Japanese)
13. Mills-Harris, M.D., Soylemezoglu, A., Saygin, C.: RFID data-based inventory management of time-sensitive materials. In: 31st Annual Conference of IEEE on Industrial Electronics Society, IECON 2005 (2005)
14. Gramling, K., Bigornia, A., Gilliam, T.: IBM Business Consulting Services EPC Forum Survey. MIT Aouto ID Center White Paper (2003)
15. Su, W., Ma, L., Hu, K.Y., Zhang, L.: A research on integrated application of RFID-based lean manufacturing. Control and Decision Conference, CCDC 2009. Chinese, pp. 5781–5784 (2009)
16. Hadley, G., Within, T.M.: Analysis of Inventory Systems. Prentice-Hall Inc., Englewood Cliffs (1963)

17. De Sensi, G., Longo, F., Mirabelli, G.: Inventory policies analysis under demand patterns and lead times constraints in a real supply chain. Int. J. Prod. Res. **46**, 6997–7016 (2008)
18. Jun'e, L., Zhang, X., Liu, B.: The application of RFID technology in the inventory management. In: 2010 2nd International Conference on Signal Processing Systems (ICSPS), vol. 2 (2010)
19. Zhang, T., Luo, Z., Wang, H., Zhang, Y.: A service platform for RFID technology adoption analysis in inventory control. In: IEEE International Conference on Service Operations and Logistics, and Informatics, vol. 2. IEEE/SOLI (2008) (2008)
20. Müller, J., Uflacker, M., Kruger, J., Scnapranow, M., Zeier, A.: noFilisCrossTalk 2.0 as device management solution—experiences while integrating RFID hardware into SAP Auto-ID infrastructure. In: 16th International Conference on Industrial Engineering and Engineering Management, IE&EM 2009 (2009)
21. Ramadan, M., Wang, Z., Noche, B.: RFID- enabled dynamic value stream mapping. In: 2012 IEEE International Conference on Service Operations and Logistics, and Informatics (SOLI) (2012)
22. Bonvik, A., Gershwin, S.: Beyond kanban-creating & analyzing lean shop. In: Manufacturing and Service Operations Management Conference (1996)
23. Singh, N., Shek, K., Meloche, D.: The development of a kanban system: a case study. Int. J. Oper. Prod. Manag. **10**(7), 28–36 (1990)
24. Lee-Mortimer, A.: A continuing lean journey: an electronic manufacturer's adopting of Kanban. Assemb. Autom. **28**(2), 103–112 (2008)
25. Kumar, C.S., Panneerselvam, R.: Literature review of JIT-KANBAN system. Int. J. Adv. Manuf. Technol. **32**(34), 393–408 (2006)
26. Agus, A., Hajinoor, M.: Lean production supply chain management as a driver towards enhancing product quality and business performance: a case study of manufacturing companies in Malaysia. Int. J. Qual. Reliabil. Manag. **29**(1), 92–121 (2012)
27. Zheng, N., Xiaochun, L.: Comparative study on push and pull production system based on Analogic. In: International Conference on Electronic Commerce and Business Intelligence, pp 455–458 (2009)
28. Frein, Y., Mascolo, M., Dallery, Y.: On the design of generalized Kanban control systems. Int. J. Oper. Prod. Manag. **15**(9), 158–184 (1995)
29. Singh, B., Garg, S.K., Sharma, S.K., Grewal, C.: Lean implementation and its benefits to the production industry. Int. J. Lean Six Sigma **1**(2), 157–168 (2010)
30. Stump, B., Badurdeen, F.: Integrating lean and other strategies for mass customization manufacturing: a case study. J. Intell. Manuf. **23**(1), 109–124 (2009)
31. Nam, V.Q., Tinh, D.T., Huy, D.T.N., Le, T.H., Huong, L.T.T.: Internet of Things (IoT), artificial intelligence (AI) applications for various sectors in emerging markets-and risk management information system (RMIS) issues. Design Eng., 609–618 (2021)
32. Nam, V.Q., Huy, D.T.N., Hang, N.T., Le, T.H., Thanh, N.T.P.: Internet of Things (IoTs) effects and building effective management information system (MIS) in Vietnam enterprises and human-computer interaction issues in Industry 4.0. In: Webology, vol. 18 (2021)
33. Tinh, D.T., Thuy, N.T., Ngoc Huy, D.T.: Doing business research and teaching methodology for undergraduate, postgraduate and doctoral students-case in various markets including Vietnam. Elem. Educ. Online **20**(1) (2021)
34. https://en.wikipedia.org/wiki/Gemba#:~:text=Genba%20(%E7%8F%BE%E5%A0%B4%2C%20also%20romanized%20as,genba%20is%20the%20factory%20floor
35. https://www.orderhive.com/blog/two-bin-Kanban-inventory-system
36. https://www.planview.com/resources/articles/lkdc-2-bin-Kanban-system/
37. https://study.com/academy/lesson/2-bin-Kanban-system-calcuation-advantages.html
38. https://staragile.com/blog/two-bin-system

39. https://Kanbanize.com/blog/two-bin-Kanban-system/
40. https://www.jotform.com/blog/Kanbanformula/#:~:text=Here's%20the%20formula%3A%20N%20%3D%20DT,measured%20in%20parts%20per%20day

Modeling and Forecasting the Post-war Economic Recovery of Ukraine's Transport Potential

Stehnei Marianna[1], Irtyshcheva Inna[2], Kramarenko Iryna[2(✉)], Boiko Yevheniia[2], Nadtochiy Iryna[3], Sirenko Ihor[2], Hryshyna Nataliya[2], and Ishchenko Olena[2]

[1] Department of Economics and Finance, Mukachevo State University, Mukachevo, Ukraine
[2] Department of Management, Admiral Makarov National University of Shipbuilding, Mykolaiv, Ukraine
irinamk86@gmail.com
[3] Department of Economics, Kherson Branch of the Admiral Makarov National University of Shipbuilding, Kherson, Ukraine

Abstract. The article's purpose is to model and forecast the post-war economic recovery of Ukraine's transport potential. The construction of dynamic models and forecasting of the constituent parameters of Ukraine's transport potential in the system of global socio-economic development was carried out. The characteristics of the periods and predictive estimates of ex-post-war dynamic models of the development of transport potential are offered. The authors developed systematic approaches to eliminate the subjectivity of the obtained results, using statistical data from the State Statistics Service of Ukraine and modern tools of the Microsoft Excel application program. It was determined that to build ex-post war dynamic models and forecast the constituent parameters of the national transport potential in the system of socio-economic development, it is proposed to carry out research based on grouping the characteristics of the transport potential according to its resource capabilities and production results, by distinguishing the following groups of indicators: material resources, human resources, investment resources, production results. Grouping and building ex-post war dynamic models are proposed, which allow structuring the resources of the transport system to achieve maximization or optimization of the production results of the transport system in the context of national socio-economic development and to determine forecast estimates for certain parameters of the transport potential of Ukraine.

Keywords: post-war economic recovery · transport potential · modeling and forecasting · post-war dynamic models

1 Introduction

The effectiveness of the socio-economic development of Ukraine largely depends on the transport potential, the unique role of which is actualized in martial law conditions and in the post-war period of reconstruction of the economy of Ukraine. Opportunities to carry out various types and volumes of transportation are essential for socio-economic development and the country's defense capability needs. Great attention should be paid to the possibilities of restoration and development of the national transport potential of Ukraine based on the use of forecasting tools, which will allow optimizing the structural relations not only of transport subsystems but also of the processes of production of the gross national product, systematizing product, passenger, investment and information flow at the level of the country and its regions.

The analysis of previous results of scientific research shows that a lot of attention at the national and regional levels is paid to the evaluation of the transport system and transport potential [1, 2], however, most of the published results are based on expert assessments, which are subjective and cannot be extended over time, especially in extreme conditions of military aggression. The impact of globalization processes on the development of socio-economic systems is determined separately [3–6].

Thus, to date, there are no uniform methodological approaches to the evaluation of the transport potential of Ukraine and the possibilities of forecasting its constituent components. In our opinion, using available statistical data and modern tools of applied programs is essential for predicting the constituent parameters of the national transport potential based on dynamic models in the system of socio-economic development. For the

Table 1. Essential definition of the categories "potential", "transport potential" and "logistic potential"

Authors	Definition
Definition A.I. Anchyshkin [7]	"potential" means certain opportunities, reserves, means that can be used to implement goals, tasks, and plans."
Marks K. [8]	"means, objects of work and labor are only opportunities, that is, potential" (interpretation of potential as a system of material and labor factors, conditions, and components that ensure the achievement of production goals)
Ansoff I. [9]	"the potential is the ability of the resource complex of the economic system to implement the tasks assigned to it" (the potential is considered as a complete system with the unity of the structure and functions of the object and their interconnection)
Alkema V.G. [10]	"transport potential of the country - quantitative and qualitative properties and resources of the country's transport system, as well as its ability to increase the level of efficiency of functioning and ensure the proper level of transport service to consumers, taking into account the interests of the state and the entire society
Uvarov S. A. [11]	"Logistics potential includes elements of the infrastructure complex of logistics that contribute to the achievement of the goals of enterprises in the field of organizing regional and interregional supplies"

objectivity of the substantiation of the proposed methodological approaches to building dynamic models of the national transport potential and making predictive assessments, it is necessary to investigate the fundamental techniques for defining the categories "potential" and "transport potential" and "logistics potential" (Table 1).

So, it is possible to generalize that the transport potential covers all possibilities (material, human resources, investment resources, etc.) that can be used to transport anyone or anything, that is, to obtain the results of the production of the transport system, which is an essential component of the national production infrastructure.

2 Discussion

To build dynamic models and forecast the constituent parameters of the national transport potential in the system of socio-economic development, we propose to carry out research based on grouping the characteristics of the transport potential according to its resource capabilities and production results, highlighting the following groups of indicators (table):

– material resources;
– human resources;
– investment resources;
– production results.

There is a relationship between the selected indicators for forecasting the components of the national transport potential: material, human and financial resources, as components of the transport potential, affect the results of the production of the transport system. Taking such interrelationships into account allows structuring the help of the transport system to achieve maximization or optimization of the production results of the transport system in the context of national socio-economic development.

One of the essential tasks of regulation of the transport potential in the design of national socio-economic development is the determination of estimated values of the necessary resources to achieve the expected (or predicted) production results of the transport system. The socio-economic development of Ukraine is characterized by the presence of natural factors (intensification of military aggression) and conditions of uncertainty. That is why it is necessary to use mathematically based means and tools to forecast the main parameters of the transport potential. A forecast in the economic sphere is considered a scientifically or expertly based definition of estimated numerical values of economic indicators, their trends, and patterns of change for future periods.

An important forecasting task for the management and administration system is to predict the consequences (results) depending on the difference in the input parameters of the influencing factors. Forecasts formulated based on experts' subjective opinions, despite having some experience, still cannot be considered objective. That is why the need to use the tools of modern application programs for making forecasts, which ensures the formalization of relationships between individual parameters of predictive dynamic models, is becoming urgent. The forecast values of the parameters of the national transport potential in the system of socio-economic development should be based on the patterns identified in previous periods and be implemented through the extrapolation (extension) of the levels of the series of dynamics for the selected indicators.

Table 2. Characteristics of groups of hands for building dynamic models and forecasting the components of the national transport potential in the system of socio-economic development

Group of indicators	Component indicators of the group
Material resources	- Initial (revalued) cost of fixed assets by type of economic activity "Transport, warehousing, postal and courier activities", UAH million (MR1); - The cost of new fixed assets received during the year, by type of economic activity "Transport, warehousing, postal and courier activities", million hryvnias (MR2)
Human resources	- The average number of full-time employees of enterprises of the economic activity "Transport, warehousing, postal and courier activities", is thousands of people (LR1)
Investment resources	- Capital investments by type of economic activity "Transport, warehousing, postal and courier activities" (IR1)
Production results (financial and transport-production)	- Profitability of all activities of enterprises of the type of economic activity "Transport, warehousing, postal and courier activities", percentages (P1); - Volume of sold products (goods, services) of enterprises by type of economic activity "Transport, warehousing, postal and courier activities", UAH million (P2); - Export of transport services and telecommunication services, thousands of dollars. USA (P3); - import of transport and telecommunication services, thousands of dollars USA (P4)

Source: grouping proposed by the authors

Phenomena and processes characterizing the national transport system have the property of changing over time, they can be described using trend equations $y = f(t) + \xi t$, where $f(t)$ is a functional representation of the primary trend, i.e. the regularity revealed in previous periods, and ξt is the degree of deviation of the actual values from the primary trend. It is believed that the trend equation has the form: "$y = f(t) + \xi t$, where $f(t)$ is the deterministic non-random component of the process (phenomenon), ξt is the stochastic random component of the process" [11].

The possibilities of building dynamic models and predictive estimates are significantly expanded and simplified due to modern application tools, among which Microsoft Excel is one of the most widely used. With the help of Microsoft Excel, it is possible to perform a functional and graphical representation of the primary trend $f(t)$, as well as to determine estimated values for predictive parameters, that is, to perform extrapolation (continuation) of the series of dynamics for the studied indicators. To extrapolate the levels of the dynamics series, the following prerequisites must be met: - the ranks of the investigated series of dynamics for previous periods should form the main pattern of change (main trend) f(t) and stochastic deviations ξt; - the arsenal of mathematical functions makes it possible to present ways of changes in any socio-economic phenomena or processes; - Microsoft Excel tools and methods of mathematical statistics make it possible to minimize stochastic deviations ξt. All the above conditions are satisfied by all groups of indicators for building dynamic models and forecasting the components of the national transport potential in the system of socio-economic development from Table 2.

In Ukraine's current martial law conditions, it is expedient to talk not just about the need to build dynamic development models but about ex-post military dynamic models. Ex-post - from Latin means "after the fact". In our case, after the end of the war, there is a period of recovery, the end of which is identified with the restoration of the previous development trends established before the war. Regarding the period of forecast estimates, in the current conditions of martial law in Ukraine, we suggest considering three periods: potentially lost, recovery period (ex-post period), and post-recovery periods (Table 3).

Table 3. Characterization of the periods and prognostic assessments of ex-post military dynamic models of the development of transport potential

Brief description period	Predictive assessment
A potentially lost period for economic development	I
Period of recovery of economic development (ex-post period)	II
Post renewable period	III

It is possible to supplement the group of indicators characterizing material resources in the national structure of transport potential with other indicators (for example, the residual value of fixed assets or wear and tear of fixed assets of the transport system), however, to demonstrate the algorithm for calculating the parameters of dynamic models and predictive estimates, it is advisable to limit ourselves to the indicators listed in Table 2.

The same opinion applies to other groups of hands that can be expanded. Most importantly, in the process of modeling, adhere to the grouping of indicators proposed above, which corresponds to the interpretation of the transport potential through the categories of opportunities (material, human resources, investment resources, etc.) and the results of the production of the transport system, which is an essential component of the national production infrastructure. The dynamics of the initial cost of fixed assets by the type of economic activity "Transport, warehousing, postal and courier activities" for 2015–2021 shows a fluctuation of values, which is characterized by a consistent increase and decrease from year to year. And the dynamics of the cost of new fixed assets are also characterized by fluctuating values but without clear systematicity. From 2015–2021, there is an increase in both the initial cost of fixed assets and the annual amount of new fixed assets (Table 4).

Table 4. Material resources in the system of the national transport potential of Ukraine by type of economic activity "Transport, warehousing, postal and courier activities"

	2015	2016	2017	2018	2019	2020	2021	Increase 2021–2015
The original (revalued) cost of fixed assets, UAH million (MR1)	7641357	8177408	7733905	9610000	9574186	10577278	10819289	3177932
The cost of new fixed assets received, UAH million (MR2)	216697	202120	237793	306147	437695	376384	462940	246243

Source: data from [12]

During the studied period of 2015–2021, the initial (revalued) value of fixed assets in the system of the national transport potential of Ukraine by type of economic activity "Transport, warehousing, postal and courier activities" increased by UAH 3,177,932 million, i.e. on average every year it increased by UAH 529,655.3 million, and the cost of new fixed assets increased by UAH 246,243 million, that is, on average, it grew by UAH 41,040.5 million every year.

For the functional and graphical representation of the regularity of changes in the indicators of dynamic models for the constituent components of the national transport potential in the system of socio-economic development, we will choose the form of the trend equation to which the most significant value of the coefficient of determination R2 will correspond and whose graphical representation will not deviate sharply from the actual data for the studied period 2015–2021 (Fig. 1).

Modeling the dynamics of material resources in the national structure of transport potential for 2015–2021 made it possible to present the pattern of changes in the original (revalued) value of fixed assets and the importance of new fixed assets with a significant value of the coefficient of determination (R2 > 0.9), which indicates a high level of approximation trend values to actual statistical data and provides grounds for calculating forecast estimates based on the obtained trend equations.

The dynamics of changes in the original (revalued) value of fixed assets by type of economic activity "Transport, warehousing, postal and courier activities" is described by the second-order polynomial $y - 6609.8x2 + 517472x + 7E + 06$, based on which forecast values for the following are calculated periods The III forecast estimate for the initial cost of fixed assets for the post-recovery period amounted to UAH 12,738,523 million.

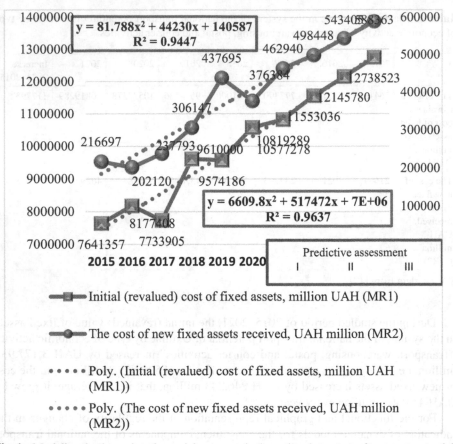

Fig. 1. Modeling the dynamics of material resources in the national structure of transport potential

Taking into account the fact that in 2022 the economy of Ukraine was greatly affected by Russian aggression, it is possible to claim that the forecast estimates for 2022 and 2023 are not realistic since the war considerably changed the main socio-economic patterns. The year 2022 can be considered potentially lost from the point of view of building dynamic models of the socio-economic sphere. After the end of the war, during the period of recovery of the country's economy, the task of restoring the previous trends and reaching the levels of the predetermined (pre-war) forecast estimate, which was derived for the years 2015–2021, that is, for the period before the beginning of Russia's invasion of Ukraine, is actualized.

Thus, it is possible to claim that the end of the period of recovery and reconstruction of the economy of Ukraine after the Russian aggression should be identified with the achievement of the level of most economic indicators, which will correspond to the predicted estimates determined based on extrapolation of trend equations constructed for regularities for the years 2015–2021 because the potential should be restored.

Of course, it is possible to change the length of the recovery period and forecast periods, but the calculation algorithm is preserved. The same can be said about the remaining parameters of the national transport potential of Ukraine, which characterize human resources, investment resources, and production results in the transport system (Tables 5, 6 and 7).

Table 5 Human resources in the system of the national transport potential of Ukraine by type of economic activity "Transport, warehousing, postal and courier activities" The same can be said about the remaining parameters of the national transport potential of Ukraine, which characterize human resources, investment resources and production results in the transport system (Tables 5, 6 and 7).

Table 5. Human resources in the system of the national transport potential of Ukraine by type of economic activity "Transport, warehousing, postal and courier activities"

	2015	2016	2017	2018	2019	2020	2021	Increase 2021–2015
Average registered number of full-time employees, thousand persons (LR1)	661,4	659,9	655,2	648,4	635,1	625,8	614.3	−47,1

Source: data from[12]

During the studied period of 2015–2021, the average number of full-time employees in the system of the national transport potential of Ukraine by the type of economic activity "Transport, warehousing, postal and courier activities" decreased by a total of 916.8 thousand people, that is, on average every year the average registered number of full-time employees decreased by 7,8 thousand people. Such a reduction in the number of employees was achieved due to optimization processes in the transport system and warehouse management.

The regularity of changes in the average accounting number of full-time employees in the system of the national transport potential of Ukraine can also be represented using the second-order polynomial $y = -0,0927x2 - 6,3863x + 671,51$ (Fig. 2).

Modeling the dynamics of human resources in the federal structure of the transport potential for 2015–2021 made it possible to present the pattern of changes in the average accounting number of full-time employees with a significant value of the coefficient of determination $R2 = 0,9854$, which indicates a high level of closeness of trend values to actual statistical data and provides grounds for calculation of forecast estimates.

The forecast estimate III for the post renewable period for the average registered a number of full-time employees in the system of the national transport potential of Ukraine by type of economic activity "Transport, warehousing, postal and courier activity" amounted to 6768.7 thousand people. The next group of indicators of the study of the national transport potential is investment resources, represented by the indicator of capital investment by type of economic activity "Transport, warehousing, postal and courier activities" (Table 6).

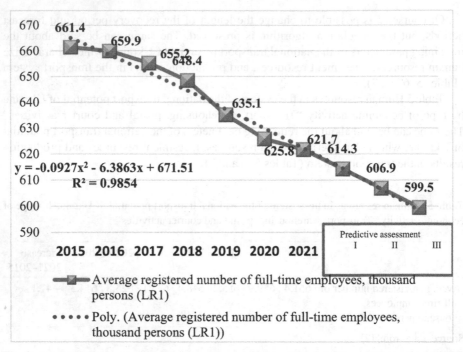

Fig. 2. Modeling the dynamics of human resources in the national structure of transport potential

Table 6. Investment resources in the system of the national transport potential of Ukraine by type of economic activity "Transport, warehousing, postal and courier activities"

	2015	2016	2017	2018	2019	2020	2021	Increase 2021–2015
Capital investments, UAH million (IR1)	273116,4	359216,1	448461,5	578726,4	623978,9	508217,0	685291,7	412175,3

Source: data from [12]

Over the studied period of 2015–2021, capital investments in the system of the national transport potential of Ukraine by type of economic activity "Transport, warehousing, postal and courier activities" increased by UAH 412,175.3 million, that is, on average, capital investments increased by UAH 68,695.9 million.

The regularity of changes in the level of capital investments in the system of the national transport potential of Ukraine can also be represented using the second-order polynomial $y = -1610.2x2 + 77896x + 219856$ (Fig. 3).

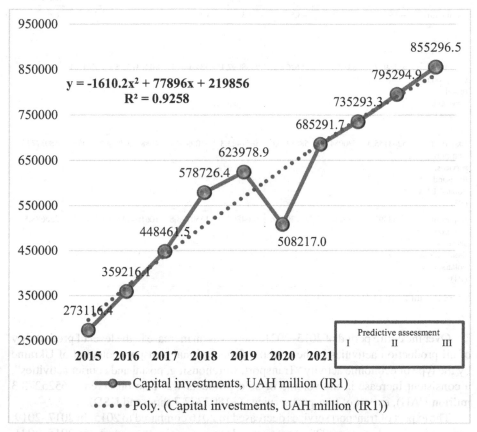

Fig. 3. Modeling the dynamics of investment resources in the national structure of transport potential

Modeling the dynamics of investment resources in the national structure of transport potential for 2015–2021 made it possible to present the regularity of changes in the number of capital investments with a significant value of the coefficient of determination $R2 = 0.9258$, which provides grounds for calculating forecast estimates. The III forecast estimate for the post-recovery period for capital investments in the system of the national transport potential of Ukraine by the type of economic activity "Transport, warehousing, postal and courier activities" amounted to UAH 855,296.5 million. As the resulting indicators of the use of all kinds of resources in the system of national transport potential, it is possible to use several indicators, including value measurement of the volume of products sold (goods, services), profitability, export, and import of transport services, etc. (Table 7).

Table 7. Production results in the system of the national transport potential of Ukraine by type of economic activity "Transport, warehousing, postal and courier activities"

	2015	2016	2017	2018	2019	2020	2021	Increase 2021–2015
Profitability of all activities, interest (P1)	−4,9	1,8	−3,5	−4,3	1,4	1,6	1,7	6,6
Volume of sold products (goods, services), million UAH (P2)	5318957,7	6387872,7	7862695,2	9388092,1	9841060,7	10273152,5	11844231	6525273,3
Export of transport services, thousands of dollars. USA (P3)	5263155,3	5300545,6	5861405,6	5851423,3	9109918,8	4988433,7	7066933	1803777,7
Import of transport services, thousands of dollars. USA (P4)	1153393,5	989274,8	1213073,6	1464807,2	1559143,8	1061043,8	1390082	236688,5

Source: data from [12]

Over the entire period of 2015–2021, there was an increase in the level of profitability of all production activities in the system of the national transport potential of Ukraine by the type of economic activity "Transport, warehousing, postal and courier activities", a consistent increase in the volume of sold products was also observed (+6525273.3 million UAH), export of transport services (+1803777.7 thousand USD).

The export of transport services decreased in 2016 compared to 2015. In 2017–2019, exports increased, and in 2020, there was a decrease again. In general, for 2015–2021, imports increased by 236,688.5 thousand dollars. Analogous to the above calculations, it is possible to determine forecast estimates of production results in the system of the national transport potential of Ukraine (Table 8) in terms of each indicator given in Table 7.

It should be emphasized again that the estimated forecast values for 2022 and 2023 are not realistic for Ukraine due to Russian aggression. Only after the recovery of Ukraine's economy will the predictive estimates built on the basis of the revealed regularities of the pre-war period become relevant again. Thus, for the post-restoration period, it is possible to assert the actualization of the issue regarding the forecasted estimates determined on the basis of extrapolation of trend equations constructed for the identified regularities for the years 2015–2021 (Table 7).

Table 8. Predictive estimates of production results in the system of the national transport potential of Ukraine by type of economic activity "Transport, warehousing, postal and courier activities"

	Predictive assessment I for a potentially lost period	Predictive assessment II for the recovery period (ex-post period)	Predictive assessment III for the post renewable period
Profitability of all activities, interest (P1)	2,6	3,5	4,3
Volume of sold products (goods, services), million UAH	12891544	13938857	14986169
Export of transport services, thousands of dollars USA	7353920	7640906	7927893
Import of transport services, thousands of dollars USA	1432927	1475773	1518618

Source: author's calculations

Within the framework of building dynamic models of the national transport potential, an interesting question is the study of relationships between its individual parameters: resources (material, investment and human) and production results (Table 9).

There is a close correlation between the above indicators, which are parameters of dynamic models of the national transport potential, which is proven by constructing a correlation table (Table 10).

The results of the calculations prove the presence of a close relationship between all the parameters we have chosen for building dynamic models of the national transport potential because all the values of the correlation coefficients are relative to 1 (Table 10).

Thus, we proved the hypothesis put forward at the beginning that material, human and financial resources, as components of the transport potential, affect the results of the production of the transport system. And the methodological approaches proposed by us to the construction of dynamic models of the national transport potential allow making predictive assessments and structuring of the resources of the transport system to achieve maximization or optimization of the results of the production of the transport system in the context of national socio-economic development.

Table 9. Dynamics of indicators of the national transport potential of Ukraine by type of economic activity "Transport, warehousing, postal and courier activities" for the study of interrelationships

	2015	2016	2017	2018	2019	2020	2021
Volume of sold products (goods, services), million UAH (P2) y	5318957,7	6387872,7	7862695,2	9388092,1	9841060,7	10273152,5	11844232
The original (revalued) cost of fixed assets, UAH million (MR1) X_1	7641357	8177408	7733905	9610000	9574186	10577278	10960292
The cost of new fixed assets received, UAH million (MR2) X_2	216697	202120	237793	306147	437695	376384	453491
The average registered number of full-time employees, thousand people (LR1) X_3	661,4	659,9	655,2	648,4	635,1	625,8	621,7
Capital investments, UAH million (IR1) X_4	273116,4	359216,1	448461,5	578726,4	623978,9	508217,0	675291,7

Source: data from [12]

Table 10. Correlation table of dependence between the volume of sold products and material, human, and investment resources in the system of the national transport potential of Ukraine by type of economic activity "Transport, warehousing, postal and courier activities"

	y	X_1	X_2	X_3	X_4
y	1				
X_1	0,974792	1			
X_2	0,968512	0,957138	1		
X_3	0,977419237	0,981358162	0,97768667	1	
X_4	0,980178	0,934403	0,958346	0,92992	1

Source: author's calculations

3 Conclusion

The great importance of the transport potential for the effective socio-economic development of the state, for ensuring the production processes of the gross product, the systematization of goods, passengers, and other flows at the level of the entire country and its regions is indisputable, which actualizes the methodical approaches proposed by us to the construction of dynamic models and the preparation of forecast estimates postwar economic recovery of the national transport potential. To implement the proposed methodological approaches and to eliminate the subjectivity of the obtained results, statistical data of the State Statistics Service of Ukraine and modern tools of the Microsoft Excel application program was used. The category "transport potential" is proposed to be understood as all the possibilities (material, human resources, financial and investment resources, etc.) that can be used to transport anyone or anything, that is, to obtain the results of the production of the transport system, which is a critical component national production infrastructure.

To build ex-post-war dynamic models and forecast the constituent parameters of the national transport potential in the system of socio-economic development, it is proposed to carry out research based on the grouping of the characteristics of the transport potential according to its resource capabilities and production results, distinguishing the following groups of indicators: material resources, human resources, investment resources, production results. The proposed grouping and built ex-post war dynamic models allow structuring the transport system's resources to maximize or optimize the transport system's production results in the context of national socio-economic development and to determine predictive estimates for individual parameters of the national transport potential.

References

1. Potapova, N.M.: Problems and features of regional transport potential development, Mechanisms for increasing the efficiency of managing the functioning of the regional economy. Series "Economics": Collection of Science Works of the Donetsk State University of Management, Volume XIV, vol. 260, pp. 166–173 (2013)

2. Kotlubai, O.M.: Theory and methodology of development of transport and technological systems of cargo transportation, p. 200. IPREED of the National Academy of Sciences of Ukraine, Odesa, Ukraine (2012)
3. Vyshnevska, O., et al.: The influence of globalization processes on forecasting the activities of market entities. J. Optim. Ind. Eng. **15**(1), 261–268 (2022)
4. Irtyshcheva, I., et al.: Efficiency of decentralization as an important instrument of Ukraine's socio-economic development. Int. J. Ind. Eng. Prod. Res. **33**(1) (2022)
5. Nadtochiy, I., et al.: Economic Diagnostics of territorial development: national dimension and experience of EU countries. WSEAS Trans. Environ. Dev. **18**, 486–495 (2022)
6. Zhuravel, Y., et al.: Management aspects in the higher education quality assurance system. In: Ahram, T., Taiar, R., Groff, F. (eds.) Human Interaction, Emerging Technologies and Future Applications IV. IHIET-AI 2021. Advances in Intelligent Systems and Computing, vol. 1378, pp. 635–642. Springer, Cham (2021). https://doi.org/10.1007/978-3-030-74009-2_81
7. Anchyshkin, A.I.: Forecasting economic growth, p. 98. Ekonomika, Moskva, Russia (1996)
8. Marx, K., Engels, F.: Capital: Soch, 2nd edn. T. 23, 24, 49 9
9. Ansoff, I.: Strategic management, p. 519. Ekonomika, Moskva, Russia (1989)
10. Alkema, V.G.: The genesis of the structure of transport potential in conditions of sustainable development. Mark. Innov. Manage. **2**, 172–180 (2012)
11. Grabovetskyi, B.E.: Basics of economic forecasting, p. 209. VF TANG, Vinnytsia, Ukraine (2000)
12. State Statistics Service of Ukraine. https://ukrstat.gov.ua/

Advances of Engineering Technology and Artificial Intelligence in Application Management

Visual Object Tracking Using Machine Learning

Ammar Odeh[1]([✉]), Ismail Keshta[2], and Mustafa Al-Fayoumi[1]

[1] Department of Computer Science, King Hussein School of Computing Sciences, Princess Sumaya University for Technology Amman, Amman, Jordan
a.odeh@psut.edu.jo
[2] Department of Computer Science, College of Applied Sciences, AlMaarefa University Riyadh, Riyadh, Kingdom of Saudi Arabia

Abstract. Visual object tracking has become a very active research area in recent years. Each year, a growing number of tracking algorithms are proposed. Object detection and tracking is a critical and challenging task in many critical computer vision applications, including automated video surveillance, traffic monitoring, autonomous robot navigation, and intelligent environments. Object tracking is segmenting an object of interest and tracking its velocity, orientation, and occlusion in a video scene to extract useful information. Over the last two decades, several object tracking approaches have been developed to design a robust object tracker that covers all practical obstacles in real-world operations. This paper reviews recent trends and advances in tracking and assesses the reliability of various trackers based on feature extraction techniques. In video processing, visual tracking has a wide range of applications. When a target is identified in one video frame, it is frequently advantageous to track that object in subsequent frames. Every successful frame in which the target is tracked yields more information about the target's identity and activity. Because tracking is more straightforward than detection, tracking algorithms can require fewer computational resources than object detectors.

Keywords: Visual object tracking (VOT) · Object Representation · Object recognition · Object Classification · Object tracking

1 Introduction

A visual object tracker's goal is to estimate the location of a target in all frames of a video sequence based on the target's initial location (or bounding rectangle) [1, 2]. The computer vision field has studied the object tracking problem for decades. However, creating a reliable and efficient visual object tracking system for all realistic real-world applications remains a challenge. Furthermore, various factors influence the object tracker's performance, including lighting fluctuations, size variations, occlusions, deformations, motion blur, rotations, and low resolutions [3–5].

Visual object tracking VOT is the method of recognizing an object of interest in a sequential manner. It comprises four implementations of this model: target preparation, body shape model, movement forecasting, and target locating [6, 7]. The process of annotating an object position or region of interest with any of the following representations: object bounding box, ellipse, centroid, object skeleton, object contour, or object silhouette is known as target initialization [8, 9].

In most cases, an object bounding box is provided in the first frame of a sequence, and the tracking algorithm estimates the target position in the subsequent frames. Appearance modeling identifies visual object characteristics to better demonstrate a region of interest and effectively builds a mathematical model for detecting objects using learning techniques [10, 11]. The target location is predicted in successive frames in motion prediction. The target positioning operation entails maximum posterior prediction, also known as greedy search. Limitations set on the appearance and motion models can help to simplify tracking problems [8, 12]. New target appearances are integrated during tracking by updating the appearance and motion models [13, 14].

The basic concept underlying visual object tracking is to follow an object in a sequence of frames, with the first frame containing the center point and surrounding box. It's worth noting that there's presently no viable tracking mechanism that works in all situations where the object's appearance changes.

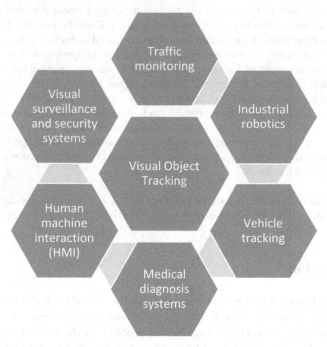

Fig. 1. Visual Object Tracking applications

Figure 1 shows some visual object tracking applications; for example, Interaction between human machines (HMI) in this emerging field, VOT can significantly improve community life by easily interacting with machinery. These systems are omnipresent visual monitoring and security systems, and VOT is an essential part of intelligent visual monitoring. Monitoring of public and defense sites and buildings to detect intruders

[15, 16]. VOT may be employed for engine and road traffic management, such as traffic monitoring, traffic accident detection, etc. [17].

The findings are based on only a few sequences with distinct attributes or factors, which is a prevalent difficulty when evaluating tracking approaches. As a result, the findings do not offer a complete picture of these methods. Conduct a thorough and fair performance evaluation [18].

2 Components of the Object Recognition System

Figure 2 shows a block diagram that shows interactions and data flows among various system components. The model database contains all known models for the system. The data in the model database is determined by the recognition method. It could be anything from a qualitative or functional description to precise geometry data on the surface. Object models are often abstract feature vectors, as mentioned later in this section. A feature is a characteristic that helps characterize and identify a thing related to other objects. Size, color, and shape are the most commonly used characteristics [19–21].

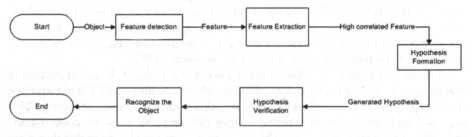

Fig. 2. Components of an object recognition

Operators use the detector on images to discover where features can be used to form hypotheses about the object. The type and organization of the model database of items to be recognized determine the system's components. The hypothesizer assigns possibilities to items in the picture based on the image's properties. With some features, this step decreases the recognizer's search space. The model base is arranged using some sort of indexing technique to make it easier to eliminate implausible item choices from consideration. The verifier then uses object models to verify the hypothesis and enhance the likelihood. The system will select the object as the correct object based on all evidence [22, 23].

All object recognition systems use templates and feature detectors based on these object models, whether explicitly or implicitly. The formulation and verification components of hypotheses vary in importance in different approaches to object recognition. Some systems rely solely on hypothesis development and select the object with the highest probability as the appropriate object. Pattern classification approaches are a good illustration of this strategy. On the other hand, many artificial intelligence systems place less emphasis on hypothesis creation and place more emphasis on checks. The typical approach of matching the template entirely skips the hypothesis generation stage [24, 25].

An object recognition system must select appropriate tools and technologies for the aforementioned phases. Many considerations must be considered while choosing the best procedures for a particular application. The following are the most important factors to consider while creating an object recognition system:

Object or representation of model: How should objects be displayed in the model database? What are the essential characteristics or characteristics of things in these templates? Geometric descriptions may be available for particular objects and can also be effective, while generic or functional characteristics may require one in another class. An object's image should capture all relevant information without any redundancies and arrange it to allow easy access to the various components of the object recognition system [26].

Extraction feature: What features must be identified, and how can they be reliably detected? Most components can be calculated in two-dimensional images but have to do with three-dimensional object characteristics. Because of the nature of the imaging process, some features can be reliably estimated, while others are very complicated [26, 27].

They are matching feature models: how are image functions compared to database models? Many functionalities and numerous objects exist in most object recognition tasks. A comprehensive combined approach solves the problem of recognition but can be too slow to work. When developing a matching system, the efficiency and the effectiveness of a matching technique must be considered [28].

Formation of hypotheses: How to select a set of likely objects based on the feature matching, and how can each possible object possibility be allocated? The construction of the hypothesis is essentially a heuristic step that reduces the space for search. This step uses application domain expertise to give different objects in the domain some probability or confidence measure. This measure reflects the likelihood that things are presently based on the detected characteristics [29].

Object confirmation: How can object designs be used to select the subject most likely in a given image from the set of likely objects? Each object can be checked for its presence by its models. Every plausible hypothesis must be limited to determine or ignore the object's presence. If models are geometric, the camera location and other scene parameters can quickly check things accurately. In other cases, a hypothesis may not be checkable [30, 31].

3   Dimension Object Classification

Multiple factors affect the object recognition task. We classify the problem of object recognition into the classes below.

3.1   Two-Dimensional

In many applications, images from a distance are obtained sufficiently for the orthographic projection. If the objects are always stable in the scene, they can be considered double-dimensional. A two-dimensional model base can be used in these applications. Two possibilities exist:

- Objects can be occluded by other items of interest or be partially visible as in a parts issue bin.
- Objects are not occluded as in remote sensing or many industrial applications.

While the objects may be remote, in some cases, they can appear in several stable views in several different positions. In those cases, the problem can also inherently be regarded as recognizing two-dimensional objects.[32].

3.2 Three-Dimensional

If images of objects from arbitrary viewpoints can be obtained, an object can appear in its two views very distinctly. The perspective effect and viewpoint of the image must be considered to recognize the object using three-dimensional models. The three-dimensionality of the models and the images containing only two-dimensional information affect the recognition of objects. Again, whether or not objects are separated from other objects is the two factors to consider [33].

The information used in the object recognition task should be considered in 3-dimensional cases. Two cases are different:

- Intensity: no surface information is explicitly available in images of intensity. Intensity values should be used to recognize characteristics that match the three-dimensional structure of objects.
- 2.5-dimensional images: In many applications, images are available or can be calculated from surface representations with viewer-centric coordinates. In object recognition, this information may be used. Pictures are 2.5 dimensional as well. These images distinguish from a particular point of view to different points in an image.

4 Object Representation

An object may be defined for further examination in a tracking scenario as anything of interest. The following things may be crucial to track in a particular domain: boats in the water, fish within an aquarium, roads, airplane vehicles, people strolling on the road, or bubbles in the water. By their forms and appearances, objects can be represented. In this part, we first discuss the representations of object shapes often used to track and then address the representations of joint form and appearance [34, 35] (Fig. 3).

4.1 Points. The object consists of one point, the center of the object, or several points. The point representation is generally suitable for the following objects in a picture, which occupy small areas [36].

4.2 Main geometrical forms. Object form is a rectangle, ellipse, etc. Object form. Object motion is usually modeled upon by translation, affinity, or projective transformation of the representations (homograph). Although early geometry forms represent simple rigid objects more appropriately, they are also used to track no rigid objects. They are more appropriate [37].

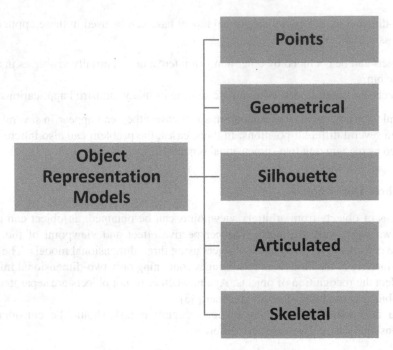

Fig. 3. Object Representation Models

4.3 Silhouette and outline of the object. The depiction of the contour defines the object boundary. The contour region is called the object's silhouette. The silhouette and contour representations are suitable [38].

4.4 Models of articulated form. Articulated objects consist of body parts held with joints. The human body is a joint object, for example, that has joints connected to its torso, legs, hands, head, and feet. The connection between the components is regulated by films, such as joint angle, etc. The component components can be modeled using cylinders or ellipses to represent an articulated object [39].

4.5 Models of the skeletal. By applying the medial axis to the object's silhouette, the skeleton can be removed. This model is usually used as a form representation for object recognition. A skeleton representation can be used for modeling articulated and rigid objects [40].

5 Object Recognition

A statistical estimation theory is used to examine the problem of identifying objects subject to the finite transformation of images from a physical angle. In an estimated six-dimensional parameter vector describing an object subject to transformation and generalizing the bundle of the one-dimensional position error previously achieved in the radar and sonar pattern recognition, we focus first on objects that occlude zero-mean scenes with additional noise and thus generalize the band on one-dimensional position error [41–43].

Objects that can be uniquely identified by six affinity criteria and a seventh parameter that specifies the class of objects will be evaluated in complex real-world settings as a problem. The joint probability distribution of our charging coupled (CCD) images for pixel brightness measurements, which are distorted by an additive gauze noise with zero mean additives, is determined using experimental data [44].

This distribution is then used to create the probability function for the refined vector parameter, which defines the object from our image data.

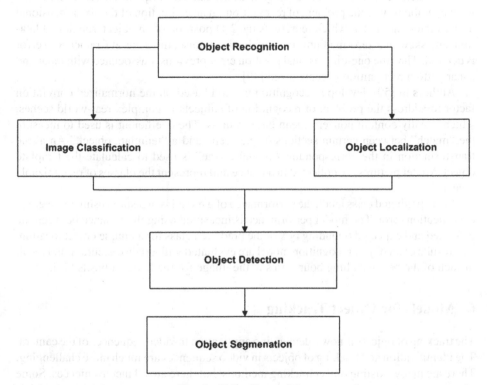

Fig. 4. Object Recognition

Figure 4 shows the object recognition block; the general term object recognition is a collection of related visual tasks involving identifying objects in digital photographs. Classification of images means predicting an object's class in an image. Object localization means identifying and drawing an abundant box around one or more objects in an image. Object detection brings together these two tasks, locates one or more objects, and classifies them in an image.

The object's Fisher information is derived from two practical image descriptors independent of the noise level and is directly calculated from the probability function. The first is a generalized consistency scale, which determines how an object is self-related to an affinity transformation, thereby providing a physical measurement of the extent to which an object can be resolved by affinity [45, 46].

The object's Fisher information is derived from two practical image descriptors independent of the noise level and is directly calculated from the probability function. The first is a generalized consistency scale, which determines how an object is self-related to an affinity transformation, thereby providing a physical measurement of the extent to which an object can be resolved by affinity. The second is the scalar measure of the complexity of an object, which is constantly undergoing affinity with a robust reverse relationship to the ambiguity of recognition [47, 48].

The practical value of this complexity measure is that it can quantitatively describe the level of ambiguity of the problem of recognition. In an estimation of the six-dimensional affine vector parameter, which represents the 2-D position of an object, rotation, dilatation, and skew in a zero-medium scene with added noise, the general Cramer-Rao error is derived. Thus the one-dimensional position error previously associated with radar and sonar pattern recognition is generalized [49].

Authors in [50] develop a recognition method based on the normalized correlation factor to address the problem of recognition of subjects in complex real-world scenes, which usually contain nonzero-mean backgrounds. The coefficient is used to measure the "match" between certain sections of the scene and a "template object." An affine transformation in the corresponding "model image" is used to calculate the template object. Model pictures are collected in advance and represent the classes of recognizable objects.

In the predicted class label, the performance of a model is measured using the average classification error. The model performance is measured using the distance between the predicted and expected bounding box of the predicted class for a unique object location. The results of an object recognition model are evaluated with precise accuracy and recall in each of the best matching boundaries in the image for the known objects [51].

6 Models for Object Tracking

The tracking of objects is now a demanding application in video sequences of the camera. The identification and tracking of objects in video sequences are much more challenging. There are many existing object tracking methods, but there are all inconveniences. Some of the existing Object Tracking models include contour, regional, and dot-based models (Fig. 5).

6.1 Contour-Based Object Tracking Model

An active contour model is used to locate an image's object contour. The objects are plotted as border contours in the contour-based tracking algorithm [52, 53].

These contours are subsequently mistakenly updated in the following frames. This approach is presented in a different version of the active contour model. The discrete approach utilizes the point distribution model to limit the shape. This algorithm, however, is highly sensitive to tracking initialization, which makes automatic tracking complicated to begin.

An object contour tracking algorithm for tracking video sequence contours of objects. The active contour was segmented using their algorithm's graph-cut image segmentation

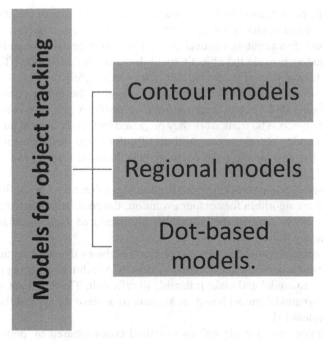

Fig. 5. Models for object tracking

method. Every frame has the resulting contour of the previous frame. The intensity of data from the current and differential frame and the previous frame is used to detect a new object contour [54].

They used the combination of the weighted gradient and contours of the object for the driver-face tracking problem. They calculated the gradient of an image in the segmentation step. They proposed an object tracking gradient-based attraction field [54].

Neural Fuzzy tracking model of an active contour-based object. The shaped model is used for the object's characteristic vector extraction. Their approach uses the self-construction neural fluids inference network to train and recognize moving objects. In this paper, they took horizontal and vertical projections of the histograms of the figurative of the human body, transforming them through a Discrete Fourier Transformation (DFT) [55].

The two-stage object tracking method. The kernel method is first used to find an object in a complex environment, such as partial occlusions, conflicts, etc. Again, they used a contour-based method to improve tracking results and precisely tracked the object contour after the target location. The initial target position is predicted and evaluated in the target localization step with the Kalman filter and Bhattacharyya coefficient [56].

The multi-hypothesis algorithm uses color and contour integration information based on the particle filter. The Sobel operator is used to detect contours. The shape similitude is assessed by corresponding points in the two contour images between the observing and sample positions [57].

Through the multi-feature fusion approach, the rough position of the object is found. They have extracted contours for accurate and robust object contour tracking using regionally-based object contour removal. A color histogram and the corner Harris feature a fusion method to provide the object's rough location in their model. They used the Harris corner fusion method for the particle filter method [58].

The region-based tempo difference model is used in the object contour detection step, which results in the rough location tracking result. A practical contour tracking framework for objects. The framework they proposed included different models, such as initialization tracking algorithms, algorithms of color-based development of contours, and the evolution of adaptive form contours and dynamic form model based on the Markov model [59].

The automatic and fast-tracking initialization algorithm uses optical flow detection. In the color-based algorithm for contour evolution, the correlations between the values of adjoining pixels to estimate the probability are measured using the Markov random field (MRF) theory [60].

Their algorithm for adaptive shape evolution combines the color feature alone and the shape priors to achieve the final outline. A new PCA technique is being implemented to update the form model and make it flexible to refresh it. The dominant set clustering is used in the dynamical model based on Markov to achieve the typical form modes of periodic movement [61].

Multiple object tracking algorithms modified contour-based by point processing. Multiple objects have the benefit of this approach. Their system is capable of detecting and tracking people in indoor videos. Their background estimation method was the Gaussian mixture model (GMM) [62].

6.2 Region-Based Object Tracking Model

The object model is based on a region based on the color distribution of the tracked object for tracking of objects. It shows the color-based object. It is therefore computer-efficient. However, its efficiency is declined when several objects move in the image sequences together. Accurate tracking is not possible when several objects move as a result of occlusion [63].

Furthermore, the object tracking depends mainly on the background model used in extracting the object outlines if no object-form information exists.

An Adaptive Kalman Filter Corner-based Method for tracking objects. The moving object corner function is used first. Then, to set up the estimate parameters automatically for the Kalman Filter, you use the number of corner points in consecutive frames. The discriminatory features were chosen using the object/background separation voting strategy. They introduced an improved mid-size algorithm for object tracking using discriminative features [64].

The FLIR Object Tracking Framework is based on a mean shifting algorithm and features matching for forward-looking infrared imagery. In the corresponding feature step, the Harris detector was used to extract template object and candidate area feature points. To measure the resemblance of feature points, they further developed a better Hausdorff distance [65].

Self-adaptive tracking panel views based on the location and NMI function of the target center. The standard inertia moment (NMI) characteristics are combined to locate the tracking object center in real-time. A mean algorithm for shifting is available to track the object [66].

The enhanced tracking method tracks both single objects and several objects in video sequences that can move the object quickly or slowly. The method proposed is based on the subtraction of the background and the matching of SIFT features. The object is detected with the aid of background subtraction. Combining motion characteristics and SIFT characteristics helps to detect and track the object [67].

The new object tracking framework combines the sift feature and the color and particle filter combinations. For target reproduction and localization, SIFT features are used. The transformation of an image produces a local feature vector. The scaling, translation rotation, and illumination changes are all subjects of the feature vectors. Approximation of the solution to the sequential estimate is found with the particulate filter (PF) [68].

Algorithm for object tracking based on Mean Shift and selection of online functionality. The objective object is defined in 4-D state space. Function space in R, G, and B channels are created according to color pixel values. The best space to track the objects and background scenes during tracking is chosen. The state estimation of the objects is done using a Kalman filter in their algorithm. The robust online tracking method applies adaptive classifiers in consecutive frames to match the detected vital points. The approach proposed shows that integrating the robust local feature and the adaptive online boosting algorithm can contribute to the adaptation of different frames [69].

Real-time picture processing on mobile devices. They use a holistic hair-like feature to track exciting objects. The robustness of their method was achieved with the help of an online feature update system. A color filtering feature detection method for tracking recovery: an algorithm combines motion detection, function extraction, and block matching background information. The four adjacent directions are detected by a series of features called Shape Control Points (SCPs). Using an adaptive background generation method, the weakness of the block matching algorithm was reduced [70].

The representative object appearances have been stored as candidate templates during tracking, and the best template is selected to match new frames. This template addition process is updated with further object appearances and changed via the online strategy. They showed that feature-based methods could be extended to objects that are not planned or undergo significant modifications. Extended their object tracking feature-based method using sparse shape points. Possible data association events with the particulate filter are sampled. The filter also helps to estimate the global position and velocity of the object. They have used time, together with partial regression of the least square, to improve the performance of the tracker [71].

A multi-part SIFT rotating object tracking feature model for tracking objects. The reference and target object are represented to extract the possible significant similarity points measurement. The filter solves the state space estimate when the state equation is non-linear and the subsequent density is non-Gaussian. A tracking particle filter that is useful for non-linear or non-Gaussian problems. They use Bhattacharyya object distance and the predicted position of the object obtained by the particle filter to find the posterior probability of the particle filter. The rear chance is used to update the filter's status. Their experiment has shown HSV to be the optimal color room for changes in scale, occlusion, and lighting [72].

New Distance Metric Learning (DML) tracking framework for Object Tracking combined with Nearest Neighbor (NN) grades. They used a canny edge detector to detect the object; the object can be distinguished from other objects by using the Nearest Neighbor Classifier. The background can be removed from the Nearest Neighbor (NN) algorithm framework. The algorithm of the closest neighbor uses the distance between the object and the background to remove it. The object is then determined based on skin color utilizing a blob detector. An abounding box is created for the identified object [73].

Enhanced Monte Carlo (MCMC) Markov chain was known as the MCMC (OF-MCMC) vehicle flow sampling algorithm. The automatic movement model has been applied to achieve the moving direction of the vehicle in the initial frames using the optical flow method, which resolves the scale change problem and the moving speed of the object. They have produced a more accurate feature template with different weighted features to handle vehicle tracking in low resolution of video data and obtain better follow-up results [74].

7 Feature Point-Based Tracking Algorithm

Feature-point models are used to describe objects. The feature-point tracking algorithm has three basic steps. The first step is to detect and track the object with elements extracted. The second step is to group them into higher levels. The last step is to match the extracted features in successive frames between images. The essential steps in function-driven object tracking are feature extraction and feature correspondence. The challenge of tracking functions is the correspondence of a feature because a point in one picture may have many similar points in a different image, which leads to ambiguity of feature correspondence [75].

New video sequence segmenting method for objects supervised. The user entry object outline is considered to be a video object in the proposed method. The model included the segmentation of the area and the motion estimation of the object in moving object tracking. The active contour model is also used [76]. The backward region-based classification video object tracking system. Their system comprises five phases, region pre-processing, region extraction, regionally-based motion estimation, area classification, and regional post-processing [77].

A combination of morphological segmentation tools and human support can be used to locate a semantic video object boundary. Motion estimates, video object compensation, and iframes border information are taken in the remaining frames to identify other video objects [78]. The object partition is initialized in the initial frame can the object tracking algorithm avoid segmentation. The tracking process is carried out with object limit forecast using block motion vectors and then updating the object contour by occlusion/discussion detection method. They used an adaptive block-based approach to estimate the motion between frames. Changes to the algorithm for dis-occlusion detection help to develop algorithms for occlusion detection by considering the duality principle [79].

Descriptors are derived from regions for segmentation and tracking. Partitioning an image into a series yields the image's homogeneous regions. As a result, the problem of object extraction shifts from pixel-based to database-based analysis. Two trackers are essentially composed of an object extraction algorithm. The pixel-wise tracker retrieves an object using the Adaboost-based global color selection function. The region-specific tracker is done at the start to regionalize each frame K-means clustering. The region tracking is performed using a two-way labeling system [80].

A backdrop image updating approach is utilized to ensure accurate object detection in a confined setting. The filter has been used to create a robust object tracking framework under challenging situations and considerably enhance the accuracy of estimates for complicated tracking challenges [81].

Automatic background modeling detection and tracking of moving objects. Instead of geometrical limits, their proposed region level-set approach was employed to detect and follow motion via statistics on image intensity within each subset. Background modeling is completed before turning to object segmentation and tracking [82].

A generic object tracking and segmentation region-based particle filter. Its approach combines a particle filter based on color and a particular filter based on region. The program reliably tracks objects and delivers a precise segmentation during the sequence. Particle filters use Multi-hypotheses to monitor things [83]. A robust 3D tracking model can extract independent item motion paths in an uncontrolled environment. Two new algorithms, including motion segmentation and Mean Shift tracking approaches based in the region, have been developed. A Kalman filter is used to integrate their tracking results from both algorithms [84].

8 Conclusion

This paper gives a literature classification and a quick survey of related subjects on visual object tracking approaches. The components of the object recognition system are made up of a series of phases that begin with feature detection and continue with feature extraction to locate highly correlated features before constructing the hypothesis system to recognize the object. Points, Geometrical, Silhouette, Articulated, and Skeletal, are the five kinds of Object Representation Models. There are three types of tracking techniques: contour, region, and function. With rich theoretical details of the tracking algorithms and bibliographic contents, we intend to contribute to research on object tracking in images and promote future studies.

Acknowledgments. This research was supported by Princess Sumaya University for Technology (PSUT) and Researchers Supporting Program (TUMA-Project-2021-14), AlMaarefa University.

Conflict of Interest. The authors declare no conflict of interest.

References

1. Xuan, S., et al.: Siamese networks with distractor-reduction method for long-term visual object tracking. Pattern Recogn. **112**, 107698 (2021)

2. Jiang, M., et al.: High speed long-term visual object tracking algorithm for real robot systems. Neurocomputing **434**, 268–284 (2021)
3. Mehmood, K., et al.: Context-aware and occlusion handling mechanism for online visual object tracking. Electronics **10**, 43 (2021)
4. Wang, Y., Ma, J.: Visual object tracking using surface fitting for scale and rotation estimation. KSII Trans. Internet Inf. Syst. **15** (2021)
5. Wu, J., et al.: Towards accurate estimation for visual object tracking with multi-hierarchy feature aggregation. Neurocomputing **451**, 252–264 (2021)
6. Rinnert, P., Nieder, A.: Neural code of motor planning and execution during goal-directed movements in crows. J. Neurosci. **41**, 4060–4072 (2021)
7. Clarence, A., et al.: Unscripted retargeting: reach prediction for haptic retargeting in virtual reality. In: 2021 IEEE Virtual Reality and 3D User Interfaces (VR), pp. 150–159 (2021)
8. Zhao, H., et al.: Deep mutual learning for visual object tracking. Pattern Recogn. **112**, 107796 (2021)
9. Guo, Q., et al.: Exploring the effects of blur and deblurring to visual object tracking. IEEE Trans. Image Process. **30**, 1812–1824 (2021)
10. Jia, S., et al.: IoU attack: towards temporally coherent black-box adversarial attack for visual object tracking. In: Proceedings of the IEEE/CVF Conference on Computer Vision and Pattern Recognition, pp. 6709–6718 (2021)
11. Zhu, J., Zhang, G., Zhou, S., Li, K.: Relation-aware Siamese region proposal network for visual object tracking. Multimedia Tools Appl. **80**(10), 15469–15485 (2021). https://doi.org/10.1007/s11042-021-10574-z
12. Chen, Y., Wang, J., Xia, R., Zhang, Q., Cao, Z., Yang, K.: The visual object tracking algorithm research based on adaptive combination kernel. J. Ambient. Intell. Humaniz. Comput. **10**(12), 4855–4867 (2019). https://doi.org/10.1007/s12652-018-01171-4
13. Lee, S.-H., et al.: Learning discriminative appearance models for online multi-object tracking with appearance discriminability measures. IEEE Access **6**, 67316–67328 (2018)
14. He, M., et al.: Fast online multi-pedestrian tracking via integrating motion model and deep appearance model. IEEE Access **7**, 89475–89486 (2019)
15. Franzoni, V., et al.: Emotional machines: the next revolution. In: Web Intelligence, pp. 1–7 (2019)
16. Li, S., Yeung, D.-Y.: Visual object tracking for unmanned aerial vehicles: a benchmark and new motion models. In: Thirty-First AAAI Conference on Artificial Intelligence (2017)
17. Cakir, S., Cetin, A.E.: Visual object tracking using Fourier domain phase information. Signal Image Video Process. 1–8 (2021)
18. Yuan, D., Zhang, X., Liu, J., Li, D.: A multiple feature fused model for visual object tracking via correlation filters. Multimedia Tools Appl. **78**(19), 27271–27290 (2019). https://doi.org/10.1007/s11042-019-07828-2
19. Chowdhury, P.R., et al.: Brain Inspired Object Recognition System. arXiv preprint arXiv:2105.07237 (2021)
20. Dawod, M., Hanna, S.: BIM-assisted object recognition for the on-site autonomous robotic assembly of discrete structures. Constr. Robot. **3**(1–4), 69–81 (2019). https://doi.org/10.1007/s41693-019-00021-9
21. Poza-Lujan, J.-L., et al.: Distributed architecture to integrate sensor information: object recognition for smart cities. Sensors **20**, 112 (2020)
22. Girish, S., et al.: The lottery ticket hypothesis for object recognition. In: Proceedings of the IEEE/CVF Conference on Computer Vision and Pattern Recognition, pp. 762–771 (2021)
23. Fu, J., et al.: A multi-hypothesis approach to pose ambiguity in object-based SLAM. arXiv preprint arXiv:2108.01225 (2021)

24. Kutschbach, T., et al.: Sequential sensor fusion combining probability hypothesis density and kernelized correlation filters for multi-object tracking in video data. In: 2017 14th IEEE International Conference on Advanced Video and Signal Based Surveillance (AVSS), pp. 1–5 (2017)

25. Wang, Q., et al.: HypoML: visual analysis for hypothesis-based evaluation of machine learning models. IEEE Trans. Visual Comput. Graphics **27**, 1417–1426 (2020)

26. Long, L., et al.: Object-level representation learning for few-shot image classification. arXiv preprint arXiv:1805.10777 (2018)

27. Hubert, C.: More on the model: building on the ruins of representation. Archit. Des. **91**, 14–21 (2021)

28. Li, Z., et al.: Self-guided adaptation: progressive representation alignment for domain adaptive object detection. arXiv preprint arXiv:2003.08777 (2020)

29. Huang, J.: Auto-attentional mechanism in multi-domain convolutional neural networks for improving object tracking. Int. J. Intell. Comput. Cybern. (2021)

30. Bekiroglu, Y., et al.: Learning tactile characterizations of object-and pose-specific grasps. In: 2011 IEEE/RSJ International Conference on Intelligent Robots and Systems, pp. 1554–1560 (2011)

31. La Porta, F., et al.: Unified Balance Scale: an activity-based, bed to community, and aetiology-independent measure of balance calibrated with Rasch analysis. J. Rehabil. Med. **43**, 435–444 (2011)

32. Du, B., et al.: A discriminative manifold learning based dimension reduction method for hyperspectral classification. Int. J. Fuzzy Syst. **14**, 272–277 (2012)

33. Hsiao, E., Hebert, M.: Occlusion reasoning for object detection under arbitrary viewpoint. IEEE Trans. Pattern Anal. Mach. Intell. **36**, 1803–1815 (2014)

34. Bajcsy, R.: Three-dimensional object representation. In: Kittler, J., Fu, K.S., Pau, LF. (eds) Pattern Recognition Theory and Applications, pp. 283–295. Springer, New York (1982). https://doi.org/10.1007/978-94-009-7772-3_17

35. Moghaddam, B., Pentland, A.: Probabilistic visual learning for object representation. IEEE Trans. Pattern Anal. Mach. Intell. **19**, 696–710 (1997)

36. Laurentini, A.: The visual hull concept for Silhouette-based image understanding. IEEE Trans. Pattern Anal. Mach. Intell. **16**, 150–162 (1994)

37. Ashok, V., Ganapathy, D.: A geometrical method to classify face forms. J. Oral Biol. Craniofac. Res. **9**, 232–235 (2019)

38. Wagemans, J., et al.: Identification of everyday objects on the basis of Silhouette and outline versions. Perception **37**, 207–244 (2008)

39. Sapp, B., et al.: Cascaded models for articulated pose estimation. In: Daniilidis, K., Maragos, P., Paragios, N. (eds.) Computer Vision – ECCV 2010. LNCS, vol. 6312, pp. 406–420. Springer, Heidelberg (2010). https://doi.org/10.1007/978-3-642-15552-9_30

40. Geldof, A.A.: Models for cancer skeletal metastasis: a reappraisal of Batson's plexus. Anticancer Res. **17**, 1535–1539 (1997)

41. Jarrett, K., et al.: What is the best multi-stage architecture for object recognition? In: 2009 IEEE 12th International Conference on Computer Vision, pp. 2146–2153 (2009)

42. Xu, G., Zhang, Z.: Epipolar Geometry in Stereo, Motion and Object Recognition: A Unified Approach, vol. 6. Springer, New York (2013). https://doi.org/10.1007/978-94-015-8668-9

43. Riesenhuber, M., Poggio, T.: Models of object recognition. Nat. Neurosci. **3**, 1199–1204 (2000)

44. Grasselli, G., et al.: Quantitative three-dimensional description of a rough surface and parameter evolution with shearing. Int. J. Rock Mech. Min. Sci. **39**, 789–800 (2002)

45. Dutton, Z., et al.: Attaining the quantum limit of superresolution in imaging an object's length via predetection spatial-mode sorting. Phys. Rev. A **99**, 033847 (2019)

46. Betke, M., Makris, N.C.: Information-conserving object recognition. In: Sixth International Conference on Computer Vision (IEEE Cat. No. 98CH36271), pp. 145–152 (1998)
47. Barrett, H.H., et al.: Objective assessment of image quality. II. Fisher information, Fourier crosstalk, and figures of merit for task performance. JOSA A **12**, 834–852 (1995)
48. Betke, M., Makris, N.C.: Recognition, resolution, and complexity of objects subject to affine transformations. Int. J. Comput. Vision **44**, 5–40 (2001)
49. Tian, T., et al.: Cramer-Rao bounds of localization estimation for integrated radar and communication system. IEEE Access **8**, 105852–105863 (2020)
50. Zheng, Y., et al.: A new precision evaluation method for signals of opportunity based on Cramer-Rao lower bound in finite error. In: 2019 Chinese Control Conference (CCC), pp. 3934–3939 (2019)
51. Lee, S., et al.: Estimation error bound of battery electrode parameters with limited data window. IEEE Trans. Industr. Inf. **16**, 3376–3386 (2019)
52. Li, X., Yang, F., Cheng, H., Liu, W., Shen, D.: Contour knowledge transfer for salient object detection. In: Ferrari, V., Hebert, M., Sminchisescu, C., Weiss, Y. (eds.) ECCV 2018. LNCS, vol. 11219, pp. 370–385. Springer, Cham (2018). https://doi.org/10.1007/978-3-030-01267-0_22
53. Gong, X.-Y., et al.: An overview of contour detection approaches. Int. J. Autom. Comput. **15**, 656–672 (2018)
54. Philbrick, K.A., et al.: RIL-contour: a medical imaging dataset annotation tool for and with deep learning. J. Digit. Imaging **32**, 571–581 (2019)
55. Dai, Y., et al.: Trajectory tracking control for seafloor tracked vehicle by adaptive neural-fuzzy inference system algorithm. Int. J. Comput. Commun. Control **13**, 465–476 (2018)
56. Guan, W., et al.: Visible light dynamic positioning method using improved Camshift-Kalman algorithm. IEEE Photonics J. **11**, 1–22 (2019)
57. Hu, B., Niebur, E.: A recurrent neural model for proto-object based contour integration and figure-ground segregation. J. Comput. Neurosci. **43**(3), 227–242 (2017). https://doi.org/10.1007/s10827-017-0659-3
58. Qin, J., et al.: An encrypted image retrieval method based on Harris corner optimization and LSH in cloud computing. IEEE Access **7**, 24626–24633 (2019)
59. Cheng, J., et al.: Hidden Markov model-based nonfragile state estimation of switched neural network with probabilistic quantized outputs. IEEE Trans. Cybern. **50**, 1900–1909 (2019)
60. Cai, D., et al.: A moving target detecting and tracking system based on DSP. In: 2017 International Conference on Optical Instruments and Technology: Optoelectronic Imaging/Spectroscopy and Signal Processing Technology, p. 106200Z (2018)
61. Dimeas, F., Doulgeri, Z.: Progressive automation of periodic tasks on planar surfaces of unknown pose with hybrid force/position control. In: 2020 IEEE/RSJ International Conference on Intelligent Robots and Systems (IROS), pp. 5246–5252 (2020)
62. Zong, B., et al.: Deep autoencoding Gaussian mixture model for unsupervised anomaly detection. In: International Conference on Learning Representations (2018)
63. Lee, H., Kim, D.: Salient region-based online object tracking. In: 2018 IEEE Winter Conference on Applications of Computer Vision (WACV), pp. 1170–1177 (2018)
64. Yu, T.T., War, N.: Condensed object representation with corner HOG features for object classification in outdoor scenes. In: 2017 18th IEEE/ACIS International Conference on Software Engineering, Artificial Intelligence, Networking and Parallel/Distributed Computing (SNPD), pp. 77–82 (2017)
65. Wang, X., et al.: Aerial infrared object tracking via an improved long-term correlation filter with optical flow estimation and SURF matching. Infrared Phys. Technol. **116**, 103790 (2021)
66. Sadegh, A.M., Worek, W.M.: Marks' Standard Handbook for Mechanical Engineers: McGraw-Hill Education (2018)

67. Chhabra, P., Garg, N.K., Kumar, M.: Content-based image retrieval system using ORB and SIFT features. Neural Comput. Appl. **32**(7), 2725–2733 (2018). https://doi.org/10.1007/s00 521-018-3677-9

68. Amaya, M., et al.: Adaptive sequential Monte Carlo for posterior inference and model selection among complex geological priors. Geophys. J. Int. **226**, 1220–1238 (2021)

69. Bae, S.-H., Yoon, K.-J.: Confidence-based data association and discriminative deep appearance learning for robust online multi-object tracking. IEEE Trans. Pattern Anal. Mach. Intell. **40**, 595–610 (2017)

70. Mbakop, S., et al.: Inverse dynamics model-based shape control of soft continuum finger robot using parametric curve. IEEE Robot. Autom. Lett. **6**, 8053–8060 (2021)

71. Liu, F., et al.: Robust visual tracking revisited: From correlation filter to template matching. IEEE Trans. Image Process. **27**, 2777–2790 (2018)

72. Kaskman, R., et al.: HomebrewedDB: RGB-D dataset for 6D pose estimation of 3D objects. In: Proceedings of the IEEE/CVF International Conference on Computer Vision Workshops (2019)

73. Xu, J., et al.: Bilevel distance metric learning for robust image recognition. Adv. Neural. Inf. Process. Syst. **31**, 4198–4207 (2018)

74. Cabeza de Vaca, I., et al.: Enhanced Monte Carlo methods for modeling proteins including computation of absolute free energies of binding. J. Chem. Theory Comput. **14**, 3279–3288 (2018)

75. Guler, Z., et al.: A new object tracking framework for interest point based feature extraction algorithms. Elektronika ir Elektrotechnika **26**, 63–71 (2020)

76. Pareek, A., et al.: A robust surf-based online human tracking algorithm using adaptive object model. In: Proceedings of International Conference on Artificial Intelligence and Applications, pp. 543–551 (2021)

77. Rejeesh, M.: Interest point based face recognition using adaptive neuro fuzzy inference system. Multimedia Tools Appl. **78**, 22691–22710 (2019)

78. Kann, K., et al.: Fortification of neural morphological segmentation models for polysynthetic minimal-resource languages. arXiv preprint arXiv:1804.06024 (2018)

79. Noyel, G., et al.: Morphological segmentation of hyperspectral images. arXiv preprint arXiv: 2010.00853 (2020)

80. Yang, X., et al.: A face detection method based on skin color model and improved AdaBoost algorithm. Traitement du Signal, vol. 37 (2020)

81. Hameed, K., et al.: A sample weight and AdaBoost CNN-based coarse to fine classification of fruit and vegetables at a supermarket self-checkout. Appl. Sci. **10**, 8667 (2020)

82. Sun, Y., et al.: Active perception for foreground segmentation: an RGB-D data-based background modeling method. IEEE Trans. Autom. Sci. Eng. **16**, 1596–1609 (2019)

83. Voigtlaender, P., et al.: MOTS: multi-object tracking and segmentation. In: Proceedings of the IEEE/CVF Conference on Computer Vision and Pattern Recognition, pp. 7942–7951 (2019)

84. Gunjal, P.R., et al.: Moving object tracking using Kalman filter. In: 2018 International Conference on Advances in Communication and Computing Technology (ICACCT), pp. 544–547 (2018)

The Application of Machine Learning on Concrete Samples

Aybike Özyüksel Çiftçioğlu$^{(\boxtimes)}$ (iD)

Department of Civil Engineering, Faculty of Engineering, Manisa Celal Bayar University, Manisa, Turkey
`aybike.ozyuksel@cbu.edu.tr`

Abstract. Machine learning is a branch of artificial intelligence that helps computers to learn from data and make predictions based on patterns identified in big data. The purpose of this study is to explore the applicability of machine learning models in classifying the compressive strength of concrete specimens with different types of ingredients. Despite the investigations in the literature about estimating concrete density, there is no relevant study on categorizing compressive strength. To address this gap, in this study, three machine learning classification algorithms (Decision Tree, Naive Bayes Classifier, and K-Nearest Neighbors) are employed to classify concrete samples. The performance of each algorithm is evaluated and compared. The results show that the Decision Tree classifier provides the best performance with an average precision and recall of 99%, f1-score of 0.99, and accuracy of 99%. Moreover, the study provides insights into the application of ML algorithms in a real-world dataset. This study demonstrates that machine learning is a powerful tool that can be used to improve the accuracy of concrete strength classification.

Keywords: Classification · Concrete · Decision Tree Algorithm · Machine Learning · Naïve Bayes Algorithm

1 Introduction

As the global economy continues to accelerate and cities continue to expand, it is necessary to design and build structures that can safely sustain the load. This involves designing, constructing, and maintaining buildings that are capable of withstanding seismic activity as well as other conditions without compromising structural integrity. To accomplish this, engineers need a robust understanding of how their designs will perform in real-world scenarios. In the field of civil engineering, this involves using compressive strength analysis to determine the structural capabilities of buildings, roads, or bridges. Engineers use compressive strength analysis because it directly relates structural performance to material properties, making it easy to compare one material against another [1, 12, 17].

Concrete is a composite material consisting of aggregate, cement, and water. Concrete compressive strength is the amount of force a sample of concrete can take before

A. Mirzazadeh et al. (Eds.): SEMIT 2022, CCIS 1809, pp. 80–90, 2023.
https://doi.org/10.1007/978-3-031-40398-9_5

breaking under pressure. It is a crucial test performed on any batch of concrete to determine its suitability for use in a project and is a vital component of ensuring the longevity and integrity of the structure. Compressive strength testing also helps to ensure that concrete performs as intended. Concrete compressive strength is a very important property for engineers to consider when designing structures. Engineers use compressive strength values to determine how much force can be safely applied to the structure, allowing designers to choose the right type of construction that will withstand the most stress [4, 22, 24, 33].

Artificial intelligence (AI) is revolutionizing our world. AI has become so prevalent that it is difficult to imagine a world where computers are not capable of solving complex problems. As the world becomes more complex and the demand for new and innovative products increases, the need for AI in research is becoming more urgent. Researchers are under pressure to find new solutions to old problems and to create new products that meet the needs of a rapidly changing world. AI helps researchers to meet these challenges by providing new ways of understanding and analyzing data, by providing new ways of creative problem solving, and by helping to create new and innovative products. AI, or more specifically, machine learning, has been at the center of many of these advancements [9, 16, 23]. Machine learning (ML) is a branch of artificial intelligence that helps computers to learn from data and make predictions based on patterns identified in big data. It is used in many applications today such as signal processing, speech recognition, search engines, and financial modeling. Using ML, engineers can train their models without needing human experts to review and test each individual dataset [10, 11, 19, 20, 27, 29].

ML is a broad term that describes the field of data analytics that seeks to automate tasks by analyzing data and making predictions about future outcomes. There are a number of different types of ML algorithms, including regression, clustering, and classification [15, 25, 26]. Regression algorithms are used to predict continuous values, such as prices or temperatures. In contrast, clustering algorithms are used to group data points together, and classification algorithms are used to assign labels to data points. Classification algorithms are algorithms that can be used to separate objects into categories. The purpose of a classification algorithm is to take an input (such as a set of data points) and output a class label for each data point. The class label is simply a name that represents the category that the data point belongs to. ML algorithms can be broadly broken down into two categories. A category of ML algorithms is supervised learning, where the algorithm receives a set of input data and produces a set of outputs. The other category of ML algorithms is unsupervised learning, where the algorithm receives a set of input data but does not produce any outputs. Instead, the algorithm simply generates a set of observations that are then used as input to another algorithm (e.g., using clustering to classify objects into different classes) [14].

In general, supervised learning is more accurate than unsupervised learning because it relies on human expertise to make judgments about whether particular classes exist in the data. However, supervised learning requires careful preprocessing of the data before it can be used. This preprocessing step can be time-consuming and difficult, particularly if the data is large and complex. In unsupervised learning, the input data is unlabeled and the output data is labeled. These algorithms employ clustering and dimensionality reduction techniques to derive insights from the raw data. The goal of unsupervised learning is to find patterns in the data that are not explicitly given. Unsupervised learning can be used to create a model, which can be used for classification or prediction [18].

The strength of concrete is a measure of how much force the concrete can resist before it breaks or deforms [21]. The higher the strength, the more resistant to cracking the concrete. In general, strength is measured by either compression or shear strength. Compression strength is basically how much pressure a material can resist before it starts to crack. Strength depends on both concrete ingredients and construction techniques. A well-made concrete mix will usually be stronger than one that is not properly mixed or made.

Three categories can be used to classify concrete: normal strength, low strength, and high strength. Low-strength concrete refers to concrete that has a compressive strength of less than 25 Mpa. It is a type of concrete with less cement content than normal, high-strength concrete. It is often used in projects that require a temporary solution, like construction sites or sidewalks. Low-strength concrete has some drawbacks - it can't be used for load-bearing structures like buildings or bridges because it doesn't have enough strength to support them.

Normal-strength concrete is the most common type. It has an average compressive strength of 25 to 50 Mpa and is also known as "Standard-Strength" concrete. This category of concrete is commonly used for residential, commercial, and industrial applications. Normal-strength concrete can also be used for foundations and other common building purposes. Extremely heavy loads are not recommended for normal-strength concrete because it may not have enough strength to hold up under the additional weight.

High-strength concrete is a type of concrete that has a compressive strength of 50 MPa or higher. This means that high-strength concrete can support more weight than concrete made with standard strengths [28]. High-strength concrete is produced using different methods depending on the desired level of strength. For example, normal-strength concrete can be strengthened by adding high-strength aggregates (rock or gravel) to the mix. Alternatively, strong mixes can be produced using additives such as fly ash or silica fume, which are produced from coal or silica sand. Other factors that affect the strength of a high-strength concrete mix include the amount of coarse aggregate used, the type of cement, and how carefully it is mixed together. High-strength concrete is most commonly used in building foundations and retaining walls, where it is required to support heavy weights such as large buildings and bridges. It is also used in roads and bridges, where its properties are needed to resist loading on the surface of the material, and in tunnels, where it is required to withstand water pressure [7].

There are various types of research on the prediction of concrete compressive strength. Gao et al. [6] studied the concrete column compressive strength prediction. They demonstrated that recycled coarse aggregate had a negligible impact on the performance of the concrete column, and steel fibers and stirrups could increase the strength and ductility of the column. They developed a model to forecast the load capacity of an axially loaded column, and it provided good agreement with the experimental findings.

Rajakarunakaran et al. [24] used machine learning-based regression models to forecast the compressive strength of self-compacting concrete. They employed linear regression, Lasso regression, ridge regression, multi-layer perceptron regression, decision tree regression, and random forest regression. They stated that the Random Forest model safely predicts the compressive strength of concrete.

Li et al. [13] employed artificial neural networks to estimate the local compression capacity for stirrups-confined concrete. They validated the ANN model using experimental data and existing models. In addition, they asserted that for determining the local compression capacity of stirrups-confined concrete, the ANN technique was both highly applicable and accurate.

On concrete-filled steel tube columns, Ci et al. [3] provide experimental and computational research. The test results demonstrate that the CFDST column outperforms existing composite columns in terms of strength and ductility. Based on the outcomes of the tests, they suggested a new reduction factor for estimating the ultimate strengths of the columns. They discovered that by implementing the newly proposed reduction factor and design approach, the design predictions are enhanced and generate accurate estimates for concrete-filled steel tube columns.

Although there are investigations in the literature on estimating concrete compressive strength, there is no relevant study on compressive strength classification. To fill this gap, in this study, three ML classification algorithms are used to classify the compressive strength of concrete samples. The performance of each algorithm is evaluated and compared.

The main contributions are summarized as follows:

1) Novel three ML algorithms are employed to classify the compressive strength of concrete as an early prediction.

2) The proposed ML-based classification model can be used to assess the strength of concrete in existing structures.

3) The Decision Tree classification model achieves 99% accuracy.

2 Database

The 1030 concrete sample test results collected from the literature [32] are used to classify the compressive strength of this research. Cement (C), blast furnace slag (BFS), fly ash (F.Ash), water (W), superplasticizer (S), coarse aggregate (C.Agg), fine aggregate (F.Agg), age (A) and compression strength (CS) are the input variables, while the class number (CS) is the output. A low-strength concrete has a compressive strength of less than 25 Mpa, normal-strength concrete has a compressive strength between 25 and 50 Mpa, and high-strength concrete has a compressive strength of more than 50 Mpa. Low-strength concrete is classified as Class 1, normal-strength concrete is classified as Class 2, and high-strength concrete is classified as Class 3. The descriptive statistics on the variables are listed in Table 1.

A visual representation of the colormap correlation matrix is provided in Fig. 1. The colormap correlation matrix of the variables reveals the inter indicators' relationships in the dataset. Dark blue is associated with a strong positive correlation, whereas yellow indicates a strong negative correlation. The correlation matrix reveals that cement, superplasticizer, and age are strongly correlated with compressive strength. In addition,

84   A. Ö. Çiftçioğlu

Table 1. Statistics of the dataset.

	C	BFS	F.Ash	W	S	C.Agg	F.Agg	A	CS
Minimum	102.00	0.00	0.00	121.75	0.00	801.00	594.00	1.00	2.33
Maximum	540.00	359.40	200.10	247.00	32.20	1145.00	992.60	365.00	82.60
Average	281.17	73.90	54.19	181.57	6.20	972.92	773.58	45.66	35.82
Std	104.46	86.24	63.97	21.35	5.97	77.72	80.14	63.14	16.70

water has a negative correlation with compressive strength. This is in line with the common knowledge that increasing cement, superplasticizer, and age will improve concrete compressive strength while increasing water will reduce it.

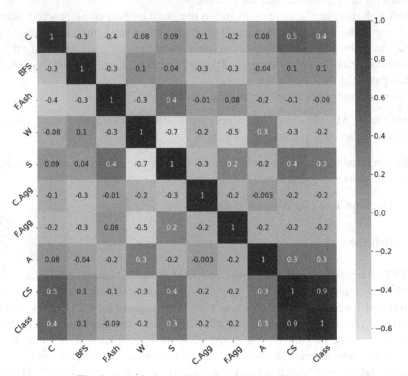

Fig. 1. Correlation matrix of variables in the dataset

Figure 2 shows a sample representation of the concrete compressive strength test. Compressive strength is the force that concrete can bear without breaking apart or giving way. The test is carried out by applying a load to the specimen and measuring the deformation of the specimen.

Fig. 2. Representation of concrete compressive strength test [8].

3 Methodology

Some of the most widely used algorithms are Decision Tree, Naive Bayes, and K-Nearest Neighbors. 1) Decision Tree is a simple, intuitive algorithm with a wide range of applicability. 2) Naive Bayes is an algorithm that can be used for classification and regression problems.3) K-Nearest Neighbors uses the K nearest neighbors to predict the class of an input value (based on their similarity). Based on this study and how well they fit the use cases being investigated, these three algorithms are chosen.

3.1 Decision Tree Classification Model

A decision tree is a classification model [30] that is used to analyze large datasets in a way that is both intuitive and efficient. The basic idea behind a decision tree is that of a branching structure in which each node represents an observation in the dataset. At each node, there is a set of possible classifications that could be made based on the features present in the data. This process is repeated until every possible classification has been considered. The resulting set of classifications can then be used to group observations into buckets for further analysis or prediction.

There are several methods for creating decision trees. The most common method is to use iterative re-weighting with the random splitting of existing instances. This approach can create numerous split clusters that can be used for further analysis. Another method is to create a random forest, which takes advantage of the enormous computational power available with modern computers to build an ensemble of decision trees using many different initializations.

A decision tree can be used to make predictions or classify new instances in many ways. For example, it can be used to create predicted labels for new instances, which allows for clustering and dimensionality reduction on new unseen data sets. A decision tree can also be used to fit models directly onto existing data sets, allowing for easy interpretation and visualization of predictions from learning algorithms. It works by splitting the data into training and test sets, then fitting a model to the training set. The model is then tested on the test set to see how well it performs. The model can be made to fit any number of scenarios by changing the values in the decision tree.

3.2 Naive Bayes Classification Model

In ML, the Naive Bayes classification (NBC) model is a Bayesian statistical technique that is used to predict the likelihood of two or more classes based on the observed data [31]. The basic approach used in Bayesian classification involves dividing your dataset into two parts: a training set and a test set. The NBC model assumes that all features are independent and identically distributed, with each feature representing a class variable. When using the NBC model, probability estimates for each feature are combined using the Bayes theorem. In its basic form, the NBC takes as input a set of observed variables and produces as output a predicted probability for each variable. This predicted probability may then be used to make a decision about whether or not the data support a specific hypothesis [2].

3.3 K-Nearest Neighbors Classification Model

The K-Nearest Neighbors (KNN) classification model [5] is a popular machine-learning technique that classifies data points into different categories using k nearest neighbors. The idea behind this approach is to predict a category given a set of classes, where k represents the number of classes. In this approach, a list of training examples is used to find the K nearest neighbors that have the same class label. Then, using these examples and their labels, the model predicts the label for new examples. It is a supervised learning technique and can be used for both categorical and continuous data. KNN classifiers use distance metrics, such as Euclidean distances, to identify possible candidates for the target category. This can be important for categorizing large data sets with many different values. The accuracy of KNN depends on how well it can identify nearby points, as well as its ability to calculate distance and find local minima. KNN is applicable to both classification and regression problems and can be used for tasks such as clustering, image segmentation, and anomaly detection.

4   Results and Discussion

In this study, the utility of machine learning for classifying the compressive strength of concrete specimens with different types of ingredients is investigated. Three ML classification models (DTC, NBC, and KNN) are used to classify the compressive strength of concrete samples. The standard scaler is implemented in all ML models to put the variables into the same range. The classifiers are then trained on 780 (75%) samples, and the remaining 260 (25%) samples are employed for validation. The evaluation metrics used to assess the performance of the classification models are accuracy, precision, recall, and f1-score. The accuracy is the percentage of observations that were correctly classified by the algorithm as shown in Eq. 1.

$$Accuracy = \frac{TruePositive + TrueNegative}{TruePositive + FalsePositive + TrueNegative + FalseNegative} \tag{1}$$

Precision is the ratio of correct predictions to total predictions as indicated in Eq. 2.

$$Precision = \frac{TruePositive}{TruePositive + FalsePositive} \tag{2}$$

The recall is the ratio of correct predictions to all possible observations as shown in Eq. 3.

$$Recall = \frac{TruePositive}{TruePositive + FalseNegative} \tag{3}$$

The harmonic mean of precision and recall is the f1-score as indicated in Eq. 4.

$$F1 - score = 2 * \frac{precision * recall}{precision + recall} \tag{4}$$

Table 2 shows the classification reports for each ML model. From the table, DTC has the highest accuracy at 99% followed by NBC at 90%. KNN has the lowest accuracy at 84%. Also from the table, the DTC and NBC models have similar performance when compared to each other and both are better than KNN. Moreover, DTC provided the best performance with average precision and recall of 99%, and an f1-score of 0.99. The findings of this study demonstrated that the compressive strength of concrete samples can be predicted with high accuracy—nearly 100%—using machine learning.

Table 2. Classification reports for ML classification models

	DTC				NBC				KNN	
	1	2	3	1	2	3	1	2	3
precision	1.00	0.99	1.00	0.87	0.93	0.88	0.86	0.86	0.78
recall	0.98	1.00	1.00	0.94	0.90	0.88	0.79	0.86	0.86
f1-score	0.99	1.00	1.00	0.90	0.91	0.88	0.82	0.86	0.82
accuracy		0.99			0.90			0.84	

The confusion matrices for each ML classification model are shown in Fig. 3. DTC has a low amount of misclassified samples in Class 2, with only one incorrect prediction. It makes no incorrect predictions in Classes 1 and 3. NBC has high accuracy when it comes to predicting the high compressive strength of concrete. NBC makes has a low amount of incorrect predictions in all classes, especially class 3, with only six incorrect predictions. KNN makes many wrong predictions in all classes, especially Class 2 with 20 incorrect predictions, which means that it is not very reliable.

When comparing the effectiveness of the techniques, it is evident that DTC is the most effective model, even though NBC performing well. The KNN method is the least effective for this dataset in terms of both classification report and confusion matrices. Moreover, DTC achieves 100% precision, recall, and f1-score ratings in at least two classes. The precision, recall, and f1-score metrics of the NBC technique are generally between 85% and 95%. The precision and recall metrics of the KNN method are less than 80% for classes 3 and 1, respectively.

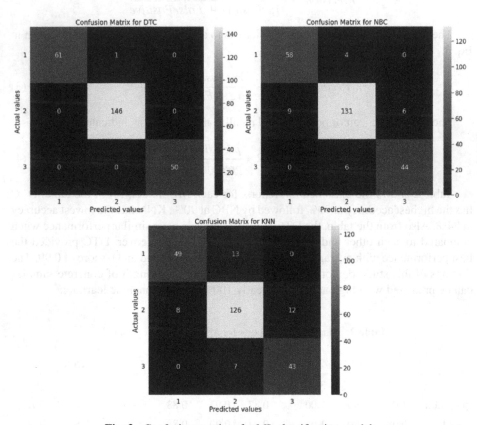

Fig. 3. Confusion matrices for ML classification models

5 Conclusions

The research provides valuable insights into the use of ML for concrete compressive strength classification. Due to the high cost of testing and repair of concrete structures, it is desirable to have a concrete strength prediction method available in real-time. Structural simulations based on empirical models can provide insight into the strength of concrete. However, these simulations are dependent on the assumptions made about the response of concrete to deformation. The purpose of this study is to explore the applicability of ML models in classifying concrete specimens with different ingredients. The compressive strength of any concrete sample, for which the quantity of components is known, can be determined using the ML model developed as part of this study, without the need for costly and time-consuming tests. This classification can help predict the quality of concrete construction and make better decisions when designing, constructing, and repairing concrete structures. Moreover, the study provides insights into the application of ML algorithms in a real-world dataset and highlights the importance of feature engineering in ML. The DTC model is found to be the most accurate, with an accuracy of 99%. The NBC and KNN models are also found to be accurate, with accuracies of 90% and 84%, respectively. This study demonstrates that ML is a powerful tool that can be used to improve the accuracy of concrete compressive strength classification. ML can be also applied to estimate the compressive strength of other concrete structures such as beams, columns, piers, and walls. Some drawbacks of the presented study that can be addressed in future research include: 1) the need to investigate new classification algorithms, 2) the examination of additional explainability metrics, and 3) studying other characteristics of concrete. .

References

1. Balaghi, S., Naseralavi, S.S., Khojastehfar, E.: Optimal design of structures under earthquake loads using basic modal displacements method enhanced by fuzzy c-means clustering. Structures. **32**, 778–791 (2021)
2. Chen, S., Webb, G.I., Liu, L., Ma, X.: A novel selective naïve Bayes algorithm. Knowledge-Based Syst. **192**, 105361 (2020)
3. Ci, J., Ahmed, M., Jia, H., Chen, S., Zhou, D., Hou, L.: Testing and strength prediction of eccentrically-loaded circular concrete-filled double steel tubular stub-columns. J. Constr. Steel Res. **186**, 106881 (2021)
4. Dabiri, H., Rahimzadeh, K., Kheyroddin, A.: A comparison of machine learning- and regression-based models for predicting ductility ratio of RC beam-column joints. Structures. **37**, 69–81 (2022)
5. Fix, E., Hodges, J.L.: Discriminatory Analysis. Nonparametric Discrimination: Consistency Properties. Int. Stat. Rev. / Rev. Int. Stat. 57 (3), 238–247 (1989)
6. Gao, D., Li, W., Pang, Y., Huang, Y.: Behavior analysis and strength prediction of steel fiber reinforced recycled aggregate concrete column under axial compression. Constr. Build. Mater. **290**, 123278 (2021)
7. Guo, Y.B., Gao, G.F., Jing, L., Shim, V.P.W.: Response of high-strength concrete to dynamic compressive loading. Int. J. Impact Eng. **108**, 114–135 (2017)
8. Karatas, M., Gunes, A.: Engineering Properties of Self-Compacting Concrete Produced by Polypropylene and Steel Fiber. Period. Polytech. Civ. Eng 59 (2015)
9. Khalilpourazari, S., Khalilpourazary, S., Özyüksel Çiftçioğlu, A., Weber, G.-W.: Designing energy-efficient high-precision multi-pass turning processes via robust optimization and artificial intelligence. J. Intell. Manuf. **32**(6), 1621–1647 (2020). https://doi.org/10.1007/s10845-020-01648-0
10. Khalilpourazari, S., Mirzazadeh, A., Weber, G.-W., Pasandideh, S.H.R.: A robust fuzzy approach for constrained multi-product economic production quantity with imperfect items and rework process. Optimization **69**(1), 63–90 (2020)

11. Khalilpourazari, S., Naderi, B., Khalilpourazary, S.: Multi-Objective Stochastic Fractal Search: a powerful algorithm for solving complex multi-objective optimization problems. Soft. Comput. **24**(4), 3037–3066 (2019). https://doi.org/10.1007/s00500-019-04080-6
12. Kwag, S., Gupta, A., Baugh, J., Kim, H.-S.: Significance of multi-hazard risk in design of buildings under earthquake and wind loads. Eng. Struct. **243**, 112623 (2021)
13. Li, S., Zheng, W., Xu, T., Wang, Y.: Artificial neural network model for predicting the local compression capacity of stirrups-confined concrete. Structures **41**, 943–956 (2022)
14. Mirjalili, S., Dong, J.: Multi-Objective Optimization using Artificial Intelligence Techniques (2020)
15. Mirjalili, S., Faris, H., Aljarah, I.: Evolutionary Machine Learning Techniques Algorithms and Applications: Algorithms and Applications (2020)
16. Moslemi, S., Mirzazadeh, A., Weber, G.-W., Sobhanallahi, M.A.: Integration of neural network and AP-NDEA model for performance evaluation of sustainable pharmaceutical supply chain. Opsearch **59**, 1–42 (2021). https://doi.org/10.1007/s12597-021-00561-1
17. Muc, A.: Design of composite structures under cyclic loads. Comput. Struct. **76**(1), 211–218 (2000)
18. Naser, M., Alavi, A.: Insights into Performance Fitness and Error Metrics for Machine Learning. Under Rev. (2020)
19. Naser, M.Z.: AI-based cognitive framework for evaluating response of concrete structures in extreme conditions. Eng. Appl. Artif. Intell. **81**, 437–449 (2019)
20. Naser, M.Z.: Mechanistically informed machine learning and artificial intelligence in fire engineering and sciences. Fire Technol. **57**(6), 2741–2784 (2021). https://doi.org/10.1007/s10694-020-01069-8
21. Naser, M.Z.: Observational Analysis of Fire-Induced Spalling of Concrete through Ensemble Machine Learning and Surrogate Modeling. J. Mater. Civ. Eng. 33 (1), (2021)
22. Naser, M.Z., Kodur, V., Thai, H.-T., Hawileh, R., Abdalla, J., Degtyarev, V.: V: StructuresNet and FireNet: Benchmarking databases and machine learning algorithms in structural and fire engineering domains. J. Build. Eng. **44**, 102977 (2021)
23. Özyüksel Çiftçioğlu, A., Naser, M.Z.: Hiding in plain sight: What can interpretable unsupervised machine learning and clustering analysis tell us about the fire behavior of reinforced concrete columns? Structures. **40**(April), 920–935 (2022)
24. Rajakarunakaran, S.A., et al.: Prediction of strength and analysis in self-compacting concrete using machine learning based regression techniques. Adv. Eng. Softw. **173** 103267 (2022)
25. Rather, S.A., Bala, P.S.: Analysis of Gravitation-Based Optimization Algorithms for Clustering and Classification. IGI Global (2020)
26. Rather, S.A., Shahid, M., Bala, P.S.: A Comprehensive Survey on Solving Clustering and Classification Problems Using Gravitational Search Algorithm. In: 2019 IEEE 9th International Conference on Advanced Computing (IACC), pp. 13–18. (2019)
27. Seitllari, A., Naser, M.Z.: Leveraging artificial intelligence to predict fire-induced explosive spalling in concrete. Comput. Concr. **24**, 271–282 (2019)
28. Sioulas, B., Sanjayan, J.G.: Hydration temperatures in large high-strength concrete columns incorporating slag. Cem. Concr. Res. **30**(11), 1791–1799 (2000)
29. Taheri, J., Mirzazadeh, A.: Optimization of inventory system with defects, rework failure and two types of errors under crisp and fuzzy approach. J. Ind. Manag. Optim. **18**(4), 2289–2318
30. Tan, P.-N., Steinback, M., Kumar, V.: Introduction to Data Mining. (2006)
31. Wu, X., et al.: Top 10 algorithms in data mining. Knowl. Inf. Syst. **14**(1), 1–37 (2008)
32. Yeh, C.: Modeling of strength of high performance concrete using artificial neural networks. Cem. Concr. Res. **28**(12), 1797–1808 (1998)
33. Zhang, X., Akber, M.Z., Zheng, W.: Prediction of seven-day compressive strength of field concrete. Constr. Build. Mater. **305**, 124604 (2021)

Analysis of Online Reviews Created by Hotel Guests

Hamid Reza Irani(✉), Farhad Oghazian, Mostafa Esmaeili Mahyari,
and Mohammad Erfan Sobhani

Faculty of Management and Accounting, College of Farabi, University of Tehran, Qom, Iran
hamidrezairani@ut.ac.ir

Abstract. Considering the importance of social media and the opportunity to share online reviews, the massive volume of user-generated content created requires the application of new methods of analysis such as data mining and text mining. Although the investigation of customer experience with this approach is welcome in the tourism and hospitality industry, but not applied in Iran appropriately. Therefore, current research utilized this approach to investigate customer experience and to accomplish this purpose used text mining to analyze online reviews about Iranian hotels written by foreign guests. The study considered 9734 reviews written by foreign guests on TripAdvisor about hotels in Tehran, Isfahan, Shiraz, and Yazd from 2004 to 2018. Findings revealed the most frequent words considering at least 10 frequencies in reviews indicating the most discussed topics and issues among travelers as following: *Staff, friendly, food, breakfast, restaurant, clean, Tehran, city, Iran, location, helpful, etc.* Other words were also revealed using the TF-IDF method: wifi, English, Shower, Quiet, Coffee, etc. According to the research results, the main words discussed in the online comments were related to hotel staff and food quality. Therefore, hotel managers should pay special attention to training the hotel staff and improving the quality of services provided by the staff to achieve customer satisfaction.

Keywords: Online reviews · Text mining · Iranian hotels · electronic WOM · User generated content · customer experience

1 Introduction

The spread of the Internet and technology has greatly influenced decision-making and purchasing processes. Increased reliance on technology in decision-making and purchasing processes has created challenges and opportunities for marketers in the tourism and hospitality industry. In particular, the advent of Web 2.0 and its development, as well as content production platforms and websites by the user have allowed consumers to share information about products and services with others, as well as information and feedback, whether negative or positive. This reliance on online information obtained from others is further due to the purchase of tourism products and services, which are intangible and perishable in nature, and it is difficult for consumers to evaluate the quality of these products and services before consuming them[1, 2, 3]. This unique feature of

A. Mirzazadeh et al. (Eds.): SEMIT 2022, CCIS 1809, pp. 91–103, 2023.
https://doi.org/10.1007/978-3-031-40398-9_6

services creates uncertainty in their choices and therefore requires a lot of information to reduce perceived risks and make informed decisions [4].

Online feedback allows potential customers to evaluate the quality of a product or service before consumption and create a related image [5]. In addition, consumers and customers find online feedback more up-to-date, informative, enjoyable, and reliable than information published by travel service providers [4]. The ability to express opinions online allows consumers to interact, and this interaction ultimately leads to the consumer's ability because it gives him the ability to make his voice heard [6]. Developing and paying attention to online reviews not only expands the effect of referrals from loyal customers but also dissatisfied customers can be beneficial to hotels. The first is that they can show hotels areas of performance that may need special attention and improvement, and the second is the paradox of service recovery. Accordingly, satisfaction among customers who did not receive good services, in other words, failed services and then experienced service recovery, is higher than customers who were satisfied in the first place and received satisfactory services [7]. In general, access to information has increased the power of customers, which has created a challenge for marketers and hotel managers, but on the other hand, online feedback has created an important learning tool for service providers that can help They helped to understand problems and identify areas for improvement [8].

Hotel managers have long recognized the value of information technology systems and business intelligence. One of the areas in which information technology has focused is the use of data mining techniques to extract patterns and identify models that predict customer relationships from numerical data. Data mining can only be used for structured and numerical databases, while much of the business information is available in the form of structured and semi-structured text documents, such as those available in the hotel's internal database or web-based data sources [9]. Text mining converts unstructured data into structured data or measurable values [10]. Text mining extracts data from text files to create valuable patterns that represent basic trends and characteristics of a particular topic [9, 11].

According to the above, a new approach has been formed in the study of consumer behavior and customer experience that the use of big data and especially online comments and their analysis methods in comparison with traditional methods that change the shape and horizon of services. It makes the need for this approach to better understand, design, and manage the customer experience of more services, which is very important and necessary for both managers and researchers [12]. Given that examining the experience of foreign customers and tourists maybe a little more difficult, this approach is even more important in studying the experience of foreign customers. However, not much attention has been paid to this new approach in studying consumer behavior and the customer experience in Iranian tourism. The main purpose of this study is to examine online comments about Iranian hotels by foreign guests on the Trip Advisor site using the text mining technique to identify the content of comments expressed by hotel guests and customers, topics, and areas of service performance important from the customer perspective because These issues can affect customer satisfaction or dissatisfaction. The present research will be in several forms of knowledge. First, it will introduce researchers and new technical activists to study the customer experience and awareness about it, and second, the research findings can help them to focus on important and effective topics and areas and further research. In each of them to help better understand the needs of the customer.

2 Research Literature

2.1 Online Comments

Online customer feedback on social media, especially those focused on the after-shopping experience, is more useful and reliable to users than information provided by companies and marketers [13, 14]. In a survey of Generation Y, the largest consumer group in the United States, eight out of 10 people said that online-generated content influenced by someone they did not know influenced their purchasing decision [15]. Customer feedback on online comment sites is an important form of word-of-mouth advertising, now called electronic word-of-mouth advertising. It is about a service or product [11]. Unlike traditional word-of-mouth advertising, online word-of-mouth advertising has a profound effect due to its speed, ease, access to large numbers, and the elimination of the pressure of face-to-face communication between humans [16]. Reducing the time to receive information and decisions and thus making a satisfactory decision are other reasons for the tendency to use online word of mouth. The wide range of electronic word-of-mouth advertising and the ease of accessing online feedback can greatly affect a company's performance. Thus, companies are increasingly seeking to understand the effects of word of mouth [17]. Evaluations placed on websites and social media have a high impact on consumer decisions that businesses should pay special attention to [8]. Although positive feedback raises business awareness and builds trust among potential consumers in online forums [18], it can be said that negative comments are considered more informative than positive comments. Because when a customer reads a negative review online, they realize the low quality of a product, while positive or neutral online reviews are less useful because such feedback about the product is ubiquitous. Thus, it can be said that negative online comments are more credible and pathological for the purchasing decision process and are therefore more useful than positive comments [19].

In the case of tourism and travel services, the content produced by tourists and travelers is widely used to share information and information source for decision making and is very important. In this regard, online customer reports are usually up-to-date, have useful and effective information [20], and many potential guests and travelers check online reviews before deciding to travel and book [8]. For example, in connection with the choice of hotel, the customer may name a hotel based on location (for example, proximity to the airport, tourist places, or the city center), brand name, the various facilities that are available in hotels (Such as swimming pool, sports field, gym), quality of service, design, and atmosphere of the hotel (atmosphere) price, customer loyalty programs, and evaluation or rating by previous customers [21]. The online comments produced about the quality of hotel services, both in writing and in numerical evaluation, are positively associated with online awareness. Research shows that users' online opinions significantly affect hotel reservations and are a kind of online certificate on the performance of service providers [18].

2.2 Text Mining

Unlike quantitative approaches that obtain structured data, technological advances provide customers with channels and platforms that can be used to obtain qualitative textual and non-structured feedback. This form of feedback includes open-ended questions, emails, online comments, and social media conversations. In this way, the customer plays a key role and actively defines the processing and timing of the feedback and the context in which the information is presented. Thus, this type of feedback is much more effective than structured approaches because its content and effectiveness better reflect customer motivation [22]. In general, user-generated content is divided into structured and non-structured categories. Structured content on comment websites includes general evaluations and items that are commented on a Likert scale, but structured content refers to content that does not have a specific format such as comments about products or forums in forums [23]. Like data mining, text mining examines data in a text file to extract valuable patterns, trends, insights, and knowledge [11]. Unlike data mining, text mining deals with a set of unstructured or semi-structured texts (such as corporate texts, web pages, or news content) [24, 9]. Text mining is different from traditional research: Traditional research seeks to understand the target population using sample statistics, while the purpose of text mining is to study the entire population instead of the sample. Also, survey questions are designed and selected based on the researcher's special interests. It is a specific theoretical framework and respondents answer questions while in the text mining approach, the data is based on individual preferences. Also, contrary to the traditional approach, there is no person-to-person interaction as a human being [9]. In addition, errors occur in traditional research, such as measurement errors such as navigation patterns or navigation vocabulary, so due to these limitations, new methods such as text mining are needed to achieve more accurate insights [25].

3 Experimental Background

O'Connor (2010) identified ten topics discussed in the comments: hotel location, room size, staff, cleaning, breakfast, in-room facilities, comfort, temperature, dirtiness, and cleaning services[26]. Stringham and Gardz (2010) also examined online customer reviews on the Expedia site and examined the main factors that lead to hotel rankings by customers. They examined users' rankings by combining ratings and opinions, extracting words with more repetition, and the pattern of using words appropriate to the high or low ranking of users. The choice of words is also examined by the guests based on whether the hotel scores are high or low [27]. Lee et al. (2011) used the text mining technique to extract descriptive comments from hotel customers to identify areas in need of service recovery or improvement [28]. Li et al. (2013) used text mining and content analysis to publish online reviews of hotels in Chinese cities. The results showed that room, ease of transportation, proximity to tourist destinations, and monetary value were the most important characteristics that affected guest satisfaction [29]. Xiang et al. (2015) used a text mining approach to analyze the comments written in Expedia and extracted the guests' experience and satisfaction by measuring and analyzing the repetition of words [30]. Also, Kim et al. (2016), using online opinions, examined the factors that create satisfaction and dissatisfaction in hotels with full service and limits, and their research findings identified key factors that affect guest satisfaction, such as location, staff, and rooms. Among the dissatisfying factors in full-service and limited-service hotels, four were common to both sections: "staff and their treatment", "dirtiness", "noise" and "bathroom". In addition, "employees and their attitude" and "dirtiness" have been identified as the most obvious causes of dissatisfaction in both departments. They also found that employees and their attitudes have the highest rank in influencing customer satisfaction and dissatisfaction [31]. Xu, F., et al. (2019) used a data-driven approach to examine the shared experience of guests, and also collected data from Airbnb and extracted the dimensions that lead to a shared experience. The results of their research showed that room facilities, as well as home experience, have an important effect on guest satisfaction [32].

4 Research Methodology

4.1 Data Collection

The present research is descriptive-analytical. In this study, data from the whole community were extracted, counted, and examined from the TripAdvisor website. The statistical population is all foreign tourists who have reviewed and commented on Iranian hotels on the Trip Advisor website. The Trip Advisor website was chosen because this reputable website allows travelers to leave comments, and experiences, and share their information about destinations, hotels, airlines, etc. [1]. According to the researcher's survey, 412 hotels with 17840 comments (on the date of the research) have been registered on the TripAdvisor website. At the time of the main research by recording the harvest time, storing the data of this website and considering it as a statistical community, and from the extracted data, select items related to non-Iranians on the website and has specifically analyzed their data. It should be noted that out of this number, 9734 comments were related to non-Iranian users, which have been specifically considered for text mining, and comments with unknown nationalities have not been examined. In terms of text review and finding different characteristics of hotels, due to the ease of analysis according to the Pareto principle, 20% of hotels that have provincially more than 80% of the total number of comments registered on the Trip Advisor website, has been studied. These hotels were located in four provinces of Tehran, Isfahan, Fars, and Yazd and therefore, hotels located in the four provinces mentioned are the subject of this study.

4.2 Data Extraction Method from Content Production Websites

Due to the huge development that has occurred in communication technology in recent years and with the huge volume of data that is constantly increasing exponentially today, various software and methods have been formed to manage all this information. Business executives and people who are interested in collecting data from the Internet for any purpose need specific and useful data for their work. Today, web scraping is considered an efficient way to collect data through software and computer coding from the Internet. Web scraping is just a modification to address the act of extracting data from websites and storing it in a specific location. The following Fig. 1 shows the general idea of obtaining structured and textual data.

Data extraction technology   Structured data
                                            from the web   and textual data

Fig. 1. General method of obtaining structured and textual data

Content Gerber software is the software used in this study. This software allows you to simply follow the automatic macro methods or directly take control of the user and code it for each component that is intended to be extracted inside the relevant factor. Content Gerber factor is a set of commands and codes that are executed sequentially. These commands can be an activity, for instance, going to a specific web address or getting specific data, such as extracting the text of a comment or the date of writing a comment, etc.

4.3 Textual Data Analysis

The method of analysis used for the text is content analysis. In this research, text mining methods have been used using the databases of software packages available for R software. The steps for extracting text from the data set are as follows:

1) Preparation: In the preparation stage, the packages and libraries required for text mining in R software are called and then the file in Excel format prepared with the data of TripAdvisor website is imported into the software as input data.

2) Extracting a column containing text: One of the columns of Excel software that we have entered in R software has the name "Review", which contains the specific comments of each commenter. Because the data removal from the TripAdvisor website has already been done regularly, there is no need to further manipulate the data and convert the format to a body text which is done in most research. Also, Tidytext and Stringr software packages accept inputs to the Dataframe form and do not need to be converted to other formats. Therefore, directly in the relevant functions, the position of comments in the relevant column is addressed and the necessary calculations are performed on the text.

3) Pre-processing of the text: In this step, the necessary steps are taken to clear the data (convert words to lowercase letters, delete punctuation marks, delete neutral words such as suffixes, pronouns, conjunctions and here hotel) and then the words to the root. They changed (for example, the words "complicated", "complication", "complicate" become the root of "Complicat").

4) Analysis through a term frequency matrix: One of the key questions at the beginning of text mining is how to numerically calculate the content within the text. This can be done by breaking the text into sentences and their constructive words. One of the indicators that can be used to determine the meaning of words is the Term Frequency (TF). The meaning of this term is how often a word is repeated in a comment. A number

of words may be repeated abundantly in the sentences and comments of online users, but they are not very important. In English, words such as the, is, of, etc., which are sometimes prepositions, definite letters, etc., can be mentioned. To solve the problem, a set of these words, known as stop words, has been prepared, which are entered into the R software before running the text mining computer programs. Therefore, due to the insignificance of these neutral words, we remove them from the text before performing the analysis. Another way to check words is to" IDF (inverse document frequency)", which reduces the weight of repetitive words in a separate comment row and increases the weight of words that are used too much in a set of comments. The latter method can be combined with the word repetition method (committees obtained from the two methods are multiplied by each other) and the frequency of words is thus better regulated and reported. The inverse repetition in the comments is indicated by the following formula:

$$IDF(term) = \ln\left(\frac{n_{documents}}{n_{documents\ containing\ term}}\right)$$

TF-IDF (term frequency-inverse document frequency) is the most popular method of weighting repetitive words in digital library recommendation systems, and today 83% of these libraries use this matrix for their calculations, and the main idea of Using the term-inverse text frequency index (TF-IDF) is to find the keywords for each comment, by reducing the weight of the most commonly used words and increasing the weight of the less commonly used words in a text or mass set. The comments used are made [33, 34]. The following Fig. 2 summarizes the path used to extract information in this paper.

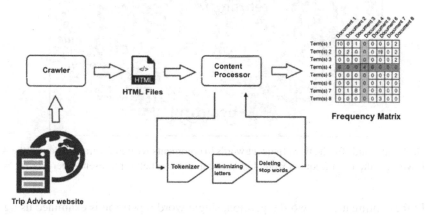

Fig. 2. The path of information extraction and frequency matrix formation

5) Exploratory analysis for the text: To perform exploratory analysis in the text of the comments extracted from the Trip Advisor website to summarize and discover different angles of data, draw repetitive word diagrams using special packages available in R software. These charts include bar charts, word clouds, and comparison charts of different groups of words (positive and negative/different emotions). Therefore, one of the ways to discover the most frequent fields is to find the frequency of words in the text of the

collected opinions for Iranian hotels. Word clouds are a common way of illustrating word groups to understand word repetition. In this method, words are displayed according to the greater or lesser frequency. Colors can also be used in this illustration method to distinguish between low and high repetition ranges. To check the repetition of words, all the comments collected from Iranian hotels were analyzed as input using dplyr, tidytext, and Stringr packages. The word clouds given in Fig. 4 are the most common words used by users to criticize Iranian hotels.

5   Results

In Fig. 3, which is a repetitive word cloud in the comments, various aspects of the hotel that are important to the users along with their repetition rate are visible. Important aspects (repetition related to word size in the figure) include breakfast, staff, hotel cleanliness, location, friendly staff, restaurant, food, service, Wi-Fi and more.

Fig. 3. Word clouds for the most frequent words in comments written for Iranian hotels (the word hotel, which is the most frequent word, has been removed to better represent other words)

In the continuation of word repetition, single word repetition is examined using TF and TF-IDF matrices. In Fig. 4 the repetition of words for 10 words with more repetition for Iranian hotels overtime for the years between 2004 and 2018 is shown by foreign users. As can be seen in the figures, the main areas that are most frequently repeated vary from year to year, indicating the dynamics of the content produced by users and the changing level of their expectations. But in general, important aspects for foreign tourists in Iranian hotels include the following:

Staff, friendly, breakfast, restaurant, clean, location, Iran, city, Tehran, helpful.

As we can see, other words like "hotel" and "stay" have been repeated a lot. As explained earlier about the TF-IDF matrix, by inverting the frequency of the text, repetitive words can be modified and replaced with words that are less frequently but specifically considered in the comments. Have also been examined. A user's opinion of a hotel involves repeating the word "hotel" several times, or users frequently referring to their stay, which is indicated by the word "Stay". In the TF-IDF method, the repetition of words in each comment is adjusted by dividing it by the total comments, and as a result, more specific words that are less mentioned in each separate comment are allowed to appear. According to the diagrams in Fig. 5, which are derived from the TF-IDF matrix, other repetitive and important words are displayed that indicate other important aspects of hotels. Therefore, the following important aspects can be added to the list obtained from the previous step: Wifi, English, Shower, Quiet, Coffee, etc.

The noteworthy point in the reviews related to repetition is that these repetitive words are related to all Iranian hotels and there may be some words that are specific to a hotel and according to the conditions and features of that hotel for tourists. Be more important.

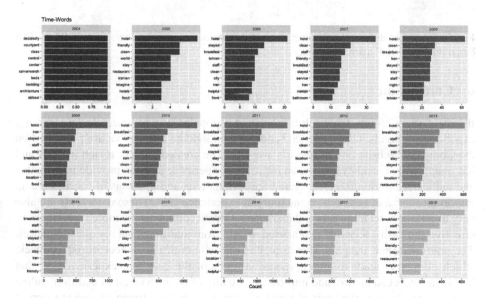

Fig. 4. Review of repetitive words in the comments of foreign users in different years

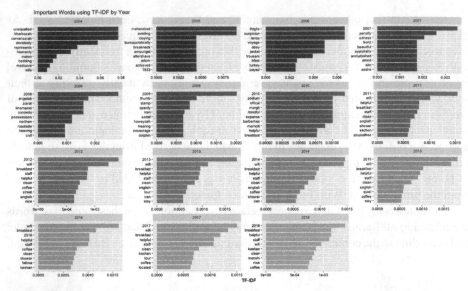

Fig. 5. Graphs of different word repetition rates expressed by foreign users from 2004 to 2018 based on the TF-IDF matrix

6 Conclusion

In recent years, online feedback has become a popular way to research the customer experience in hotels. User-generated content is individual ratings that are published on the Company Website or a third-party website. The created content is rich in itself and has a rapid impact and evaluation on the tourist experience and can provide informative and authentic information [35]. Numerical evaluations and opinions of tourists are an important source of research on the tourism experience [36]. These comments are also very useful for hotel managers and marketers. Online comments are more realistic, cost-effective and easily accessible compared to data from traditional survey questionnaires. They can create new insights. Therefore, it is very economical to collect tourist feedback, which ultimately leads to a comprehensive view of the customer experience, so that hotel managers can control and improve the quality of their services. In addition, online customer feedback is the basis of word-of-mouth marketing strategies, and the impact of online customer feedback is crucial. Therefore, companies need to manage online feedback in a way that leads to positive results [18]. The most advanced decision support systems and business intelligence usually integrate machine learning techniques that are mostly used for data mining to identify hidden patterns in the data that can be turned into useful knowledge. The most advanced decision support systems and business intelligence usually integrate machine learning techniques that are mostly used for data mining to identify hidden patterns in the data that can be turned into useful knowledge. Text mining is a special method of data mining that focuses on analyzing the value of unstructured data such as raw texts. These can be documents, comments, or any other form of information [37].

Therefore, in a highly competitive market for tourism and hospitality, continuous monitoring of online customer feedback is essential to identify important and core problems in customer experience and measure customer satisfaction to ultimately create a unique and memorable experience for them. Online opinion mining can provide useful insights. Based on this, the present study studied the content of 9734 online comments written on the Trip Advisor site by foreign guests about hotels in Tehran, Isfahan, Shiraz, and Yazd provinces from 2004 to 2018, and collected these comments using Gerber content software, and examined with R software. The results of the research revealed the most frequently discussed words in the comments of hotel guests, which are: staff, friendly, breakfast, food, restaurant, clean, location, Iran, city, Tehran, helpful. Other words were also revealed using the TF-IDF method: wifi, English, Shower, Quiet, Coffee, etc. According to the research results, the main words discussed in the online comments were related to hotel staff and food quality. Therefore, hotel managers should pay special attention to training the hotel staff and improving the quality of services provided by the staff to achieve customer satisfaction.

The present study examines the content of words and their repetition. Future research can use emotion analysis as a complementary analysis to express customers' feelings about each of the repetitive words and the role of each in customer satisfaction or dissatisfaction. A more complete review can also be provided by combining numerical evaluations and written comments. The present study has examined all hotels with different quality degrees and also without dividing the four provinces. Although this may increase the generalizability, in future research it is necessary to use hotels of the same quality in a special province and even study a specific hotel to provide more detailed insights into the subject matter. Also, because the data was collected only from the Trip Advisor site, the results are limited to the same site. In addition, this study examines foreign travelers and guests. Future studies can identify and compare the experiences of the two travelers and their differences and needs by examining Iranian travelers and comparing them with the opinions of foreign travelers. It is also possible to review online opinions related to other sectors of the tourism industry in Iran to gain a more complete insight into the travelers' experience.

References

1. Sezgen, E., Mason, K.J., Mayer, R.: Voice of airline passenger: a text mining approach to understand customer satisfaction. J. Air Transp. Manag. **77**, 65–74 (2019)
2. Yang, Y., Mao, Z., Tang, J.: Understanding guest satisfaction with urban hotel location. J. Travel Res. **57**(2), 243–259 (2018)
3. Yang, Y., Mueller, N.J., Croes, R.R.: Market accessibility and hotel prices in the Caribbean: the moderating effect of quality-signaling factors. Tour. Manag. **56**, 40–51 (2016)
4. Yang, Y., Park, S., Hu, X.: Electronic word of mouth and hotel performance: a meta-analysis. Tour. Manag. **67**, 248–260 (2018)
5. Filieri, R.: What makes an online consumer review trustworthy? Ann. Tour. Res. **58**, 46–64 (2016)
6. Duan, W., Yu, Y., Cao, Q., Levy, S.: Exploring the impact of social media on hotel service performance: a sentimental analysis approach. Cornell Hosp. Q. **57**(3), 282–296 (2016)

7. Berezina, K., Bilgihan, A., Cobanoglu, C., Okumus, F.: Understanding satisfied and dissatisfied hotel customers: text mining of online hotel reviews. J. Hosp. Mark. Manag. **25**(1), 1–24 (2016)
8. S. Melián-González, J. Bulchand-Gidumal, and B. González López-Valcárcel, "Online customer reviews of hotels: As participation increases, better evaluation is obtained," Cornell Hosp. Q. **54**(3), 274–283 (2013)
9. Lau, K.-N., Lee, K.-H., Ho, Y.: Text mining for the hotel industry. Cornell Hotel Restaur. Adm. Q. **46**(3), 344–362 (2005)
10. Park, S.B., Jang, J., Ok, C.M.: Analyzing Twitter to explore perceptions of Asian restaurants. J. Hosp. Tour. Technol. **7**(4), 405–422 (2016)
11. He, W., Tian, X., Tao, R., Zhang, W., Yan, G., Akula, V.: Application of social media analytics: A case of analyzing online hotel reviews. Online Inf. Rev. **41**(7), 921–935 (2017)
12. Roy, S.: Effects of customer experience across service types, customer types and time," J. Serv. Mark. **32**(4), 400–413 (2018)
13. Bickart, B., Schindler, R.M.: Internet forums as influential sources of consumer information. J. Interact. Mark. **15**(3), 31–40 (2001)
14. Chen, W.-K., Riantama, D., Chen, L.-S.: Using a text mining approach to hear voices of customers from social media toward the fast-food restaurant industry. Sustainability **13**(1), 268 (2020)
15. Voice, B,: talking to strangers: Millennials trust people over brands. Whitepaper, January (2012)
16. Sun, T., Youn, S., Wu, G., Kuntaraporn, M.: Online word-of-mouth (or mouse): an exploration of its antecedents and consequences. J. Comput. Commun. **11**(4), 1104–1127 (2006)
17. Schiffman, L.G., Kanuk, L.L.: Consumer behavior, 7th, NY Prentice Hall, pp. 15–36, (2000)
18. Ye, Q., Law, R., Gu, B., Chen, W.: The influence of user-generated content on traveler behavior: an empirical investigation on the effects of e-word-of-mouth to hotel online bookings. Comput. Human Behav. **27**(2), 634–639 (2011)
19. Lee, M., Jeong, M., Lee, J.: Roles of negative emotions in customers' perceived helpfulness of hotel reviews on a user-generated review website: a text mining approach. Int. J. Contemp. Hosp. Manag. **29**(2), 762–783(2017)
20. Gretzel, U., Yoo, K.H.: Use and impact of online travel reviews. Inf. Commun. Technol. Tour. **2008**, 35–46 (2008)
21. McCarthy, L., Stock, D., Verma, R.: How travelers use online and social media channels to make hotel-choice decisions (2010)
22. Ordenes, F.V., Theodoulidis, B., Burton, J., Gruber, T., Zaki, M.: Analyzing customer experience feedback using text mining: a linguistics-based approach. J. Serv. Res. **17**(3), 278–295 (2014)
23. Zhang, X., Yu, Y., Li, H., Lin, Z.: Sentimental interplay between structured and unstructured user-generated contents: an empirical study on online hotel reviews. Online Inf. Rev. **40**(1), 119–145 (2016)
24. Usai, A., Pironti, M., Mital, M., Mejri, C.A.: Knowledge discovery out of text data: a systematic review via text mining. J. Knowl. Manag. **22**(7), 1471–1488 (2018)
25. Kwon, H.-J., Ban, H.-J., Jun, J.-K., Kim, H.-S.: Topic modeling and sentiment analysis of online review for airlines. Information **12**(2), 78 (2021)
26. O'connor, P.: Managing a hotel's image on TripAdvisor. J. Hosp. Mark. Manag. **19**(7), 754–772 (2010)
27. Stringam, B.B., Gerdes, J., Jr.: An analysis of word-of-mouse ratings and guest comments of online hotel distribution sites. J. Hosp. Mark. Manag. **19**(7), 773–796 (2010)
28. Lee, M.J., Singh, N., Chan, E.S.W.: Service failures and recovery actions in the hotel industry: a text-mining approach. J. Vacat. Mark. **17**(3), 197–207 (2011)

29. Li, H., Ye, Q., Law, R.: Determinants of customer satisfaction in the hotel industry: an application of online review analysis. Asia Pacific J. Tour. Res. **18**(7), 784–802 (2013)
30. Xiang, Z., Schwartz, Z., Gerdes, J.H., Jr., Uysal, M.: What can big data and text analytics tell us about hotel guest experience and satisfaction? Int. J. Hosp. Manag. **44**, 120–130 (2015)
31. Kim, B., Kim, S., Heo, C.Y.: Analysis of satisfiers and dissatisfiers in online hotel reviews on social media. Int. J. Contemp. Hosp. Manag. **28**(9), 1915–1936 (2016)
32. Xu, F., La, L., Zhen, F., Lobsang, T., Huang, C.: A data-driven approach to guest experiences and satisfaction in sharing. J. Travel Tour. Mark. **36**(4), 484–496 (2019)
33. Beel, J., Gipp, B., Langer, S., Breitinger, C.: Paper recommender systems: a literature survey. Int. J. Digit. Libr. **17**(4), 305–338 (2016)
34. Salton, G., Fox, E.A., Wu, H.: An Automatic Environment for Boolean Information Retrieval. In: IFIP Congress, pp. 755–762 (1983)
35. Zhou, L., Ye, S., Pearce, P.L., Wu, M.-Y.: Refreshing hotel satisfaction studies by reconfiguring customer review data. Int. J. Hosp. Manag. **38**, 1–10 (2014)
36. Rhee, H.T., Yang, S.-B.: Does hotel attribute importance differ by hotel? focusing on hotel star-classifications and customers' overall ratings. Comput. Human Behav. **50**, 576–587 (2015)
37. Calheiros, A.C.D.D.: Sentiment analysis in hospitality using text mining: the case of a Portuguese eco-hotel (2015)

Technology-Aided Decision-Making: Systems, Applications, and Modern Solutions

Deep Reinforcement Learning at Scramble Intersections for Traffic Signal Control: An Example of Shibuya Crossing

Serap Ergün[✉]

Isparta University of Applied Sciences, Isparta, Turkey
serapbakioglu@isparta.edu.tr

Abstract. In vehicular networks, one of the traffic light signal parameters is the current inefficient traffic light control and causes problems such as long delay and energy waste. To improve traffic efficiency, dynamically adjusting the traffic light duration, taking into account real-time traffic information, is a logical and reasonable method. In this study; a deep reinforcement learning model is proposed to control the traffic light. In order to reduce the waiting time of the intersection users, the model and timing of the changes were optimized using deep reinforcement learning for the signals. In addition to the existing studies, Shibuya Crossing is chosen as an exemplary intersection application, focusing on encrypted intersections as the application target of traffic control with deep reinforcement learning. A traffic simulation SUMO is used to create the perimeter of Shibuya Crossing. Traffic signals are optimized using DQN, A2C and PPO algorithms. As a result, by using reinforcement learning, the waiting time has been reduced by about four times compared to the signal patterns currently used. In the study, the behavior of the optimized signal is also analyzed, explaining how the accuracy of the learning process changes when the method or condition observation is changed.

Keywords: Vehicular network · traffic signal control · deep reinforcement learning · SUMO

1 Introduction

The existing road junction management in cities is done with traffic lights. And countless pedestrians and vehicles pass by at these intersections. Inadequate traffic light control causes many problems, such as long delays for passengers, a huge waste of energy and worsening air quality [1, 2].

Some parts of major cities use encrypted intersection structures to allow large numbers of pedestrians to cross safely and efficiently. At such intersections, all vehicles will be stopped during the signal cycle and only pedestrian crossing time is provided so that crossings are possible. By doing this, it has become possible to simultaneously handle large-scale flows of people and improve pedestrian comfort and safety [3]. On the other hand, it is observed that the comfort of vehicles is deteriorated due to the priority given to pedestrians at mixed intersections [4].

A. Mirzazadeh et al. (Eds.): SEMIT 2022, CCIS 1809, pp. 107–120, 2023.
https://doi.org/10.1007/978-3-031-40398-9_7

A pedestrian scramble, sometimes referred to as an intersection scramble, a corner scramble, a diagonal crossing, or a crossing scramble, is a traffic signal movement that temporarily stops all vehicular traffic to allow people to cross an intersection in all directions, even diagonally.

It is thought to put the movement of pedestrians ahead of the flow of automobile traffic. In recent years, new examples have been installed in several nations due to its advantages for pedestrian comfort and safety [5].

Many cities in developing countries, as well as contemporary cities in affluent countries, require an effective transportation system. Optimizing the traffic light signal characteristics at intersections with high levels of congestion is one method for reducing the congestion issue. This strategy is a short-term solution, one of the most widely used ones since it avoids the expensive and time-consuming need to reconstruct the road system. Less vehicle stopping, little delay, and maximum network throughput all point to the best solution [6].

Such a system needs "eyes" to track current road conditions and "brain" to process them. The most recent advancements in sensor and network technology allow real-time traffic information, such as the number of vehicles, their locations, and waiting times, to be input for the "eyes" component that performs the detecting function. Reinforcement Learning (RL), a type of machine learning technology, is a promising approach to the issue for the "brain" portion. The goal of the RL system is to give an action agent the ability to discover the best course of action for interacting with their surroundings in order to maximize reward, such as the least waiting time in our intersection control scenario. State of the environment, agent action space, and reward for each action are typically its three main parts [7], can be seen in Fig. 1.

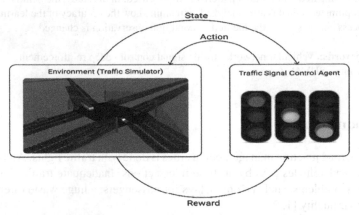

Fig. 1. RL based traffic signal control [8]

Traffic Signal Control (TSC), which controls traffic signals to optimize intersections, is a numerous method for improving the convenience of intersection users. In the past, the mainstream method for TSC was to set a signal with a fixed time length and adjust the cycle to optimize the signal [9]. However, since the advent of methods using RL, it has been shown to outperform conventional methods in terms of performance, and a RL-based approach has been introduced to his TSC.

In recent years, Deep Q-Network (DQN), a method for estimating Q values using neural networks by combining RL with deep learning, has appeared [10] and has been applied to the field of TSC to control traffic signals at intersections. Also, achieved remarkable performance improvements in [11] can be seen.

In this study, Deep RL (DRL)—which has emerged recently—is used to deal with TSC. As a result, a way for optimizing the chaotic intersection in a large metropolis with plenty of pedestrians—specifically, the Shibuya scrambled intersection—is suggested. One of the busiest crossings in the world, the Shibuya Scramble Crossing (Fig. 2) sees 30,000 automobiles and about 500,000 pedestrians each day.

Fig. 2. The Shibuya Crossing

Outside Shibuya station in Tokyo, Shibuya Crossing is the biggest and most well-known scramble crossing in all of Japan. In a single scramble, more than 3,000 pedestrians can cross [5], and it has come to represent Tokyo and all of Japan [2].

In this study, SUMO (Simulation of Urban MObility) to build the simulation environment. We created and imitated the Shibuya intersection's scrambled layout. In order to decrease the overall waiting time for users in the built environment, we implemented a large-scale simulation of human flow based on actual traffic volume data and trained traffic lights. As a consequence, compared to the fixed pattern signal, the waiting time for both pedestrians and automobiles was reduced, and the overall improvement was increased by more than 4 times.

The organizational of the paper as follows. The related works on TSC, RL, DRL are given in Sect. 2. We give some basic preliminaries of RL in Sect. 3. Also the traffic conditions, state, action and reward designs are given in Sect. 3.4. Evaluation experiment with some comparing results are given in Sect. 4. And finally the conclusion part is given Sect. 5.

2 Related Works

In [9], the value distribution of state-action pairs is estimated using a neural network in order to build a risk-sensitive strategy to traffic signal regulation. Congestion in the network is effectively reduced using a novel control strategy that assigns varying weights to the risk of an activity based on the system's level of congestion. The outcomes demonstrate that the algorithm outperforms both traditional and traditional RL-based techniques.

A variety of car flows, detection velocities, and types of road networks are handled by the authors' system [12]. Even with a low detection rate, the technology is effective in cutting down on how long cars spend on average waiting at a junction, which cuts down on how long cars have to drive.

Authors in [13] suggest an algorithm establishes the ideal placement of a blue signal. The suggested approach uses throughput and the standard deviation of the queue length as reward factors in order to optimally distribute the signals and optimize throughput.

A multi-agent RL-based traffic signal control model is suggested by the authors in [14]. In order to build state representation and reward function, they introduce a new biased pressure method that takes into account both the phase pressure and the number of incoming automobiles. They also take into account limits from the real world and define action space to enable cyclic phase management with a minimum and maximum time for each phase. It has been demonstrated that allocating separate action spaces for various phases allows for safe pedestrian crossing while maximizing throughput.

To investigate the role of Broad Learning Systems in Multi-Agent Systems, the authors of [15] propose the Multi-Agent Broad RL (MABRL) framework. Each agent is modeled using extensive networks. The "3W" information—when to interact, which agents to take into account, and what information to transmit—is then confirmed by the introduction of a dynamic self-cycling interaction mechanism. They conduct experiments based on an intelligent traffic light control scenario, and the outcomes of those studies on three datasets confirm the MABRL's efficacy.

Authors in [16] propose a framework which uses an intersection-agnostic representation to support Federated RL across traffic lights controlling heterogeneous intersection types. They evaluate Federated RL approach against Centralized and Decentralized RL strategies. They compare the reward-communication trade-offs of these strategies. The results show that Federated RL is able to reduce the communication costs associated with Centralized training by 36.24%; while only seeing a 2.11% decrease in average reward.

A DRL-based signal control system is suggested by the authors of [9] so that traffic signals can be dynamically adjusted in response to the level of congestion at intersections. Rerouting is a strategy used to load balance the vehicles on road networks in order to relieve congestion on the routes behind the intersection. They dismantle data silos and combine all the data from sensors, detectors, vehicles, and roads to generate long-lasting outcomes in order to reap the true benefits of the suggested approach.

DRL is used by the authors of [17] to make an early attempt at controlling the traffic signal for emergency vehicles. This enables a quick response to emergencies in a variety of situations and reduces the impact that competing directions have on traffic efficiency. They do accurate simulations utilizing traffic data from a network with several crossings in the real world under various testing conditions. The results show that the strategy significantly outperforms in terms of various performance indicators, confirming the model's viability and efficacy.

The Q-learning method is used in the system that the authors of [18] have presented, and the action space is defined as all potential phase lengths. The state is redesigned to condense the state space, and the incentive mechanism is altered to direct the agent to balance more traffic metrics. By using equal, unequal, and complex traffic scenarios, the suggested system is assessed. The proposed system performs better than previous approaches in controlling traffic lights, according to the results, even in scenarios with complicated traffic patterns.

A DRL system based on edge computing is demonstrated in [19]. For the purpose of maximizing various goals, a multi objective reward function is developed. The technique aims to get over the difficulty of judging activities with a straightforward number reward. The choice of reward functions significantly affects an agent's capacity to learn the best behavior for controlling multiple traffic signals in a vast road network. The agent is trained utilizing the proximal policy optimization method in several deep neural network models in order to determine efficient reward functions. Utilizing both fictitious scenarios and actual traffic maps, the system is tested. The thorough simulation results show how effective the suggested reward functions are.

[20] describes the implementation of a DRL traffic light control at a crossroad utilizing real-time traffic data with a focus on emergency vehicles. The agent learns to modify its procedures to give the emergency vehicles precedence over all other vehicles. Less waiting time and faster car movement are the results. It also shows how quickly emergency vehicles pass through intersections. The average delay employing RL is reduced by 2 to 16 percent overall with 200 to 600 autos and one emergency vehicle. There is a 27–40% reduction in the average delay for emergency vehicles when there are more of them.

3   Method

3.1   Preliminaries of *RL*

RL is a subfield of machine learning in which one or more agents learn by interaction with their environment and the experiences they create to solve problems. Creating computers with artificial intelligence that behave like people is one of its objectives [5, 7]. To do this, it is essential to act appropriately, make informed judgments, and learn through interactions with the environment. RL is one of the capabilities of artificial intelligence that allows for independent and experiential learning. By engaging with the environment and getting rewards, RL teaches behavior [2, 10, 12].

Q learning, a typical RL method, is a table of Q-values (Q-states). However, when the state-behavior space is too large, the table becomes large, making learning more difficult. Therefore, introducing a deep neural network to update the Q value makes more sense for complex systems. DRL method is used in RLs where deep neural networks are used. One of the DRL methods is DQN.

In DQN, the neural network weight θ and the state behavior value $Q_\theta(s, a)$ are set as parameters for $Q(s, a)$. Then, learning is performed to minimize the following loss function (Fig. 3).

$$L(\theta) = \mathrm{E}[(r_t + \gamma \, max_\alpha Q_\theta(s_{t+1}, a)) - Q_\theta(s_t, a_t))^2]$$

(a)   (b)

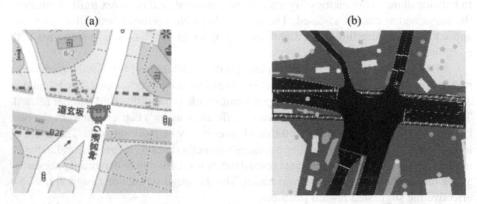

Fig. 3. OpenStreetMap diagram (a) and SUMO map (b) of Shibuya scramble crossing

The Actor-Critical method is another technique for simultaneously learning the value and policy functions. In the Actor-Critic algorithm, the Actor chooses the agent's behavior based on the strategy $\pi(a|s)$, while the Critic determines the behavior the Actor should pick by calculating the state value $V_\pi(s)$. . It contributes to helping when acting. Actor-Critic algorithms are the ancestors of algorithms like Advantage Actor Critic (A2C) and Proximal Policy Optimization (PPO) [22].

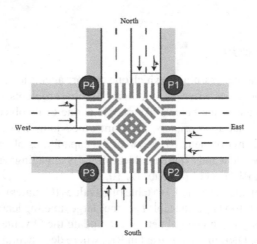

Fig. 4. Schematic diagram of Shibuya scramble crossing

3.2   Traffic Conditions at Shibuya Scramble Crossing

The Shibuya crossing is depicted schematically in Fig. 4. The Shibuya Scramble intersection has two lanes on each side and extends to the next signal at 109 m, 62 m, 71 m,
and 60 m in the north, south, east, and west, respectively. Phases 1, 2, and 3 are repeated
by the signal. In Phase 1, pedestrians are free to move in either direction.

Phase 2 is east-west in orientation. Phase 3 is open to traffic traveling in a north-south
direction. Shibuya Center-Gai, a little one-way alley that can only be entered from the
intersection side, is located between the west and the north in Fig. 4, yet its traffic flow
is higher than that of the other four directions of northeast.

It is determined based on the statistics for traffic volume, traffic strategy near Shibuya
Station, local traffic data, and the Shibuya scramble crossing [23]. The Poisson distribution is used to describe the amount of both vehicular and pedestrian traffic. The Asson
distribution is used to express it, and each hour's average value is used. Tables 1 and 2
provide examples of these.

Shibuya's scramble crossing's signal is managed by a predetermined sequence. Next,
repeat Phases 1, 2, and 3 in that order. The expressions for each period (seconds) are
(blue, yellow, red), (37, 10, 4), (44, 3, 3), and so on (33, 3, 3).

Table 1. Vehicle traffic volume (units / h)

Departure Direction	Arrival Direction			
	North	East	South	West
North	0	0	216	144
East	108	0	0	396
South	252	0	0	216
West	144	216	288	0

Table 2. Pedestrian traffic volume (people / h)

Departure Point	Arrived			
	P1	P2	P3	P4
P1	0	0	216	144
P2	108	0	0	396
P3	252	0	0	216
P4	144	216	288	0

3.3 State Expression

For each of the four directions—north, south, east, and west—is Shibuya Scramble Crossing. There are two lanes, for a total of eight lanes. L represents the set of lanes, and $|L|$ equals 8.

To describe the traffic conditions, the agent observed at time t, the next six variables are described.

Vehicle queue $Q^{(t)} \in \mathbb{R}^{|L|}$ is the density of stopped cars in each lane.

Vehicle density $D^{(t)} \in \mathbb{R}^{|L|}$ is the number of pedestrians stopped.

The number of pedestrians having a waiting time larger than zero is represented by $D^{(t)} \in \mathbb{R}$.

The total time that a vehicle must wait in each lane is represented by $S^{(t)} \in \mathbb{R}^{|L|}$.

The average speed of the vehicle in each lane is $V^{(t)} \in \mathbb{R}^{|L|}$, and the total time that pedestrians must wait is $W^{(t)} \in \mathbb{R}$.

3.4 Action Choice

The next state of the signal is selected from Phases 1, 2, and 3 every 5 s by RL agent. However, in order to prevent the signal from changing too often, the blue state shall remain for at least 10 s in each direction, during which the agent selection is not reflected in the traffic light. Also, if another state is selected after the blue light has passed for 10 s or more. When transitioning from Phase 1 to another state, a yellow traffic light for 10 s and a red traffic light for 5 s. When transitioning from Phases 2 and 3 to another state, a yellow signal for 3 s and a red signal for 2 s are created. Since the direction of the next blue light is determined in the yellow light and red light states, the agent selection in this state is not reflected in the traffic light.

3.5 Reward Design

Equation (2) uses $W^{(t)}$, vehicle waiting time $S^{(t)}$, and pedestrian waiting time to define the immediate reward $r^{(t)} \in \mathbb{R}$.

The total amount of time that pedestrians and automobiles had to wait is this. The coefficient α describes how much weight is given to the pedestrian; the higher this number, the more the pedestrian is prioritized over the automobile.

$$r^{(t)} = -\sum_{l \in L}^{L} S_l^{(t)} - \alpha W^{(t)}$$

4 Evaluation Experiment

4.1 Experiment Environment

The SUMO traffic simulator [24] is used in this investigation. An evaluation experiment is carried out to replicate the traffic situation at the Shibuya Scramble intersection mentioned in Sect. 3.2. DRL signal control involves the observation of the six variables specified in Sect. 3.3 as states. The agent decides on a course of action as outlined in

Sect. 3.4 based on the observation state. Controlled signals are used. Following that, the instantaneous reward mentioned in Sect. 3.5 is granted, and learning continues. Assuming there are typically two people per car so that intersection users will be compensated for their overall waiting time. The weight of pedestrians is set to 0.5 in Sect. 3.5. The reward is the value increased by 1/100 for the sake of clarity.

4.2 Comparison of Algorithms

First, a comparative experiment is undertaken to gauge how well the strategy we suggested performed. In the setting of Sect. 3.1, we evaluated the outcomes of four episodes, each lasting 2 million seconds, for the three algorithms DQN, A2C, and PPO, as well as the fixed-length algorithm as the reference method. The current signal control at the Shibuya scrambled junction described in Sect. 4.1 is replicated using the fixed length technique. Repetition of the predefined signal control pattern occurs. Stable Baselines3 implemented DQN, A2C, and PPO [25].

In order to compare these algorithms; the median data for 4 episodes of the average total waiting time for the most recent 400,000 s is utilized to examine variations in immediate rewards over time and their 95 percent confidence intervals (Fig. 5 and Fig. 6).

According to Fig. 5, DQN increases immediate rewards the quickest. However, because of the fluctuation range, it was only partially steady. PPO, on the other hand, is running fairly swiftly and steadily. We received a higher immediate payout than the baseline right away. A2C's operation is unsteady up until it converged, but it eventually became stable.

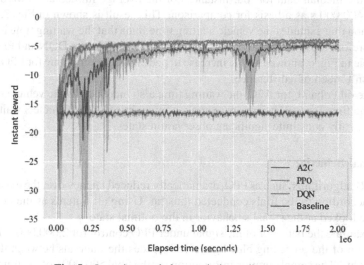

Fig. 5. Over time and changes in immediate rewards

Any algorithm will finally be relative to the baseline, according to Fig. 6. The performance is discovered to have greatly improved. It is determined that, among them, PPO cut waiting times by 76% compared to the baseline. Additionally, similar to immediate rewards, it considerably decreased compared to the baseline for both automobiles and people.

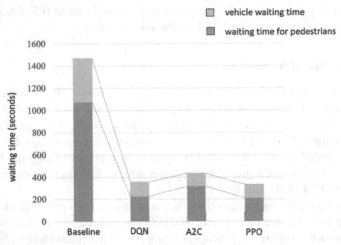

Fig. 6. Average waiting times of RL algorithms

4.3   Comparison of Observation Conditions

We used the median data for four instances of the average immediate reward over the previous 400,000 s as a basis for comparison. This result is shown in Fig. 7, 8 and 9. Any method that excludes the vehicle waiting time finds that the waiting time is growing and is therefore the most crucial observation state. The results for DQN and PPO, which were stable in Fig. 6, showed a little increase in pedestrian waiting time for PPO. Overall, there wasn't much of a difference.

On the other hand, for A2C, the waiting time also increases as the vehicle speed and the waiting time for pedestrians are overtaken, in addition to the vehicle's waiting time. These evidently constitute significant observation states.

4.4   Signal Behavior

Using DRL algorithms, such as PPO, dramatically reduced latency over the existing fixed pattern, according to the trials conducted thus far. Using all 6 items as the observation status, we looked at the signal's behavior in the optimal state.

We examine the behavior of the signal under PPO control for 2,000,000 s. However, the duration of the preceding blue light also includes the intervals between the yellow and red lights. The signal duration information for the final 500,000 s of the four episodes is presented in Table 3. The total of the blue light, yellow light, and red light of each Phase described in Sect. 4.3 determines the table's shortest duration.

According to Table 3, the average duration of Phase 1 (a pedestrian signal) and Phase 3 (a north-south signal), where there is a relatively low volume of vehicle traffic, is close to the shortest continuation length.

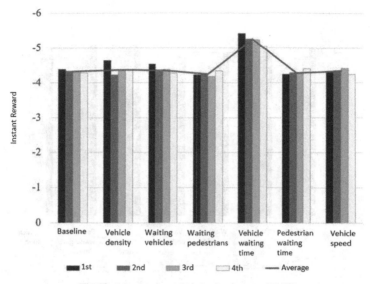

Fig. 7. Monitoring observation state of DQN

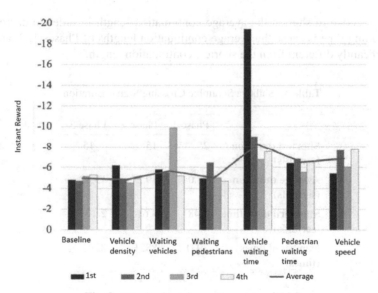

Fig. 8. Monitoring observation state of A2C

Phase 2 is an east-west signal with rather significant vehicle traffic, and its average continuation length is longer than its shortest counterpart.

Additionally, in Phase 2, both the standard deviation of the length of the continuation and the number of times it went blue are very high, and it is evident that the traffic volume affects both the length of the continuation and the frequency of the signal.

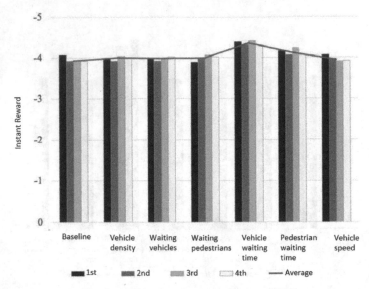

Fig. 9. Monitoring observation state of PPO

It is effective to shorten the average continuation length in order to decrease the user's waiting time because the average continuation lengths of Phases 1, 2, and 3 are not significantly different from the shortest continuation length.

Table 3. Shibuya Scramble Crossing Signal Duration

	Phase 1	Phase 2	Phase 3
Shortest duration (seconds)	25	15	15
Average duration (seconds)	25.04	19.26	15.87
Standard deviation (seconds)	0.48	4.61	2.17
Number of times **(times)**	7931	8821	8293

5 Conclusion

In this study, we use a computer simulation to recreate the Shibuya Scramble crossing. Using DRL, we looked at traffic signal optimization. In the experiment, we created a special simulation environment with a large-scale human flow, rewards, and observation conditions for RL in order to replicate the scrambled junction. We suggested the best approach for the user by contrasting and analyzing the learning algorithms.

We also examined how the improved signal behaved. The assessment experiment shown that by managing the signal by the PPO algorithm, the waiting time for every user could be reduced by a factor of more than 4.

As a result, a system that decreases waiting times for both vehicles and pedestrians has been created for chaotic crossings where a significant number of pedestrians can pass safely.

Although simulation is optimized in this study, the cost of setting up observational equipment and training will be a concern given that it will eventually be used in the actual world.

References

1. Liang, X., Du, X., Wang, G., Han, Z.: Deep reinforcement learning for traffic light control in vehicular networks (2018). arXiv preprint arXiv:1803.11115
2. Juozevičiūtė, D., Grigonis, V.: Evaluation of exclusive pedestrian phase safety performance at one-level signalized intersections in vilnius. Sustainability **14**(13), 7894 (2022)
3. Qi, W., Shen, B., Yang, Y., Qu, X.: Modeling drivers' scrambling behavior in China: an application of theory of planned behavior. Travel Behav. Society **24**, 164–171 (2021)
4. Lonkina, L.C., Carril, C.C., Lima, M.S., De La Cruz, F.C. : Evaluation of road intersections in areas of high commercial activity through the identification of vehicle-pedestrian conflicts using the black spots methodology. In :2021 Congreso Internacional de Innovación y Tendencias en Ingeniería (CONIITI), pp. 1–6. IEEE
5. Pedestrian scramble, (2022). In : Wikipedia. https://en.wikipedia.org/wiki/Pedestrian_scramble
6. Jamal, A., Al-Ahmadi, H.M., Butt, F.M., Iqbal, M., Almoshaogeh, M., Ali, S. : Metaheuristics for Traffic Control and Optimization: Current Challenges and Prospects (2012)
7. Mekrache, A., Bradai, A., Moulay, E., Dawaliby, S.: Deep reinforcement learning techniques for vehicular networks: recent advances and future trends towards 6G. Vehicular Commun. 100398 (2021)
8. Kim, D., Jeong, O.: Cooperative traffic signal control with traffic flow prediction in multi-intersection. Sensors **20**(1), 137 (2019)
9. Anirudh, R., Krishnan, M., Kekuda, A.: Intelligent Traffic Control System using Deep Reinforcement Learning. In : 2022 International Conference on Innovative Trends in Information Technology (ICITIIT), (pp. 1–8). IEEE (2022, February).
10. Kirk, R., Zhang, A., Grefenstette, E., & Rocktäschel, T.: A survey of generalisation in deep reinforcement learning. *arXiv preprint* arXiv:2111.09794
11. Wu, Q., et al.: Distributed agent-based deep reinforcement learning for large scale traffic signal control. Knowl.-Based Syst. **241**, 108304 (2022)
12. Zhang, R., Ishikawa, A., Wang, W., Striner, B., Tonguz, O.K.: Using reinforcement learning with partial vehicle detection for intelligent traffic signal control. IEEE Trans. Intell. Transp. Syst. **22**(1), 404–415 (2020)
13. Joo, H., Lim, Y.: Intelligent traffic signal phase distribution system using deep q-network. Appl. Sci. **12**(1), 425 (2022)
14. Ibrokhimov, B., Kim, Y.J., Kang, S.: Biased pressure: cyclic reinforcement learning model for intelligent traffic signal control. Sensors **22**(7), 2818 (2022)
15. Zhu, R., Li, L., Wu, S., Lv, P., Li, Y., Xu, M. : (2022). Multi-Agent Broad Reinforcement Learning for Intelligent Traffic Light Control. *arXiv preprint* arXiv:2203.04310

16. Hudson, N., Oza, P., Khamfroush, H., Chantem, T. : Smart Edge-Enabled Traffic Light Control: Improving Reward-Communication Trade-offs with Federated Reinforcement Learning. In : 2022 IEEE International Conference on Smart Computing (SMARTCOMP), (pp. 40–47). IEEE (2022)
17. Mushtaq, A., Sarwar, M. A., ul Haq, I., Khan, A., & Shafiq, O. : Traffic Management of Autonomous Vehicles using Policy Based Deep Reinforcement Learning and Intelligent Routing (2022). arXiv preprint arXiv:2206.14608
18. Cao, M., Li, V. O., Shuai, Q.: A Gain with No Pain: Exploring Intelligent Traffic Signal Control for Emergency Vehicles. In : IEEE Transactions on Intelligent Transportation Systems (2022)
19. Liu, J., Qin, S., Luo, Y., Wang, Y., Yang, S.: Intelligent Traffic Light Control by Exploring Strategies in an Optimised Space of Deep Q-Learning. In : *IEEE Transactions on Vehicular Technology*
20. Paul, A., Mitra, S.: Exploring reward efficacy in traffic management using deep reinforcement learning in intelligent transportation system. ETRI J. **44**(2), 194–207 (2022)
21. Shamsi, M., Rasouli Kenari, A., Aghamohammadi, R.: Reinforcement learning for traffic light control with emphasis on emergency vehicles. J. Supercomput. **78**(4), 4911–4937 (2022)
22. Szepesvári, C.: Algorithms for reinforcement learning. Synth. Lect. Artif. Intell. Mach. Learn. **4**(1), 1–103 (2010)
23. Shibuya Station. (2021). Traffic conditions in the area around Shibuya Station https://www.city.shibuya.tokyo.jp/assets/kankyo/000050292.pdf
24. Lopez, P.A., et al.: Microscopic traffic simulation using sumo. In : 2018 21st International Conference on Intelligent Transportation Systems (ITSC), pp. 2575–2582. IEEE.
25. Raffin, A., Hill, A., Gleave, A., Kanervisto, A., Ernestus, M., Dormann, N.: Stable-baselines3: Reliable reinforcement learning implementations. Journal of Machine Learning Research (2021)

Does the Firms' Size Affect the Decision-Making Capability of BI? A Case Study in Türkiye

Çiğdem Sıcakyüz[(⊠)] [iD]

Ankara Science University, 6570 Çankaya, Ankara, Türkiye
cigdem.sicakyuz@ankarabilim.edu.tr

Abstract. Business intelligence (BI) is one of the most evident indicators of digitization, assisting firms in better managing and executing their operations. Since Türkiye is still a developing country, recent attempts by the Ministry of Industry and Technology of the Republic of Türkiye to digitalize SMEs highlight the significance of business intelligence for the country. Thus, this research aims to determine whether the decision-making capabilities of BI software vary with organization size and BI users in various positions in the firms. To analyze the decision-making capabilities of BI software used in their businesses, a survey was designed for 50 enterprises participating in the Efficiency and Technology Fair in June 2021. The enterprises' perspectives on business intelligence capacity were acquired using a Likert scale ranging from 1 to 7. The Kruskal-Wallis test was used to analyze the differences between various business sizes, such as micro, small, medium, and large. The findings demonstrated that BI decision-making skills differ with neither enterprise size nor BI firm users. Another finding is that around 68.9% of firms use business intelligence, and 30% regard it favorably. 4% of enterprise reps need to learn who utilizes business intelligence in their organization. Furthermore, it has been observed that the most popular business intelligence software is SAP Business Objects and ORACLE, even though some firms use more BI software simultaneously. This study contributes to the literature by investigating whether the organization's size and the BI user impact BI effectiveness, providing an overview of particularly the small firms in Türkiye.

Keywords: Business Intelligence · Decision-making · Software Capability · SMEs

1 Introduction

Technological breakthroughs, communication advancements, the globalization of the workforce, and various customers' needs make the business environment complicated, competitive, and ever-changing. A company needs to be competitive for its sustainability among its rival in the market. The firms have a sustainable competitive advantage when their return on investment exceeds the industry standards [1] and if they maintain their competitive standing. Making practical, efficient, timely, fast, and high-quality decision affects the firms' competitiveness [2]. According to Davenport (2010), it is essential to focus consciously on better decisions in order to improve processes as well as to approach the effort as decision-oriented so as to develop new products [3].

A. Mirzazadeh et al. (Eds.): SEMIT 2022, CCIS 1809, pp. 121–142, 2023.
https://doi.org/10.1007/978-3-031-40398-9_8

Additionally, the dynamics and complexity of the business environment impact managers' choices negatively. Because they are struggling with overloading information, this situation beclouds just-in-time decision-making. Despite the abundance of available knowledge and technology solutions in significant corporations, Gigerenzer claims that 50% of managers covertly rely on their business choices on gut instinct. However, a lack of faith in themselves or others' gut instincts prevents CEOs from acting on it [4].

Typically, the ability to optimize company performance depends on the decision-maker's ability to analyze and control business performance and take appropriate action based on the data. Furthermore, the researchers state that today's global business community suffers from business source analysis and information overload. Indeed, 61% of managers consider that their workplace suffers from information overload, and more than half of managers ignore information in their current judgment process due to it [5]. According to a study in 2012, more than 35 percent of the top 5,000 global firms would regularly fail to make wise decisions regarding significant changes in their business and markets due to a lack of information, processes, and tools [6].

BI can be a solution for this. Institutions need to employ intelligence for two primary reasons. First, they must do an analysis that will assist them in making better selections. The analysis enables them to identify sales patterns, care for clients, and crucial concerns. Second, it greatly aids them in forecasting future consumer behavior and market need [7]. Hence, many companies use BI systems in decision-making.

BI directs to techniques, processes, architectures, and technologies that can perform and convert accumulated datasets into meaningful and helpful information and are used as valuable reports for business purposes, applications, and services [8]. In a typical BI System, data are collected from disparate sources, transformed, cleansed, loaded, and stored in a warehouse.

These data can be in various forms, from structured ones, such as data extracted from ERP (Enterprise Resource Planning) or CRM (Customer Relationship), to unstructured ones, such as images, spreadsheets, and business processes [9]. Then data is analyzed for specific aims. Many technics are used to diagnose, such as multidimensional cube analysis, exploratory data analysis, time series analysis, inductive learning models for data mining, and optimization models. Finally, the choice and adoption of a specific decision are taken and reported.

Crucial segments of proactive BI include real-time data warehousing, data mining, automated detection of anomalies and exceptions, prescient warning with automatic recipient resolution, seamless follow-through workflow, automated learning and advancement, geographic information systems, and data visualization [10].

Some studies prove the benefits of BI implementation, such as improved performance, efficiency, productivity, business growth, resource planning, supplier-buyer relationship, and cost lowering, which can eventually direct to a competitive advantage [11]. Because BI could help organizations' profitability by improving managers' decision power, the organizations commenced investing in it with annual growth of 10%. However, only 24% of these investments have been booming in recent years [9]. For instance, succeeding companies, such as Continental Airlines, have seen BI investments increase revenue and yield cost savings equal to a 1000% ROI (Return on Investment) [12]. In 2014, Indian BI software revenue was predicted to be a 15 percent increase over 2014 revenue of $133.8 million. This forecast contains payment for BI platforms, cutting-edge analytics, analytic applications, and CPM (Corporate Performance Management) software [13]. Many industries use BI applications to reach beyond the enterprise and share insights off the platform with vendors and customers of IT. Because the demand for BI and analytics technology is rising fast as more enterprises are leaning on data for decision-making, the software market is anticipated to reach $13 billion by 2025 [14].

However, the praxis exhibits that the success of BI is still debatable because the implementation of numerous BI applications fails. Organizations need to achieve the fitting benefits from BI use [15]. Understanding what BI is, applying it, and the related benefits are essential in implementing BI across the enterprise [16] because failing companies have spent more resources than their competitors with a smaller ROI, all while monitoring their market share and client base shrink continuously [12]. Hence, researchers began to solve the dilemma, and several studies have lately been driven to successful implementation. Implementing BI within the organization is a journey toward an ideal enterprise, not a destination. [16].

There is a high grade of the direct correlation between the quality of the system used in BI systems and usage at the level of significance (0.05), and the correct and reliable use of BI systems affects the quality and validity of decision-making in humanitarian organizations operating in Türkiye [17].

1.1 Digitalization and Competitiveness

Türkiye is a developing country with 3.228.421 enterprises of varying sizes, with an economic value of 5,305,543,653,183 TL in 2019. Compared to 2019, the proportion of enterprises that used ERP software increased by 7.5%, and CRM was used by 10.6%. 41.0% of enterprises with 250 or more employees used cloud computing services. The proportion of enterprises using robot technology was 4.8%. 2.7% of enterprises stated that they use artificial intelligence [18]. Figure 1 demonstrates that Türkiye's production volume consists mainly of large-scale enterprises.

But, according to the report of MID, Türkiye has been lagging in digital competitiveness worldwide.

Türkiye has moved to 48th place in the Global digital competition ranking, which includes 64 countries, by decreasing 4 points in 2021 compared to 2020 [19]. This ranking shows how far Türkiye is in the world ranking in terms of digital competitiveness. Figure 2 below shows how Türkiye's digitalization and level have changed over the years.

However, based on the graph above, it can be said that Türkiye's competitiveness level is even lower than its digitalization level. This result might indicate that Türkiye needs help to utilize technology to its advantage.

Several studies were done to examine the importance of digitalization worldwide. In a study, researchers examined the influence of digitalization on the growth of the global economy, using the economies of EU (European Union) member states as an example. It has been discovered that digitalization is a crucial element in global economic growth. Several methodologies have been established to research its influence on global economic growth, according to which the level of digitalization of the nations' economies is measured [20].

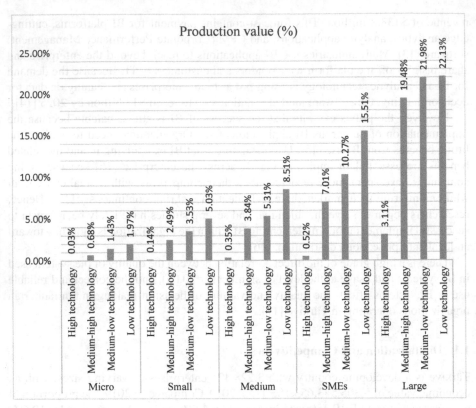

Fig. 1. The production volume of firms in Türkiye (derived from the data of TUIK, 2021).

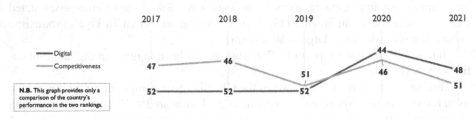

Fig. 2. Türkiye's Level of digitalization and Level by years.

Core Technologies such as 3D Print, Industrial Internet of Things (IoT), Big Data, AI (Artificial Intelligence), Collaborative Robots, and Virtual Reality have had a 68% influence on Industry 4.0 and provide predictive analytics for making high-value decisions [11].

From the perspective of Türkiye, some studies were done to find out the organization's approach in the Türkiye. For example, in a study, interviewees are asked how and how much they use analytical tools, techniques, methods, and strategies for marketing, production, and other areas. The analysis and findings indicate that most firms need to catch up in using analytical tools or techniques for business purposes, even though they all accept that data mining, digital marketing, database marketing, and extensive data analysis are significant for businesses [21].

In another study conducted in 2012 on the use of information systems to support competitive information among SMEs in Istanbul, it is seen that companies' IT (Information Technology) usage rate is low. The respondent firms' Level of IT help to manage their competitive information was the subject of this Section 56.1% declared that they did not use any systems to collect their competitive information, agreeing with the statement that it was in their thoughts and they relied on their memory. Only 12.7% said they used IT systems to manage competitive information. However, they preferred paper records and did not like relying on computers or others to protect their data [22]. Another study was conducted to determine the tendency of firms at the management level to use BI in decision-making. The result showed that all enterprises utilize IS for operational purposes. In addition, many managers think that it is either not fit for their industry or that their company needs to be more significant to implement such technologies. They all recognize the value of big data and computerized systems but still plan and make judgments based on their experience, intuitions, and views. However, they agreed they could be utilized when shown instances of intelligent systems, big data, and artificial intelligence in action [23].

According to comparative research on firm variables in BI studies, a fully designed BI system gives differential value to various businesses. The size, scope, and absorptive ability of an organization all contribute to the effective adoption of BI. For example, firm size will impact the organization's capacity to turn BI Resources into BI Benefits because large companies are more likely than small firms to harness BI's potential [24]. Another variable is that information exchange and cooperation between management across many departments are required for organizational information transfer and strategic decision-making around significant business activities. Consequently, as an organization's size grows, so does the interdependence and complexity of the process, causing managers to struggle with collaborating and sharing information to complete perceiving, decision-making, and performing duties in a timely way. As a result, based on their size, businesses may take different approaches to attain agility [25]. At the individual level, user acceptance and successful utilization are one of the most challenging difficulties for BI systems. The objective of an organization to achieve high returns on BI investments is strongly dependent on the proper usage of a BI system, which is dependent on end-users. On the other hand, user resistance to or underutilizing BI systems can lead to workflow issues, strategy blindness, and poor business performance. As a result, it is critical to recognize and fix individual-level difficulties to reap the maximum pension of BI systems and limit the chance of failings [26].

2 Literature Review

It is vital to notice that many methodologies and tools could be employed in BI creation. They have a significant influence on the functioning and capabilities of BI applications and hence on the quality of decision-making, personalization of goods and services, and process improvement [27].

BI capacity derives from IT capability, which has been extensively researched in the information systems (IS) literature. IT competence is related to the quality of IT infrastructure, the business-related expertise of the IT group, and the quality of the inter-action between IT and management groups. At the same time, BI capacity concerns information distribution and analysis for management use. BI systems facilitate analytical decision-making instead of operating systems such as ERP and E-commerce, which focus on rapid and efficient transaction processing [28].

Some researchers analyze capabilities such as data sources, data kinds, dependability, user access in terms of authorization and authentication, system flexibility, interface with other systems, and the amount of risk the system provides [29]. Others give three classification groups for BI capacity in organizations:

- BI innovation infrastructure is the fundamental capability of mobilizing and deploying BI features to support organizational innovation through infrastructure, culture, and technological improvements;
- BI process capability is the incorporation of BI into the firm's customer-centric and B2B (Business-to-Business) processes; and
- BI integration capability is how the organization builds and integrates such capability and develops ways to use it [30].

Furthermore, Olszak (2014) has presented a complete, dynamic BI capabilities framework that considers six capability areas: governance, culture, technology, people, processes, and change & innovation. According to this dynamic capacity paradigm, the talents required greatly depend on the environment's dynamics [27]. Dynamic capabilities are higher-level competencies that indicate a company's capacity to integrate, create, and restructure internal and external resources/competencies to handle and perhaps shape a fast-changing business environment. Dynamic capabilities may be conceived of as three clusters of activities and adjustments:

- opportunity detection and evaluation (sensing),
- mobilization of resources to address an opportunity and capture value from doing so (seizing), and
- ongoing regeneration (transforming) [31].

Hostmann et al. also outlined eight fundamental BI skills divided into organizational and technological components: Information Source, Information Type, Data Dependability, Adaptability, Intuition in Analysis, Communication with Other Systems, Level of Risk, User Access (web-centric or desktop app) [9].

Organizations understood that they required various business intelligence capabilities to meet the demands of their users. Finally, this variety of applications might be divided into five main groups or "Styles of Business Intelligence" applications. The five types of BI applications are as follows:

1. Advanced Data Mining and Analysis
2. Visual and OLAP Analysis
3. Business Reporting
4. Scorecards and Dashboards
5. Mobile Apps and Alerts [32].

A comprehensive literature review yielded 34 BI evaluation criteria, which were incorporated into the second part of the study. The interviewees assigned ranks to the requirements from these 34 variables to determine their relative importance. After that, factor analysis was used to extract the six main factors for evaluation. These were "Analytical and Intelligent Decision-support," "Provision of Related Experimentation and Integration with Environmental Information," "Model Optimization and Recommendation," "Reasoning," "Enhanced Decision-making Tools," and "Stakeholder Satisfaction." These structural factors demonstrate the breadth of enterprise system intelligence and its relationship to BI competence [33].

In terms of BI software, Tableau, QlikView, Microsoft Power BI, SAP Business Objects, IBM Cognos, and other leading BI products are examples. On the other hand, top analytics tools include SAS, Python, Microsoft R, IBM SPSS, Minitab, and others [34]. The primary BI tools have database query and reporting software, multidimensional data analysis tools (e.g., OLAP), and data mining tools (e.g., predictive analysis, text mining, and web mining. BI provides interactive visualization for data exploration and discovery. Indeed, BI and big data analytics emphasize valuable data, information, or knowledge [35]. Robust scheduling, sharing, cutoff point notifications, data, object-level security, and report bursting are all elements of critical BI applications.

Additionally, all major BI products include access to BI material via web portals or mobile devices and the ability to set up LDAP and entry authorization with SSO options [34]. Some prominent vendors, such as SAP, are developing analytical solutions such as SAP HANA, which will provide "predictive analytics, text, and big data in a single package" (SAP 2014). However, the Big Data job market requires experts using these tools, and BI capabilities are still considerably more remarkable than the demand for Big Data competencies [36].

BI is now built on four cutting-edge technological pillars: cloud, mobile, big data, and social networking. All of them are current online services or the Internet of services [37]. Cloud BI is a solution that enables on-demand access to software and hardware resources while requiring minimum administration work. According to a report, cloud BI is a breakthrough concept for offering BI capabilities "as a service" via cloud-based architecture at a reduced cost while allowing for faster deployment and customization. Cloud BI solutions appeal to enterprises that want to boost agility while lowering IT expenses and reaping the benefits of cloud computing [15]. For example, BI systems may employ daily operations conducted by investment banks as an alternative. Another advantage is that BI systems can interface with other technologies, such as Cloud Computing, to provide more added value to organizations [8]. On the other hand, collecting and evaluating a significant volume of timely comments and opinions from varied social media users may draw a wide range of social and business insights critical for social policy formation, customer relationship management, and product creation. Advanced information extraction, topic identification, opinion mining, and time-series analysis techniques can be applied to traditional business information as well as the new BI contents for a variety of accounting, finance, and marketing applications such as enterprise risk assessment and management, credit rating and analysis, corporate event analysis, stock, and portfolio management, and so on [38].

Considering dynamic capabilities and organizational growth concepts, Chen and Lin (2021) constructed the STD structural framework for BI capabilities. Based on the STD conceptual model, they investigate the interaction mechanics of BI capabilities and

128   Ç. Sıcakyüz

the influence of the BI application on company performance. The study showed that integrated BI capacity's sensing, transforming, and driving capabilities are essential. BI application in the real economy should yield a positive outcome and high potential considering the quick advancement of information technology and business model modifications [39].

The capability of decision-making of used BI firms might be related to the adoption and effective use of BI. Indeed, a study resulted that organization size, absorptive capacity, relative advantage, complexity, and commitment - emerged as key drivers of a firm's Data Warehouse adoption choice [40]. In a study, six dynamic capability categories related to BI were identified, which are associated with the agility of BI. Organization and governance refer to a company's ability to manage its (BI-related) resources. All operations connected to an organization's goods and services are included in business processes. Change management and change behavior are concerned with how an organization handles change. Persons and an organization's "personality" are represented through people and culture. Technology and infrastructure are terms that define broad IT items (hardware and software) and how they are used. IS portfolio and architecture describing the IS applications and their architecture, such as data models or tiered architecture [41].

BI is also crucial in agile management. As such, some studies [42] indicate that agile manufacturing offers a process for responding quickly to changing markets, producing high-quality goods, shortening supply delays, and increasing customer value. Organizations should benefit from the most recent information technology advances while continually developing their own. The capacity of management and employees to adjust to changes quickly and error-free is critical to the success of agile manufacturing.

Decision-making is especially important in emergency or disaster management. Agile risk management, as well as the use of artificial intelligence systems and data analytics, will enable an organization and its service supply chain networks to access relevant information and data in real-time, discover patterns in data, recognize uncertainty, opportunities, threats, and risks, and make effective decisions [43].

When the recent pandemic is taken into consideration, COVID-19 has a significant influence on e-commerce. One of the world's heavyweights, Walmart, increased its e-commerce transactions by 74% in the global market [44]. During COVID-19, many medical products, such as drugs, medical devices, and herbal goods, have been critical. These products must be just in time and in the right amount transported, and the demand priority must be clear. The exact needs must be apparent in the hospitals. COVID-19 is a game-changer that necessitates new operational, manufacturing, and service procedures, resulting in significant transformations and transformations of organizations worldwide. The supply chain for the services sector is a crucial business supporting most economies during these challenging times through increased job demand, material acquisition, production, storing of goods, inventory control, distribution, and delivery of necessary products and services [43].

The capability of DM (Decision maker) plays a vital role in the success of the SC (Supply Chain) companies. The main components of supply chain management are location problems, solid transportation problems, and inventory management. Finding optimal locations for retail outlets, plants, terminals, workplaces, fire stations, and railroad stations is a critical and complex issue in inventory management. Choosing the best locations for facilities and optimizing overall logistics costs, delivery times, and inventory costs by various modes of transportation can significantly impact the management system [45]. Considering today's competitive health market, corporations must maximize profit while minimizing costs and considering drug manufacture and supply time [46].

However, in many real situations, products are not directly shipped from plants to customers. In a TS (Transportation system), goods are transferred from plants to clients through a series of phases in the SCN (Supply Chain Network) [47]. Especially time is a critical factor in the process. If the items are not delivered on time, it directly impacts the entire system. As a result, employing such TP (Transportation Period), all ordered items should be delivered to the destinations on time. In SC, the transportation period of products must be completed within the set time; otherwise, items may be degraded or have a storage problem, and the client may cancel the desired goods [46].

Recent studies handle the problems in the SC to make better decisions related to the. For example, the MMFSTP (Multi-stage Multi-Objective Fixed-Charge Solid Transportation) issue delivers products from factories to customers via DCs (Distribution Centers), retailers, etc. The parameters of MMFSTP are inherently unpredictable because of factors such as a lack of input information, a shifting financial market, road conditions, poor statistical analysis, etc. In this instance, it is necessary to seek the advice of decision-makers or specialists to anticipate the probable values of the parameters. In most circumstances, decision-makers provide parameter values as an interval value, a linguistic word, or another type. For example, the demand for a DC is "14–19 tons/day" [47]. Unfortunately, correct values of the parameters cannot be obtained, and only probability distributions are insufficient to estimate the parameters. Hence, the DM must provide such uncertainty, a blending of historical information and perception degree, to define the parameters [48].

Because of insufficient information related to cost, fixed cost, supply or production, demand, and conveyance are only sometimes correct in real-life situations. As a result, uncertainty emerges in various applications because the market condition varies, and demand cannot be accurately predicted at any stage. When ambiguity arises, the decision-maker DM is limited in his or her ability to address the associated costs in the industry. Due to unforeseen circumstances, DM may be unable to make up the delivery time [49].

2.1 Contribution and Aim of Study

As mentioned above, decision-making is an essential process in well-managing companies. While the success of BI is known worldwide, there still needs to be more information about Turkish companies, whether they are aware of this technology and why digitalization in Türkiye is low. The studies in the literature were conducted mainly on the usage of IT in firms and the performance of BI. Moreover, the enterprises may need to apply BI appropriately, or the BI system they employed was unsuccessful in various sizes of firms in Türkiye.

Some of these investigations have evaluated the implementation of BI from the organizational viewpoint. However, scarcely any of them considered the influence of decision-making style as a factor in BI success [9]. Although several prior research has found that size significantly impacts the adoption of innovations, the results have proven inconclusive [40].

Hence, to fill this gap in the BI literature, the study aimed to clarify whether the low digitalization of Türkiye, an indicator of BI, has arisen from SMEs, considering the production values and quantity of the SMEs or from the capabilities of BI used. To achieve the aim, the following research questions are to be answered:

– Do firms in Türkiye use BI in their business processes?
– Which BI systems are used in Türkiye's firms?
– Who uses BI systems in the firms mostly?
– Does using BI differ from the size of enterprises?
– Is there a significant difference in the decision-making skills of BI software in different company sizes?
– Is there a significant difference in the decision-making skills of BI software in different users in companies?
– The BI system used in the firms specialized to the users?

3   Method

3.1   Sample

One hundred twenty-three firms attended the Efficiency and Technology Fair held in June 2021. One hundred surveys were handed out to 85 enterprises that agreed to contribute to research at the Fair. After one hour, the surveys were collected. Hence, the response rate is 0.85. Due to missing data, 11 of them are excluded. Twenty of 74 surveys did not use BI-Software in their company, while three were unaware if the firm uses BI. Therefore, 50 enterprises were assessed in this research.

3.2   Data Analysis

The questionnaire was adopted by [39]. Fifty enterprises were categorized into their number of employees, and there were four groups, namely, micro, small, medium-sized, and large. From the literature, four items were determined to measure decision-making capability. Decision-making capabilities were measured with four items on a 7-point Likert scale. Then the average value of items was calculated and used to test group differences. The measurement items are as follows:

• C1.BI matches with rational business planning,
• C2.BI improves the efficiency of business planning,
• C3.BI can align strategic planning and changes in the business environment,
• C4.BI ensures the practicability of business action plans.

However, to use the Anova test, normality and homogeneity of variances are to meet. In the case of violation of assumptions, the nonparametric test is used equivalently. The data conformity to the normal distribution was tested with the Shapiro-Wilk test ($W = 0.94751$, p-value $= 0.02931 < 0.05$). Hence, it was decided to use a nonparametric test

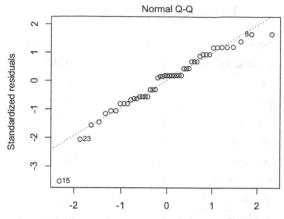

Fig. 3. Normal Q-Q plot of Group Size.

instead of a parametric one. It was determined that they were not normally distributed (Fig. 3). Hence, the one-way Kruskal-Wallis test was applied instead of the one-way Anova test. The test was run in the R studio. When an ordinal, interval or ratio level of data is provided, three or more independent groups are identical or different on some variable of interest. Because the Kruskal-Wallis test estimates variance among participants based on variation among the ranking sample means rather than variation among sample means, the normality assumption is not required in the H test, and the sample distribution may even be arbitrary.

The Kruskal-Wallis (H) test is used to examine whether there are variations in BI capacity amongst enterprises of different sizes and BI users. The test hypothesis is set as follows:

H1: The decision-making capability of the BI used in firms does not differ from the firm's size.

H2: The decision-making capability of the BI used in firms does not differ from the type of BI users.

4   Results and Discussion

The number of businesses per business varied greatly. Table 1 displays the 50 replies from 85 Turkish enterprises across various industries. The industries represented by the 50 firms who attended the show and replied to the survey are in the table below.

According to Table 1, the firms that responded to the survey mainly function in the service sector, with the majority of these enterprises coming from the defense industry (%26). Firms in the software and informatics industries are ranked second (%20), followed by organizations in the education (%16) and energy sectors (%10).

Twenty-four businesses that are BI users included in the research have been functioning for more than 15 years, and ten companies have just started their businesses as shown in Fig. 4.a. The six BI users who have been active for between 7 and 11 years have yet to encounter the company. One firm did not give information about the use of BI.

Table 1. Industry Breakdown of firms.

Sector	Number of firms	% of Total
Defense industry	13	0.26
IT	10	0.20
Education	8	0.16
Energy	5	0.10
Aviation	4	0.08
Advertising	2	0.04
Certification	2	0.04
Audit	1	0.02
Furniture	1	0.02
Iron-steel	1	0.02
Manufacturing	1	0.02
Security equipment	1	0.02
Textile	1	0.02
Total	50	

Figure 4.b shows the number of firms surveyed. The respondents were mainly from large companies, and sixteen companies act as medium-sized businesses. The number of respondents from the small and micro companies was almost equal.

The following pie chart (Fig. 5) shows the share of BI-user in firms. Users in various positions in firms use BI systems at different levels.

Most users were from different hierarchical levels, and they could mobilize and utilize business intelligence features BI programs in enterprises when needed—following that, it is used by senior and middle-level managers. While business analysts or specialists use the BI system in eleven companies, the six respondents do not know who uses these programs in the enterprise. Two firms stated that the BI systems were used solely by top managers.

BI and BA (Business Analytics) software were determined from the literature. The BI software and BA tools used by businesses are shown in Fig. 6.

Some firms' representatives added the BI software type they use in their firms which is not listed in the questionnaire. Some firms, especially large-scale enterprises, prefer more than one program for different units. It is seen from Fig. 6 that the most preferred software is the SAP business, and Oracle is in second place.

It has been determined from the survey that some companies have prepared special programs suitable for their business processes. In addition, some firms were using different BI systems simultaneously at varying operations for purposes.

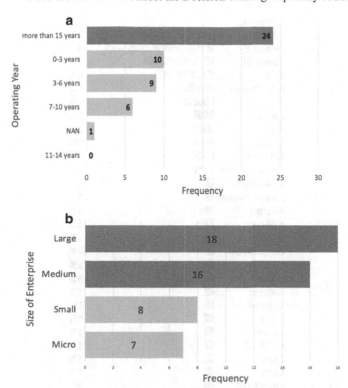

Fig. 4. a The operating years of the surveyed firms. b The number of companies to their firm size.

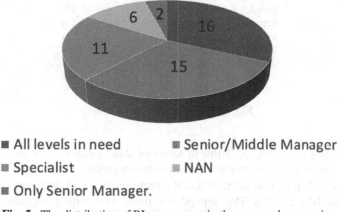

■ All levels in need   ■ Senior/Middle Manager
■ Specialist   ■ NAN
■ Only Senior Manager.

Fig. 5. The distribution of BI user groups in the surveyed companies.

4.1 Descriptive Statistics

Frequencies, averages, and standard deviations are shown in descriptive statistics relating to firm sizes and BI-user groups in firms (Table 2). The means of BI decision-making capability in different firm sizes range from 5.41 to 5.81, and they appear to approximate

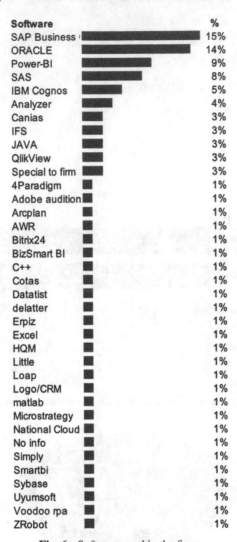

Software	%
SAP Business	15%
ORACLE	14%
Power-BI	9%
SAS	8%
IBM Cognos	5%
Analyzer	4%
Canias	3%
IFS	3%
JAVA	3%
QlikView	3%
Special to firm	3%
4Paradigm	1%
Adobe audition	1%
Arcplan	1%
AWR	1%
Bitrix24	1%
BizSmart BI	1%
C++	1%
Cotas	1%
Datatist	1%
delatter	1%
Erpiz	1%
Excel	1%
HQM	1%
Little	1%
Loap	1%
Logo/CRM	1%
matlab	1%
Microstrategy	1%
National Cloud	1%
No info	1%
Simply	1%
Smartbi	1%
Sybase	1%
Uyumsoft	1%
Voodoo rpa	1%
ZRobot	1%

Fig. 6. Software used in the firms.

each other. They do, however, differ in terms of standard deviation. Remarkably, the variance is seen in small enterprises but not between groups.

From Table 2, it can be inferred that the representatives of firms are generally satisfied with the BI capability. The respondents' opinions in large companies are close to each other regarding BI capability in decision-making. Because large and medium-sized companies account for mainly of respondents, their opinion can reflect the reality of BI-capability. However, there is an opinion gap among respondents in small firms. The considerable gap was also in special BI users, which can be understood from the standard deviation. There was no consensus among them. Nevertheless, it is not remarkable for which size of the companies these specialists work.

Table 2. The summary statistics related to the firms according to their size.

No	Group	Frequency	mean	Std. Deviation
1	Micro	7	5.61	0.827
2	Small	8	5.41	1.76
3	Medium	16	5.81	0.973
4	Large	18	5.57	0.685
1	All levels in need	16	5.83	0.561
2	Specialist	10	5.25	1.43
3	Senior/Middle	17	5.47	1.09

The boxplot in Fig. 7a shows the general distribution of firms' sizes, such as the median, first quartile, and third quartile of the group's means.

Here, it is prominently noticed that the opinion of the respondent in small-sized firms related to BI-capability has a minimum value of about 2. This value indicates that the respondent is not satisfied with BI's competence in decision-making.

The opinions in the small firms were inconsistent about BI's competence because some found BI's ability in decision-making better than others. This inconsistency might be caused by different BI used in small firms or different BI users. Since there was no information about who uses BI in small firms, it cannot be explained precisely.

The jitter diagram is shown in Fig. 7.b. The goal of the jitter is to move the pointers slightly and randomly.

A jitter diagram is drawn to minimize or mitigate the effect of overplotting, which happens when numerous points are plotted at virtually the same spot. Figure 7.b shows the jitter diagram of groups' means according to firm sizes. As seen in Fig. 7.b, although there were different opinions in the groups, it is remarkable that an outlier in the small firms causes variance, which can also be seen in Table 1 from the standard deviation column. It means that only one small-sized firm thinks BI is ineffective in decision-making while other small-sized mainly assessed the capability of BI used quite well in decision-making. Again, this variability in respondents' opinions can depend on the BI software or users in the companies. However, the thoughts were primarily wide apart in small firms. The reasons for different opinions about BI's competence could be either improper integration of BI into the small firms' business processes, or BI could not be used effectively in these firms when BI software is effective.

Regarding the BI expert groups, the boxplot graph and jitter diagram (Fig. 8) explain their distribution. The variances in the BI specialist group were higher than the others, and this can also be understood from the outlier in the jitter diagram Fig. 8.b.

Moreover, the median in the group of specialists is almost equal to the first quartile. The mean of BI capabilities to system users at various levels for specific functions is greater than the other groups of BI users. In other words, variations in the groups of senior or middle managers' assessments about the capability of BI that are used in their firms are considerable. BI specialist user groups significantly differ in the group in terms of BI capabilities in their decision-making processes.

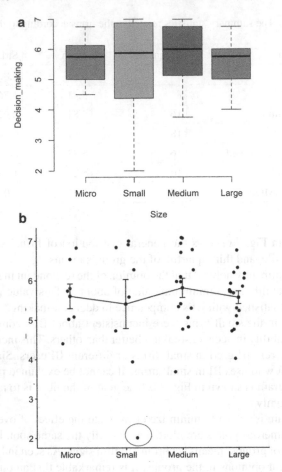

Fig. 7. a Boxplot of the firms' sizes. b Jitter diagram of the firms' sizes.

The groups of BI specialists are supposed to be the wiser group because they have the know-how of how to gain information and where to use it. Despite the BI specialists in the firms, respondents' opinions are diverse in the groups. In that case, it means the problems are related to BI software or its incompliance with the firm's processes.

These differences can be also seen in the management-level users. Nevertheless, In the firms of the BI users in the group that uses it for a specific purpose at any level of the company, the respondents feel that BI is capable of decision-making.

4.2 Hypothesis Test Results

The H test p-value is not smaller than the critical p-value (0.05), as shown in Table 3. Hence there is no evidence that the groups' means are different, and the hypothesis must be accepted. In other words, the decision-making capability of BI software does not make a difference among the enterprises' sizes. In the same way, the second hypothesis is also accepted.

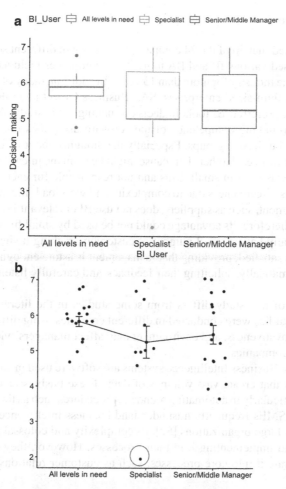

Fig. 8. a Boxplot of the firms' BI-users-groups. b Jitter diagram of the firms' BI-users-groups

Table 3. The test results of the hypotheses.

	Kruskal-Wallis chi-squared	df	p-value	Result
H1	0.93203	3	0.8177	Accept
H2	1.4607	2	0.4817	Accept

Then, it can be concluded that the decision-making capability of BI software does not make a difference among the different BI users in enterprises. Although there was no relationship between the groups in both hypotheses, the jitter diagrams and boxplots revealed that BI capability might differ in groups.

5 Conclusion

This study revealed that 50 of the 74 companies operating in different sectors participating in the Fair used various BI and BA tools. Most companies included in the research have worked in the industry for more than 15 years. In addition, many of these companies are large and medium-sized enterprises. SAP Business Object and ORACLE were the companies' most preferred BI tools in decision-making. This study also demonstrated that the decision-making competence of the software used does not differ according to the firm's size but in size groups. Especially the thoughts about BI capability among small firms differ from each other. This cause might be from the integration of BIs. When the complex BI was used in small firms and not responsible for each module, it could not be used for its effectiveness due to complexity and workload. Indeed, if small firms' business environment, such as suppliers, does not use BI or relevant IT, then BI might be inefficient, and therefore, its advantage could not be used by small firms. Because small businesses typically have a small number of customers, making it simple to determine whether they are satisfied, providing that management is astute enough to communicate with them systematically, soliciting their feedback and carefully listening to what they suggest [50].

The finding of this study differs from some studies in the literature [40, 50–52]; however, these studies were conducted in different countries using different techniques. The culture, innovativeness, and environment may affect managers' views of the recent technologies in companies.

Nevertheless, Business Intelligence systems are software used in small and medium-sized businesses that create vast volumes of data. These businesses employ Business Intelligence, particularly in automating mundane procedures such as finance, production, etc. [51]. Since SMEs frequently misunderstand business intelligence as a technology only suitable for large organizations [52], its complexity and colossal price make some small firms avoid implementing it in their processes. However, they can benefit from BI if they integrate it into core processes, such as customer relationship management systems.

The other findings of this study showed that the use of BI systems in firms did not vary to users' positions. This result indicates that big companies have complex business processes and need specialists to use, control or manage BI systems. Apart from that, the operations in big companies might be executed at the horizontal structural level; hence the user might use BI in their department, which they solely have access to and are responsible for the tasks and duties. On the other hand, small and medium-sized firms can hire specialists because of both the newness of BI to the firms and the fact that they have yet to experience it.

In the digital age, firms must integrate BI into their business processes, adopt intelligent systems such as BI, and stay digital to compete in the digital ecosystem. In addition, managers should use BI in their daily and strategic decision-making.

The digital entrepreneurship ecosystem comprises government, industrial firms, technology vendors, schools and universities, investors (including financial companies), and other businesses in the value stream. It is critical to establish a technological infrastructure, collaborate among institutions, facilitate technical and financial support, boost research and development, and create legal arrangements to stimulate the creation of novel products and services to contribute to the rise and growth of the intelligent entrepreneurship ecosystem [53]. BI can also help managers in disaster and risk management. The requirement for service supply chain integration through effective agility methods, artificial intelligence, and data analytics to enable managers to make profitable and resilient decisions inside the various supply chain networks is particularly critical during COVID-19 [43].

In summary, as discussed earlier, the performance of BI is shown in many types of research. To be competitive, firms should enhance all real-time and accurate information relevant to suppliers, consumers, rivals, services, products, business environment, and technology to make better decisions.

This study clearly demonstrated that small firms must be assisted in broadly presenting BI and its possible advantages, purchasing appropriate BI, and using it effectively. The government should support small firms notably. And take the initiative for them. To level up digitalization, at least to a global degree, the government should provide some incentives and encourage firms to use new technologies. Thus, digitalization impacts partially or the entire SC. The owner of companies should be convinced of the performance of their rivals using BI.

Limitations and Future Studies. This study has some limitations due to the missing information. For instance, the impact of the software on the business profit or performance could not be examined. Taking an example of two or three BI software, the software modules could be separately analyzed and compared in the following studies.

This study only measures the decision-making ability of software used by 50 companies operating in Türkiye. Therefore, generalization cannot be made. Some companies use more than one software together. Thus, decision-making competence at the software level needs to be made apparent. The result covers four items measuring decision-making capability, but different items can be added, more samples can be taken, and the test can be rerun. In this study, the effect of the software on business performance has not been measured. For this reason, the impact of decision-making capability on the performance of enterprises based on software can be investigated in future studies.

In the study, the jitter diagrams and boxplots illustrated that might be some differences in the groups; hence, the following study can examine the relationship between the groups by taking more samples.

Apart from that, in a future study, the opinion of BI users in firms could also be taken, and the weaknesses of BI could be identified. As such, the software could be improved or adapted to the firms' systems.

The performance and impact of BI in the risk management of firms in Türkiye could be examined after that, and the related comparisons could be made among the firms with BI users and nonusers in the future.

References

1. Ahmad, A.: Business intelligence for sustainable competitive advantage. In: Sustaining Competitive Advantage Via Business Intelligence, Knowledge Management, and System Dynamics, pp. 3–220. Emerald Group Publishing Ltd. (2015)

2. Muayad Younus, A., Shakir Mahmoud, D., Najeeb Zaidan, M., Shakir Mahmood, D.: The strategic impact of business intelligence in terms of essentials, techniques, and services. Eur. Sch. J. (ESJ) **3**, 26–37 (2022)
3. Davenport, T.H.: Business intelligence and organizational decisions. Int. J. Bus. Intell. Res. **1**, 1–12 (2010). https://doi.org/10.4018/jbir.2010071701
4. Delen, D., Moscato, G., Toma, I.L.: The impact of real-time business intelligence and advanced analytics on the behaviour of business decision makers. In: 2018 International Conference on Information Management and Processing, ICIMP 2018, pp. 49–53. Institute of Electrical and Electronics Engineers Inc. (2018)
5. Sharon, J.A., Juliet, S.: Efficient business intelligence implementation: a systematic review. In: Proceedings of the International Conference on Applied Artificial Intelligence and Computing (ICAAIC 2022), pp. 144–149. Institute of Electrical and Electronics Engineers (IEEE) (2022)
6. Elena, C.: Business intelligence. J. Knowl. Manag. Econ. Inf. Technol., 1–12 (2011)
7. Jalal Haghighat, M., Zahra, A.: Using business intelligence capabilities to improve the quality of decision-making: a case study of Mellat bank. World Acad. Sci. Eng. Technol. Int. J. Econ. Manag. Eng. **13**, 159–170 (2019)
8. Chang, V.: The business intelligence as a service in the cloud. Future Gener. Comput. Syst. **37**, 512–534 (2014). https://doi.org/10.1016/j.future.2013.12.028
9. Mohammadi, F., Hajiheydari, N.: How business intelligence capabilities contributed managerial decision making styles. Int. J. e-Educ. e-Bus. e-Manag. e-Learn. **2**, 28–33 (2012)
10. Negash, S.: Business intelligence. Commun. Assoc. Inf. Syst. **13** (2004). https://doi.org/10.17705/1CAIS.01315
11. Tavera Romero, C.A., Ortiz, J.H., Khalaf, O.I., Ríos Prado, A.: Business intelligence: business evolution after industry 4.0. Sustainability (Switzerland) **13** (2021). https://doi.org/10.3390/su131810026
12. Jourdan, Z., Rainer, R.K., Marshall, T.E.: Business intelligence: an analysis of the literature. Inf. Syst. Manag. **25**, 121–131 (2008). https://doi.org/10.1080/10580530801941512
13. Gartner: Gartner Forecasts Indian Business Intelligence and Analytics Software Revenue to Reach $150 Million in 2015. https://www.gartner.com/en/newsroom/press-releases/2015-06-09-gartner-forecasts-indian-business-intelligence-and-analytics-software-revenue-to-reach-150-million-in-2015
14. Gartner: Software Market Insights: Business Intelligence (BI) and Data Analytics. https://www.gartner.com/en/digital-markets/insights/software-market-insights-business-intelligence-and-data-analytics
15. Olszak, C.M.: Toward better understanding and use of business intelligence in organizations. Inf. Syst. Manag. **33**, 105–123 (2016). https://doi.org/10.1080/10580530.2016.1155946
16. Gangadharan, G.R., Swami, S.N.: Business intelligence systems: design and implementation strategies. In: 2nd International Conference Information Technology Interfaces IT1 2004, Croatia, pp. 139–144 (2004)
17. Aldaher, H., İşcan, Ö.F.: The role of business intelligence in promoting decision-making in humanitarian organizations operating in Turkey, Orange organization as a sample. Glob. J. Econ. Bus. **12**, 385–405 (2022). https://doi.org/10.31559/GJEB2022.12.3.7
18. TUIK: Survey on Information and Communication Technology (ICT) Usage in Enterprises (2021). https://data.tuik.gov.tr/Bulten/Index?p=Survey-on-Information-and-Communication-Technology-(ICT)-Usage-in-Enterprises-2021-37435&dil=2
19. IMD: IMD World Digital Competitiveness Ranking 2021 (2021)
20. Bezrukova, N., Huk, L., Chmil, H., Verbivska, L., Komchatnykh, O., Kozlovskyi, Y.: Digitalization as a trend of modern development of the world economy. WSEAS Trans. Environ. Dev. **18**, 120–129 (2022). https://doi.org/10.37394/232015.2022.18.13
21. Silahtaroğlu, G., Şaykol, E., Doğan, İ., Kocamaz, A.: On the use of analytics in Turkey: a data mining study, 1–9 (2014)

22. Wright, S., Bisson, C., Duffy, A.P.: Applying a behavioural and operational diagnostic typology of competitive intelligence practice: empirical evidence from the SME sector in Turkey. J. Strateg. Mark. **20**, 19–33 (2012). https://doi.org/10.1080/0965254X.2011.628450
23. Silahtaroğlu, G., Alayoglu, N.: Using or not using business intelligence and big data for strategic management: an empirical study based on interviews with executives in various sectors. In: 12th International Strategic Management Conference, ISMC 2016, pp. 208–215. Procedia Social and Behavioral Sciences, Antalya (2016)
24. Trieu, V.-H.: Getting value from business intelligence systems: a review and research agenda. Decis. Support Syst. **93**, 111–124 (2017). https://doi.org/10.1016/j.dss.2016.09.019
25. Park, Y., el Sawy, O.A., Fiss, P.C.: The role of business intelligence and communication technologies in organizational agility: a configurational approach. J. Assoc. Inf. Syst. **18**, 648–686 (2017)
26. Ain, N., Vaia, G., DeLone, W.H., Waheed, M.: Two decades of research on business intelligence system adoption, utilization and success – a systematic literature review. Decis. Support Syst. **125**, 1–13 (2019). https://doi.org/10.1016/j.dss.2019.113113
27. Olszak, C.M.: Towards an understanding business intelligence. A dynamic capability-based framework for business intelligence. In: Proceedings of the 2014 Federated Conference on Computer Science and Information Systems, pp. 1103–1110. ACSIS, Varsaw (2014)
28. Kulkarni, U.R., Robles-Flores, A.J., Popovič, A.: Business intelligence capability: the effect of top management and the mediating roles of user participation and analytical decision making orientation. J. Assoc. Inf. Syst. **18**, 516–541 (2017)
29. Isik, O., Jones, M.C., Sidorova, A.: Business Intelligence (BI) success and the role of BI capabilities. Intell. Syst. Acc. Finan. Manag. **18**, 161–176 (2011). https://doi.org/10.1002/isaf.329
30. Ramakrishnan, T., Khuntia, J., Kathuria, A., Saldanha, T.J.V.: Business intelligence capabilities. In: Deokar, A.V., Gupta, A., Iyer, L.S., Jones, M.C. (eds.) Analytics and Data Science. AIS, pp. 15–27. Springer, Cham (2018). https://doi.org/10.1007/978-3-319-58097-5_3
31. Teece, D.J.: Dynamic Capabilities: Routines versus Entrepreneurial Action (2012)
32. Nedelcu, B.: Business intelligence systems. Database Syst. J. (2013)
33. Ghazanfari, M., Jafari, M., Rouhani, S.: A tool to evaluate the business intelligence of enterprise systems. Scientia Iranica. **18**, 1579–1590 (2011). https://doi.org/10.1016/j.scient.2011.11.011
34. Saeed, K., Sidorova, A., Vasanthan, A.: The bundling of business intelligence and analytics. J. Comput. Inf. Syst., 1–12 (2022). https://doi.org/10.1080/08874417.2022.2103856
35. Sun, Z., Zou, H., Strang, K.: Big data analytics as a service for business intelligence. In: Janssen, M., et al. (eds.) I3E 2015. LNCS, vol. 9373, pp. 200–211. Springer, Cham (2015). https://doi.org/10.1007/978-3-319-25013-7_16
36. Debortoli, S., Müller, O., vom Brocke, J.: Comparing business intelligence and big data skills. Bus. Inf. Syst. Eng. **6**(5), 289–300 (2014). https://doi.org/10.1007/s12599-014-0344-2
37. Sun, Z., Sun, L., Strang, K.: Big data analytics services for enhancing business intelligence. J. Comput. Inf. Syst. **58**, 162–169 (2018). https://doi.org/10.1080/08874417.2016.1220239
38. Lim, E.P., Chen, H., Chen, G.: Business intelligence and analytics: research directions. ACM Trans. Manag. Inf. Syst. **3** (2013). https://doi.org/10.1145/2407740.2407741
39. Chen, Y., Lin, Z.: Business intelligence capabilities and firm performance: a study in China. Int. J. Inf. Manage. **57** (2021). https://doi.org/10.1016/j.ijinfomgt.2020.102232
40. Ramamurthy, K. (Ram), Sen, A., Sinha, A.P.: An empirical investigation of the key determinants of data warehouse adoption. Decis. Support Syst. **44**, 817–841 (2008). https://doi.org/10.1016/j.dss.2007.10.006

41. Knabke, T., Olbrich, S.: Exploring the future shape of business intelligence: mapping dynamic capabilities of information systems to business intelligence agility introduction and motivation: the need for speed. In: Twenty-First Americas Conference on Information Systems, Puerto Rico (2015)

42. Uçaktürk, A., Uçaktürk, T., Yavuz, H.: Possibilities of usage of strategic business intelligence systems based on databases in agile manufacturing. Procedia Soc. Behav. Sci. **207**, 234–241 (2015). https://doi.org/10.1016/j.sbspro.2015.10.092

43. Asare, A.O., Addo, P.C., Sarpong, E.O., Kotei, D.: COVID-19: optimizing business performance through agile business intelligence and data analytics. Open J. Bus. Manag. **08**, 2071–2080 (2020). https://doi.org/10.4236/ojbm.2020.85126

44. Bhatti, A., Akram, H., Basit, H.M., Khan, A.U., Raza, S.M.: E-commerce trends during COVID-19 Pandemic. Int. J. Future Gener. Commun. Network. **13**, 1449–1452 (2020)

45. Das, S.K., Pervin, M., Roy, S.K., Weber, G.W.: Multi-objective solid transportation-location problem with variable carbon emission in inventory management: a hybrid approach. Ann. Oper. Res. (2021). https://doi.org/10.1007/s10479-020-03809-z

46. Mardanya, D., Maity, G., Kumar Roy, S.: The multi-objective multi-item just-in-time transportation problem. Optimization, 1–32 (2021). https://doi.org/10.1080/02331934.2021.1963246

47. Midya, S., Roy, S.K., Yu, V.F.: Intuitionistic fuzzy multi-stage multi-objective fixed-charge solid transportation problem in a green supply chain. Int. J. Mach. Learn. Cybern. **12**(3), 699–717 (2020). https://doi.org/10.1007/s13042-020-01197-1

48. Mondal, A., Roy, S.K.: Multi-objective sustainable opened- and closed-loop supply chain under mixed uncertainty during COVID-19 pandemic situation. Comput. Ind. Eng. **159** (2021). https://doi.org/10.1016/j.cie.2021.107453

49. Ghosh, S., Roy, S.K., Ebrahimnejad, A., Verdegay, J.L.: Multi-objective fully intuitionistic fuzzy fixed-charge solid transportation problem. Complex Intell. Syst. **7**(2), 1009–1023 (2021). https://doi.org/10.1007/s40747-020-00251-3

50. D'Arconte, C.: Business intelligence applied in small size for profit companies. In: 8th International Congress of Information and Communication Technology (ICICT-2018), pp. 45–57. Procedia Comput. Sci. **131** (2018)

51. Kubina, M., Koman, G., Kubinova, I.: Possibility of improving efficiency within business intelligence systems in companies. In: 4th World Conference on Business, Economics and Management, WCBEM, pp. 300–305. Procedia Econ. Finan. (2015)

52. Raj, R., Wong, S.H.S., Beaumont, A.J.: Business intelligence solution for an SME: a case study. In: Proceedings of the 8th International Joint Conference on Knowledge Discovery, Knowledge Engineering and Knowledge Management (IC3K 2016), pp. 41–50. SciTePress (2016)

53. Ballı, A.: Digital entrepreneurship and digital entrepreneurship approach in Turkey: Ankara case. J. Bus. Res. Turk. **12**, 1058–1071 (2020). https://doi.org/10.20491/isarder.2020.895

Analysis of Effects of Tiktok Short-Video on Gen Z's Perceptions Toward Purchase Intention

Le Thi Diep Anh[✉], Pham Van Tuan, and Bui Thi Hong Viet

Faculty of Marketing, National Economics University, Hanoi, Vietnam
anh.ltd97@gmail.com, phamvantuan@neu.edu.vn

Abstract. On the basis of the theory of technology acceptance (TAM), this study has extended and proposed a model with the impact of two new factors - Perceived entertainment and perceived the prestige of KOC. The study used the quantitative method with a dataset including 406 young people aged 18–25 in Hanoi, then processed data by Cronbach's Alpha analysis, Exploratory Factor Analysis (EFA), Confirmatory Factor Analysis (CFA) and Structural Equation Modeling (SEM). As a result, all independent variables had an impact on Attitude towards Use, in which Perceived Usefulness has the strongest influence on the mediating variable. Based on the results, the author provided some suggestions for businesses/marketers regarding creating an effective online marketing campaign.

Keywords: Theory of Technology Acceptance · the prestige of KOC · attitude towards using · purchase intention · Tiktok

1 Introduction

Until now, Tiktok is known as the fastest growing explosive application of all time. Accordingly, in less than 5 years, by 2021, Tiktok (version for global audience) and Douyin (version for China) have accumulated more than 3 billion downloads - a figure close to equal to 1/3 of the total number of social network users. At the same time, it is also ranked 7th in the list of the most used social networks in the world.

Despite bans from some countries, Tiktok has continued to grow strongly from 2020 until now and is now present in more than 50 countries worldwide, including Vietnam. According to a report by We Are Social (2021), Vietnam is currently on the TOP6 countries with the highest growth rate of TikTok users in Southeast Asia with the number of users above 39.65 million (after the US, Indonesia, Brazil, Russia, and Mexico).

In particular, Tiktok is considered the domain of GenZ when more than half of its users are between the ages of 13 and 20. According to experts, the platform has a strong appeal to Gen Z audiences because of the way it works. The platform focuses on short-form video content (under 1 min), which is easier to use and go viral than other social media platforms. For businesses targeting Gen Z, the strong growth of short-form videos

A. Mirzazadeh et al. (Eds.): SEMIT 2022, CCIS 1809, pp. 143–152, 2023.
https://doi.org/10.1007/978-3-031-40398-9_9

on Tiktok has become a useful marketing tool in increasing brand awareness, building trust and impact to users' buying behavior. In addition, according to a report by Nielson (2021), 91% of users find content on Tiktok unique; 89% of them have made an unplanned purchase after watching short-videos on Tiktok – which is the highest purchase rate on all social networking platforms available. Moreover, the report of Tiktok (2021) showed that the challenge "Tiktok Made Me Buy It" (*Tiktok made me buy that product*) received a lot of participation and interaction, sharing of human products - 3.6 billion views in total. Hence, Tiktok is seen as a significant platform for enterprises to approach and motivate Gen Z to purchase.

Nonetheless, many experts believe that businesses are currently being "dissolved" into the platform and following "the old way of thinking". Generally, majority of campagins on Tiktok is related to Dance Challenge (Brandvietnam, 2021). Although the campaigns are highly pervasive and accessible to young people, but some experts say that they are for entertainment purpose only, not revenue. After the campagin, nothing but a large number of views left. Sadly, the target public quickly forgot the brand, products and messages conveyed.

In conclusion, businesses need to buid a Marketing campaign, which positively influences on customers' attitudes and purchase intentions, by understanding their perception toward your content. However, the number of studies on this topic is limited, especially in Vietnam. Therefore, the topic "Analysis Of Effects Of Tiktok Short-Video On Gen Z's Perceptions Toward Purchase Intention" is essential, which will not only provide useful knowledge for businesses to create more effective Marketing campaign in the future, but it also would help researchers to have an in-depth understanding regarding the relationship between Gen Z's perception and intention, particularly in local Vietnam.

2   Theoretical Basis

The author takes the Technology Acceptance Model (TAM) as the base model for this study, as previous studies (Zhao and Wang, 2020; Xiao et al., 2019). Guritno and Siringoringo (2013) stated that the online purchasing behavior of consumers is shaped by the acceptance of the advertising technology/platform that the brand uses. Therefore, Technology (Technology Acceptance Model (TAM)) can be used to explain the impact of Tiktok promotional videos on Gen Z's online purchase intention (Fig. 1).

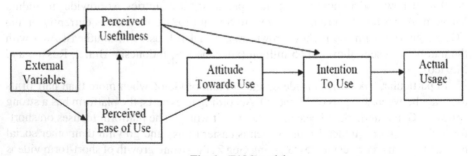

Fig. 1. TAM model

The TAM technology model is actually developed based on the Theory of Reasoned Action (TRA) and Theory of Planned Behavior (TPB). Accordingly, attitude is an important factor determining consumer's willingness, directly affecting their intention and final behavior. Regarding factors affecting the attitude, Davis et al. (1989) identified that perceived usefulness and perceive ease of use are those influence positively on attitudes and behavior of consumers. Hence, it can be said that if consumers perceive the usefulness and ease of use of a product advertised on Tiktok short video, they would have a positive attitude toward it, thereby influencing their purchase intention.

3   Proposed Model and Hypothesis

The proposed model is developed from TAM, TRA, TPB models, and extended Perceived Enterntainment and Perceived Key Opinion Consumer's prestige (known as KOC) as two new antecedents to Attitude towards Use due to the change of environment, technology (Tiktok) and research time.

In terms of the variable "Perceived Entertainment", the author has inherited the research results of Hoang et al. (2022) due to equivalence in research objectives and subjects (young people), technology used (Tiktok). Additionally, Tiktok becomes a source of daily entertainment, motivation and joy (Tiktok report, 2022). If young consumers feel entertaining while watching video, they tend to have a positive attitude and purchase intention.

"Perceived KOC's prestige, whose original idea was the Percevied credibility of Influencers, has become a virtal issue, resulting in a large numbers of study examining, particularly the relationship to purchase intentions on the Internet (Sharma et al., 2017; Lim et al., 2017; Kumar and Polonsky, 2018). Nonetheless, few researchers have studied the relationship between Perceived Influencers' Credibility and Use Intention through the meditating factor. Therefore, the current study would adapt a proposition that Attitude towards Use could mediate the relationship between Perceived Influencers's Credibility and Intention. In addition, the author proposed this variable into the model because of the development of Tiktok KOCs in Vietnam market. KOCs are regular consumers who love to share their true product reviews online. Even though most of KOC don't have a big fan base, as Xiao et al. (2019) indicated, "the professionalism and popularity of influencers/KOCs in social media have a significant positive correlation with the purchase intention of customers" (p.420). Consequently, the proposed model is shown Fig. 2.

Hypotheses
Perceived usefulness is defined when individuals find short video content on Tiktok to bring them certain values (informational, social interactivity), and assist them in improving their effectiveness and work performance (Zhao and Wang, 2020). Accordingly, if consumers think the product advertised on Tiktok short form video content is useful,

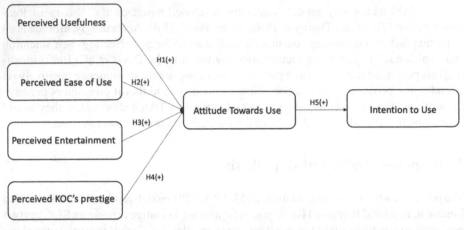

Fig. 2. Proposed Model

they are more likely to have a positive attitude in using it (Lin and Kim, 2016). From there, hypothesis H1 is put forward:

H1: Perceived usefulness of the product through Short-form video content on Tiktok has a positive impact on Gen Z's attitude towards using products.

Perceived ease of use can be understood in two aspects: Firstly, the ease of use in viewing short video content on Tiktok without spending as much time and effort as other types (Zhao and Wang, 2020). Secondly, through short videos, consumers feel the ease of use of the product. Either way, consumers perceive the ease of experience and the product may lead to their positive attitude towards the advertised product. Hence, author hypothesized:

H2: Perceived ease of use of the product through Short-form video content on Tiktok has a positive impact on the attitude towards using the product of Gen Z.

According Advertising Vietnam (2021), entertainment is one of the most important elements of videos on Tiktok. Perceived entertainment, according to Okazaki (2005), indicates comfort and enjoyment through media experiences. On Tiktok, users perceive entertainment from displayed content, special effects, or a continuous surfing experience to discover similar contents. Also, as mentioned, if the product itself is entertaining, users would feed joyful. As Hoffman et al., (1996); Shavitt et al. (2017); Nguyen Dinh Yen Oanh and Quach Ly Xuan An (2018), the higher entertainment consumers perceive, the more positive the consumer's attitude towards using the product advertised is. From there, the author hypothesized:

H3: Perceived entertainment through Short-form video content on Tiktok has a positive impact on Gen Z's attitude towards using products.

Perceived KOC's prestige means that customers have confidence and trust in KOC's expertise in a certain field. According to a report by Brand Vietnam (2021), "72.6%

of consumers will look to online reviews and consider them before making a purchase decision". Through the reviews of KOC, consumers may evaluate that the product is less commercial from advertising, reducing the "precaution" in accessing information. Customers often have a positive attitude to trust and choose a product if KOC has a good assessment of the quality, and vice versa. Therefore, the author proposes a hypothesis to test:

H4: Perceived KOC's prestige has a positive impact on attitudes towards product use of Gen Z

The relationship between attitude and intention is a classic one in studies. Many researchers have shown that purchase intention is affected by many factors, one of them is attitude towards advertising and products (Lin and Kim, 2016; Dehghani et al., 2016; Du et al., 2017). The more positive the consumer's attitude towards us through Tiktok short-form video content, the clearer the purchase intention and vice versa. From there, the author hypothesized:

H5: Attitude towards use has a positive impact on Gen Z's intention to use

4 Research Methods

4.1 Sampling Method and Sample Size

The least size to use EFA is 50, which is preferable to from 100+ onwards, according to Hair et al. (2014). The terms "measure variable" and "number observation" refer to the methyl gauge that was queried in the panel survey, respectively. In this research, the model has 24 measurement variables. Therefore, according to the principle of 5 observations per measured variable, the minimum sample size is $N = 120$.

For this study, data were collected using convenience sampling method. The target was young people aged 18–25 who were living and working in Hanoi. The author conducted a survey on Facebook and received 430 responses, of which 406 respondents were in the Gen Z, which the topic aimed, which also determined to be a reliable sample size (Hair et al., 2014). Then, the author processed all data by Cronbach's Alpha analysis, Exploratory Factor Analysis (EFA), Confirmatory Factor Analysis (CFA) and Structural Equation Modeling (SEM).

4.2 Description of the Study Sample Size

The research sample has 406 relevant observations, of which 142 were male (35%) and 264 were female (65%). Most of the respondents had bachelor's degree (364 respondents, accounting for 89.7%), and their income was mainly in the range of 3 to 10 million VND because they were mainly students/newly employed. Meanwhile, the results also show that Tiktok was the platform that the respondents watched and surfed every day, mainly from 3 to less than 5 h (recorded by 85.2% of the respondents).

5 Research Results and Discussion

5.1 Evaluation of the Scale by CROnbach's Alpha Coefficient

The author tests Cronbach's Alpha coefficient of the component variables included in the scale. Except for the variable PE4, which was excluded because the correlation coefficient of the total variable is less than 0.3, the all scales have Cronbach's Alpha coefficient greater than 0.6, satisfactory and the correlation coefficient of the total variable greater than 0.3. Therefore, all observed variables are eligible to conduct exploratory factor analysis (EFA) in the next step (Table 1).

Table 1. Evaluation of the scale by Cronbach's Alpha coefficient

No	The scale	Number of observed variables that meet the requirements	Cronbach's Alpha	Total variance extracted	Conclusion
1	Perceived usefulness (PU)	5	0.824	58.87%	Scale is reliable
2	Perceived ease of use (PEU)	3	0.791	64.211%	
3	Perceived entertainment (PE)	3	0.774	74%	
4	Perceived KOC's prestige (PKOC)	4	0.810	74.605%	
5	Attitude towards use (AT)	3	0.783	77.47%	
6	Intention to Use (IN)	5	0.827	75.98%	

5.2 Evaluation of the Scale by Exploratory Factor Analysis (EFA)

The results of exploratory factor analysis with 4 independent variables and 1 intermediate variable were performed with Principal Axis Factoring method and Promax rotation. The analysis results show that, after removing the variable PKOC3 (load factor less than 0.5), the coefficient KMO = 0.859 > 0.5, so factor analysis is appropriate. Besides, the coefficient sig = 0.000 < 0.05 shows that the observed variables are correlated with each other in the population. The total variance extracted also reached 67.811%, proving that 5 factors in the model explain 67.811% of the variation of market data.

The results of factor analysis to explore the purchase intention scale were performed with the Principal Components method and Varimax rotation. The analytical results show that the KMO value = 0.82 (0.5 < KMO = 0.82 < 1) and Barlett's test on the correlation of the observed variables has the value Sig = 0.000 < 0.05, proving that the variables are closely related. The value of total variance extracted = 60.399% (>50%) meets the requirements and shows that the component variables in the intention scale explain 60.399% of the variability of the data and are explained by the same variables as the original.

5.3 Confirmatory Factor Analysis (CFA)

The author continues using AMOS software version 20.0 to perform CFA for measuring scales after preliminary testing, evaluating the adequacy of the study model and research hypotheses. Testing criteria used include CMIN/df; Goodness of Fit Index; Tucker & Lewis Index; Comparative Fit Index; Root Mean Square Error Approximation. The model is considered suitable when testing Chi-square with P value $\geq$ 0.05. Therefore, besides P-value, CMIN/df is also used. Some practical studies indicate that when $\chi 2$/df < 5 (with sample size N > 200); or < 3 (with sample size N < 200), the model is considered to be suitable (Kettinger and Lee, 1995). In this study, the sample size is N = 409 (N > 200), according to Kettinger and Lee (1995); CMIN/df < 5; TLI, CFI $\geq$ 0.9 (Bentler and Bonett, 1990); GFI $\geq$ 0.8 (Baumgartner and Homburg, 1995); RMSEA $\leq$ 0.08, which shows that the research model is suitably.

CFA results of the above measurement scales are presented in Table 2.

Table 2. CFA test results for measurement scales

No	Indicator	Result
1	Chi-square/df	2.025
2	GFI	0.92
3	TLI	0.935
4	CFI	0.943
5	RMSEA	0.053

5.4 Structural Equation Modeling

SEM model analysis results show that the value of the test: Chi-square/df = 2.188; GFI = 0.914; TLI = 0.925; CFI = 0.935; RMSEA = 0.054. From the figures, the research model is suitable with the data conducted (Table 3).

5.5 Discussion

This study examines the effects of perceived usefulness, perceived ease of use, perceived entertainment and perceived KOC's prestige on purchase intention with the mediating

Table 3. Standardized Regression Weights

Hypothesis		Estimate	S.E	C.R	P-value	
H1	AT ← PU	0.405	0.067	6.759	0.00	Accepted
H2	AT ← PEU	0.144	0.074	3.282	0.00	Accepted
H3	AT ← PE	0.104	0.076	1.239	0.02	Accepted
H4	AT ← PKOC	0.309	0.073	3.058	0.00	Accepted
H5	IN ← AT	0.516	0.047	13.195	0.00	Accepted

role of attitudes towards use. In detail: The results demonstrated that the relationship between perceived usefulness and attitude is positive and most important, which coincides with the study of Zhao and Wang (2020); Lin and Kim (2016). From that, it can be seen that, for Gen Z consumers in Vietnam, if they feel that short videos on Tiktok provide useful knowledge, help them solve problems and make purchases easier, they may have a positive attitude towards use.

Also, research results showed that attitude towards use is also affected by perceived ease of use, which coincides with the study of Zhao and Wang (2020). It can be said that young consumers often prefer applications and products that are easy to manipulate and use. In particular, on the Tiktok platform, when a customer can directly make a purchase on it, they may have higher positive attitude towards use the products advertised, thereby promoting further intentions/behaviors in the future.

Moreover, the study found that perceived entertainment has a positive influence on consumer's attitudes (H3) and this is consistent with the research of Hoffman et al. (1996); Shavitt et al. (2017); Nguyen Dinh Yen Oanh and Quach Ly Xuan An, (2018). Especially, on platform such Tiktok, businesses should integrate some entertainment elements in videos to attract Gen Z. However, enterprises should still focus on showing usefullness and benefits of products, so consumers would purchase items they really need/want.

Furthermore, the relationship between perceived KOC's prestige and attitude towards use proved to be positive in this study (H4). Since people often have anxiety when buying products that are not same as advertising, they need reputable KOCs' review before making purchase decisions. From personal experiences, KOCs provide positive feedbacks about a product/service, then their followers would have a sense of security, feel the usefullness of products/services. Therefore, the positive attitude towards use would be clearer.

Last but not least, the positive relationship between attitude towards use and intention to use once again confirmed in this study through the regression analysis, which coincides with the study of Dehghani et al., (2016); Du et al., (2017). Obviously, a positive attitude may push Gen Z customers to purchase, conversely, they would not to purchase if their attitude towards the advertising is negative. As a result, businesses should manage customer's experience on platform such Tiktok and create value advertising video to deliver to their target customers.

6 Implications and Limitations

Based on the results of the research paper, the author has some suggestions for enterprises in term of implimenting short-form video content marketing. First, the content of the video should focus the usefullness and the ease of use and buy products online. Noticbly, there is a function called "Shopping" on Tiktok short video, that is, people may just click the button when they are interested in the products advertised to proceed to the purchase page and buy them instantaneously, which greatly improving their perception of ease of buy and their shopping experience. Furthermore, entertainment features in Tiktok videos should be added in. For instance, some unique stickers, game, or trendy music/dance/film should be taken into consideration. The key role of KOCs should be bear in mind, too. To attract the attention, build trust and positive attitude in target consumers, businesses should select some reputable KOCs to be brand ambassadors. Before hand, some evaluation criterias KOCs: Relevant to the field, Performance on their platforms, their Growth in creativity, contents,…

For Gen Z's consumers, since KOC's review has an significant impact on their attitude and purchase intentions, as the results demonstrated, unless they "follow" inappropriate KOCs. In essence, KOC is also considered a job, and they would give good feedback about the product they are "promoting". Another aspect, each person's experience and perception is different. Therefore, instead of relying entirely on online KOCs, individuals should see the usefulness of the products to their life.

Nonetheless, the study has still existed limitations. First, because of the convenience sampling method, the results of this study showed that the representativeness of Gen Z's behavior in Vietnam is not high. Secondly, there are many other factors influencing consumers's attitude towards use and purchase intention on online platforms which have not mentioned here. Therefore, they will be suggestions for the author's next research direction.

References

Davis, F.D., Bagozzi, R.P., Warshaw, P.R.: User acceptance of computer technology: a comparison of two theoretical models. Manage. Sci. 35(8), 982–1003 (1989)

Dehghani, M., Niaki, M.K., Ramezani, I., Sali, R.: Evaluating the influence of YouTube advertising for attraction of young customers. Comput. Hum. Behav. 59, 165–172 (2016)

Du, B., et al.: Exploring representativeness and informativeness for active learning. IEEE Trans. Cybern. 47, 14–26 (2017)

Ducoffe, R.: Advertising value and advertising on the web. J. Advert. Res. 36, 21 (1996)

Dwinanda, B., Syaripuddin, F.A., Hudaifi Hendriana, E.: Examining the extended advertising value model: a case of TikTok short video ads. Mediterranean J. Soc. Behav. Res. 6(2), 35–44 (2022)

Guritno, S., Siringoringo, H.: Perceived usefulness, ease of use, and attitude towards online shopping usefulness towards online airlines ticket purchase. Procedia Soc. Behav. Sci. 81, 212–216 (2013)

Hair, J., Hult, T., Ringle, C., Sarstedt, M.: A Primer on Partial Least Squares Structural Equation Modeling (PLS-SEM). Sage Publications, Inc, Thousand Oaks (2014)

Long, H.C., Uyen, N.H.D., Phuong, D.T.L., Phuong, N.H., Ngan, N.H.T., Tam, L.T.T.: The impact
    of TikTok advertising on young people's online shopping behavior during the covid-19 pan-
    demic. Int. J. Smart Bus. Technol. **10**(1), 145–162 (2022). https://doi.org/10.21742/IJSBT.
    2022.10.1.10
Hoffman, D.L., Kalsbeek, W.D., Novak, T.P.: Internet and Web use in the US. Commun. ACM
    39(12), 36–46 (1996)
Indarsin, T., Ali, H.: Attitude towards using m-commerce: the analysis of perceived usefulness,
    perceived ease of use, and perceived trust: case study in Ikens wholesale trade, Jakarta –
    Indonesia. Saudi J. Bus. Manag. Stud. **2**, 995–1007 (2017)
Jain, G., Rakesh, S., Chaturvedi, K.R.: Online video advertisements' effect on purchase intention:
    an exploratory study on youth. Int. J. E-Bus. Res. **141**(2), 87–101 (2018)
Kumar, P., Polonsky, M.J.: In-store experience quality and perceived credibility: a green retailer
    context. J. Retail. Consum. Serv. **49**, 23–34 (2018)
Lim, X.J., Radzol, A.M., Cheah, J., Wong, M.W.: The impact of social media influencers on
    purchase intention and the mediation effect of customer attitude. Asian J. Bus. Res. **7**(2),
    19–36 (2017)
Lin, C., Kim, T.: Predicting user response to sponsored advertising on social media via the
    technology acceptance model. Comput. Hum. Behav **64**, 710–718 (2016)
Oanh, N.D.Y., An, Q.L.X.: Attitudes to online advertising and consumers' intention to repurchase:
    a study in the FMCG industry. Sci. J. Open Univ. Ho Chi Minh City **13**(2), 116–136 (2018)
Okazaki, S.: Mobile advertising adoption by multinationals: senior executive initial responses.
    Internet Res. **15**(2), 160–180 (2005)
Sharma, S.K., Govindaluri, S.M., Al-Muharrami, S., Tarhini, A.: A multi-analytical model for
    mobile banking adoption: a developing country perspective. Rev. Int. Bus. Strategy **27**(1),
    133–148 (2017)
Shavitt, S., Lowrey, P., Haefner, J.: Public attitude towards advertising: more favorable than you
    might think. J. Advert. Res. **38**(4), 7–22 (2017)
Xiao, Y., Wang, L., Wang, P.: Research on the influence of content features of short video marketing
    on consumer purchase intentions. In: Proceedings of the 2019 4th International Conference on
    Modern Management, Education Technology and Social Science (MMETSS 2019) (2019)
Yuksel, H.F.: Factors affecting purchase intention in Youtube videos. J. Knowl. Econ. Knowl.
    Manag. **9**(2), 33–47 (2016)
Zhao, J., Wang, J.: Health advertising on short-video social media: a study on user attitudes based
    on the extended technology acceptance model. Int. J. Environ. Res. Publ. Health **17**(5), 1501
    (2020)

Restructuring the Industry and Technology System

Mete Gündoğan[(⊠)], Nurullah Güleç, Selen Dilara Kırklar, Ömer Gençdoğmuş, and Alp Eren Başsoy

School of Engineering and Natural Sciences, Department of Industrial Engineering, Ankara Yıldırım Beyazıt University, Ankara, Turkey
metegundogan@ybu.edu.tr

Abstract. This article reconsiders a system configuration with the Geometric Ratio Technique (GRT). In this context, the Ministry of Industry and Technology and the industrial establishment within the jurisdiction of the country were examined. In order to visualize the restructuring of the Ministry, the pyramid model, which seems suitable for the GRT method and can also use the golden ratio, was chosen. The created model is divided into four horizontal layers according to the functions that the elements in the system should have. In the created model, in the system layers, respectively, management; regulation, control, security and remediation; training & R&D and production. When the relationships of the layers are examined, a change in the first layer affects the other layers three, twelve and forty-eight times, respectively. The effect of changes in other layers on the system is determined in line with these ratios. In addition, in this study, the manpower constituting the system under the authority of the Ministry of Industry and Technology was determined as 12.7 million. This population was divided into strata with rates of 1.562%, 4.687%, 18.75% and 75%, respectively. With the proposed model, a resizable structuring has been created so that the system can continue to exist without deteriorating its functional structure in case of a possible contraction or expansion. The sectors in the system were examined on the relationship matrix and placed in the lower layers in the 3rd and 4th layers. The article has been prepared with reference to open sources. The potential of the presented model to meet the needs of the current system is quite high. Access to wider resources and opportunities related to the Industry and Technology system will make the proposed system more beneficial to the needs of the current system.

Keywords: Geometric Ratio Technique (GRT) · Restructuring · Industry and Technology · Resizing

1 Introduction

Studies related to industry and technology are of great importance for institutions, countries and companies to be leaders in the competitive environment. Investments are made in the fields of industry and technology in order to provide economic wealth, increase productivity, facilitate human life and increase the level of welfare. The ministry of industry and technology is a state institution that works on the management, audit, regulation and improvement of industrial and technological activities [1]. The Ministry of Industry and Technology constitutes the administrative part of a holistic system with all the industrial sectors it covers, R&D and education establishments and studies.

System restructuring is important in order to get the best efficiency by operating the systems properly and with the least errors. System restructuring ensures that the systems are carried out in more efficient and sustainable conditions by solving the problems arising from the economic, environmental and administrative resources in the current state of the system. The use of model-based methods in the structuring of systems produces more consistent, logical and scientifically based solutions. Meeting the solution needs is possible with the restructuring and layout management of all personnel, equipment and organization of the systems. With the layout management, the positions and sizes of the system parts are determined and the restructuring process of the system is carried out. In this study, the relations of all institutions and organizations, system parts and sub-systems in the industry and technology system were arranged and restructured with the GRT technique. The system is composed of four different but interrelated layers. All industry, energy and agriculture institutions and organizations, stakeholders and system elements in this system were analyzed layer by layer and their relations with each other were evaluated. Horizontal and vertical layers were created by taking into account the information, material, product and service exchanges between these stakeholders. The number, type and qualitative distribution of personnel in the system were determined by means of the model. According to the model, the shrinkage and growth situations that can be experienced in the system have been realized proportionally. This will ensure the proportional change of the elements of the system and cause the integrity of the system to be affected in the least way. In addition, industry sub-institutions/branches, which are of vital importance and enable the system to survive, will be least affected by the changes in the system. Triangular modeling for the application of the method to the system has been examined and exhibited in detail in the article. Various open sources were used in the study. The study is open to expert opinions and expert opinions should be taken in the further stages. In the study, the model principle, horizontal layers, sector relations, vertical layers, layer analysis, system downsizing and results are examined in detail under the headings.

2 Model

In this study, a model proposal is presented for the restructuring of the Ministry of Industry and Technology and the Geometric Ratio Technique is used. Gündoğan and Yıldırım (2018) [2], with their study, proposed a system for the State of the Republic of Turkey to maintain its existence in a healthy way. The Geometric Ratio Technique, which was used in the modeling of the system they presented, inspired this study.

Geometric structures are used while modeling with the Geometric Ratio Technique. The determined geometric structure is quite successful in visually expressing the placement of the elements in the system and their relations with each other.

Equilateral triangular pyramid was used as the geometric structure to be used in the study. Since the apex is narrow and widens towards the base, the pyramid is the most ideal geometric structure for the industry and technology system studied.

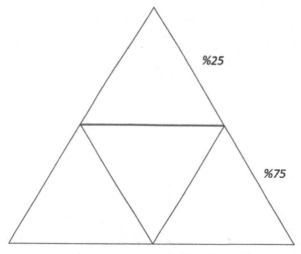

Fig. 1. Equilateral Triangle

The triangular pyramid structure also provides significant benefits for creating the layers that make up the system. When the pyramid is cut in the middle, the triangle at the top constitutes 25% of the entire structure. In the lower area, it forms three equilateral triangles. This part constitutes 75% of the entire structure. Thus, two layers can be obtained. The pyramid cut in the middle is given in Fig. 1. When the triangle at the top is cut in the middle again, it is divided into 25% and 75% areas as in the previous stage. The ratio of these areas to the general structure is 6.25% and 18.75%, respectively. The ratio of these areas is given in Fig. 2. Four horizontal layers are needed to represent the prepared model. For this reason, the top triangle was again divided in the middle and system layers were formed. The first layer represents a triangle forming 1.5625% of the entire structure at the apex of the triangle. The areas covered by the other layers are multiples of 1.5625%. The 1.5625 number we obtained for the first layer is very close to the golden ratio with a 3.55% margin of error. Placing the system layer sizes in harmony with the golden ratio is also very important for the ideality of the model.

The volume ratios of the horizontal layers in the triangular pyramid also provide areas for the system stakeholders to be placed. Each layer contains a number of small triangles directly proportional to the volume size it occupies. The formula "(2N + 1)" is used to find the number of triangles. The expression 'N' in the formula refers to the horizontal rows in the model. When the formula is applied, the number of lower triangles in the layers is 1, 3, 12, and 48, respectively. These ratios also give the "Force Multiplier", which expresses the effect power of the layers on the system. The force factor is directly proportional to the volume ratios of the layers. The force factor of the first layer is 1. The force factors of the other layers are 3, 12 and 48, respectively. To give an example of the effect of the force multiplier, a development in the first layer affects the second layer 3 times. An improvement in the second layer affects the first layer 1/3 of the time. Triangle numbers in each row is given in Fig. 3.

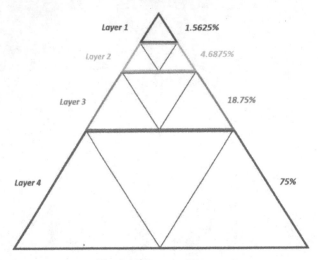

Fig. 2. Volumes of Layers

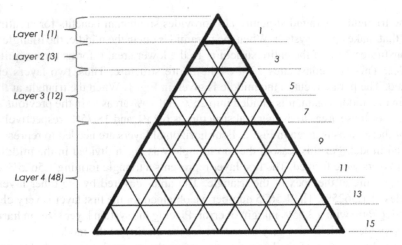

Fig. 3. Triangle numbers in each row

Having a strong industry makes an important contribution to the economic and social welfare of societies. Investments in industry and technology ensure the sustainability and prominence of countries and organizations in the competitive environment. This situation leads to investment and development of industry and technology systems. For countries with developed economies, the industry and technology system has an important place. According to open sources, the countries with the highest manufacturing output in dollar terms are China, the United States, Japan and Germany [3]. In addition, the countries with the highest value-added output in the industry are China, the United States, Japan and Germany, respectively [4]. The ratio of employment in the industry to the total population of these four countries has been examined. These rates are respectively 15.98%

in China, 11.23% in the United States, 13.11% in Japan, and 15.86% in Germany [5]. In the calculation of these ratios, data such as the populations of the countries, the labor force they have, the labor force participation rates, the employment rate and numbers and the ratio of the number of workers in the industry to employment were used. The results obtained about these four countries were evaluated as a reference in the restructuring of the industry and technology system. When the data of the ratio of the number of employees in the industry to the population are evaluated, the reference value is determined as 15%. This rate means that 15% of the population of a country works in the industry and technology system. This ratio was used in the restructuring of the industry and technology system in Turkey. The population of Turkey in 2021 is 84,680,273 [6]. As a result, the number of employees in the industry and technology system in Turkey has been determined as 12,700,000.

When the determined personnel power was distributed to the layers, the following numbers were reached:

First Layer: 198,437 s Layer: 595,313, Third Layer: 2,381,250, Fourth Layer: 9,525,000.

When the Industry and Technology System is designed according to the above-mentioned model, the layers and their tasks are as follows:

Layer 1: Management.

- Layer 1A: Senior Management
- Layer 1B: Sub-Management

Layer 2: Regulation, Audit, and Improvement.

- Layer 2A: Regulation
- Layer 2B: Audit and Security
- Layer 2C: Improvement

Layer 3: R&D and Education.

- Layer 3A: Security Sector, Health Sector, Electronic & Communications Sector, Manufacturing Sector, Logistics-Transportation Sector, Plastic Sector, Recycle Sector, Chemical Sector, Energy Sector
- Layer 3B: IT Sector, Defense Sector, Automotive Sector, Glass and Ceramics Sector, Mining Sector, Maritime Sector, Construction Sector, Aerospace Sector
- Layer 3C: Agriculture, Animal Husbandry, Forestry Sector, Food & Beverage Sector, Furniture Sector, Textile Sector, Medical Sector, Service Sector, Tourism Sector

Layer 4: Production.

- Layer 4A: Manufacturing Sector, Chemical Sector, Plastic Sector and Electronic & Communications Sector

- Layer 4B: Defense Sector, Automotive Sector, Glass and Ceramics Sector, Aerospace Sector, IT Sector and Maritime Sector

Layer 4C: Textile Sector, Medical Sector, Furniture Sector, Food & Beverage Sector and Service Sector (Fig. 4).

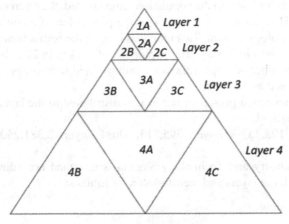

Fig. 4. Proposed Model

There are also strong relationships between system stakeholders in different layers. Secondary layers called "Vertical Layer" are used to show these relationships. The vertical layers in the system are as follows (Fig. 5):

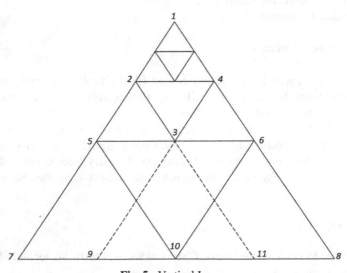

Fig. 5. Vertical Layers

- Top Layer: Covers the (1-2-3-4) area
- Center Layer: Covers the (1-5-10-6) area
- Right Layer: Covers the (2-11-8-4) field
- Left Layer: Covers the (2-7-9-4) area

3 Layer 1L

This layer represents the vertex of the triangular model representing the system. The management part of the system is located in this layer. The most authorized institution in the field of industry studied is the Ministry of Industry and Technology. Therefore, the first layer consists of the Ministry of Industry and its affiliated institutions. This is the layer with the strongest force multiplier. Every activity that occurs here causes a threefold, twelvefold and forty-eightfold impact on the lower layers, respectively. According to the GRT model used, the personnel power of this layer constitutes 1.562% of the entire system. This ratio is equal to the manpower of 198,437 people. The estimated number of staff is the ideal number offered by the model and may vary according to the adopted strategies.

The first layer is divided into two sub-layers, Layer 1A and Layer 1B. While making this distinction, the ratios offered by the GRT model were adhered. When dividing the first layer into four sub-layers in accordance with the GRT model, the first layer forms Layer 1A. Other sub-layers form Layer 1B (Fig. 6).

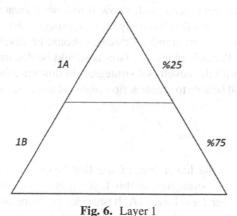

Fig. 6. Layer 1

3.1 1A

Layer 1A, which is the upper part of Layer 1, represents the top-level management of the system. The strategies required for the survival and growth of the industrial system are decided in this layer. In addition, the relations of the industrial system with other government institutions in the country and the management of foreign industries are managed in this layer. The workforce of Layer 1A consists of ministers, deputy ministers, senior ministry units and employees.

Layer 1A is the most important part for the management of the system. Therefore, the internal placement of the layer is also important. The triangular shape with the minister at the top and the deputy minister responsible for legal affairs or the directorate in the center would be the ideal layout for Layer 1A. The minister is positioned at the top as he is the final decision maker. The legal unit is positioned in the middle to confirm the legality of the strategies or legislation to be prepared. Due to the fact that the law is in the center, legal problems cannot be ignored in the decisions to be taken.

In Layer 1A, the minister of industry and technology and general directorates responsible for eight main topics are located. The general directorates are listed by evaluating the benefits they provide for the Ministry of Industry and Technology. If there is a shrinkage situation in Layer1A, the general directorates at the top of the list are the units that should be affected last. The aforementioned general directorates are:

1. General Directorate of Law
2. General Directorate of Industry
3. General Directorate of Technology
4. General Directorate of R&D
5. General Directorate of Strategic Studies
6. General Directorate of Foreign Relations
7. General Directorates of Development Agencies
8. General Directorate of Administrative Affairs

In order to maintain the existence of the industrial system in a healthy way, the current period and future trends should be followed closely. The fact that the system can act in accordance with these trends will allow it to have a greater share in the global market. In addition, a country that has a say by increasing its share in the global market can lead in the creation of new trends. Strategies should be developed in Layer 1A in line with these goals. Periodic plans and targets should be determined in order for the system to act in line with the developed strategies. In this way, the elements that make up the lower layers will be able to create action plans related to their own responsibilities (Fig. 7).

3.2 1B

Layer 1B, which forms the lower part of the first layer, plays an important role in the realization of ministry strategies. In this layer, it is the element that completes the connection between Layer 2 and Layer 1A. It provides guidance and support to the lower layers for the implementation of the strategies determined in Layer 1A, which constitutes the top management of the Ministry. It can also make suggestions for new strategies of the ministry's senior management by using the feedback provided by the lower layers.

There are management staff of the units and institutions in Layer 1B, which is one of the management layers. Of these, Provincial Directorates of the Ministry of Industry, as the local representative of the ministry, help companies within the system to solve their problems. Shares incoming requests with senior management. Development Agencies and KOSKEB provide support for the growth of companies in the system and for the inclusion of new companies in the system. TÜBİTAK and TÜBA, which are affiliated with the Ministry of Industry and Technology, carry out activities for the development

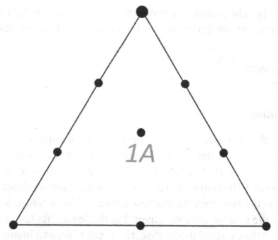

Fig. 7. Placement of Directorates

of R&D activities. These institutions provide financial support to the R&D activities of the companies, and they also have important R&D activities for the system with their own teams. The Turkish Patent Institute is responsible for registering the developments and new products obtained as a result of the R&D studies of the companies. In this way, the copyrights of companies are protected. TSE enables companies to set standards for their products and services. In this way, high quality and standard products and services can be produced within the system.

4 Layer 2L

This layer is the layer that performs the tasks of arranging and preparing the laws in the industry and technology system, supervising the adherence of the system elements and system stakeholders to the legislation, ensuring that the system is improved and developed. This layer is vital for the survival of the system. The creation and arrangement of regulations is a basic need that ensures the functioning of the system and structures the activities of all units and elements. The management and sustainability of the system depends on the legislation. Therefore, the regulation, audit and improvement layer is the main layer that ensures the integrity and functioning of the system. In addition, the regulation, audit and improvement layer has a great say in the operation and direction of research, development and training activities related to industry and technology.

The main areas of responsibility of this layer are the necessary arrangements for the continuation of the system, the regulations, audit and improvement of the elements that make up the lower layers of the system, chambers, unions, legal units. The 2L layer has a volume ratio of 4,687% within the triangular pattern. It has a direct relationship with the 1L and 3L layers. The force factor is 1/3 for the 1L layer, 4 for the 3L layer, and 16 for the 4L layer. That is, a change in the 2L layer affects the other layers 1/3, 4 and

16 times, respectively. The number of personnel in this tier is 595,313 in total. Layer 2 consists of three different sub-layers in itself. These are as follows, respectively.

2A – Regulation
2B – Audit and Security
2C – Improvement

4.1 2A – Regulation

This layer is the sub-layer where legal arrangements are made in the 2L layer. The number of employees in this tier is 198,437. The 2A has a volume ratio of 1.562% in the triangular pattern. Layers that Layer 2A is directly related to are 2B (Audit), 2C (Improvement), Layer 1 (ministry) and 3A layers, which are neighbors in the triangular model. This layer is the one with the highest degree of importance among the Layer 2 sub-layers. In case the system shrinks, Layer 2 is the least affected sub-layer.

Laws, decrees, statutes, regulations, directives, circulars and instructions on industry and technology are prepared in this layer and used by managers. Responsibilities, rights, rules and procedures to be followed by each unit in the system are found in the regulations created in the regulation layer. The way to be followed in any situation where the system elements live is provided by the actions to be taken, the regulations and the organizations in the layer. In this layer, there are relevant government institutions, chambers, exchanges, unions and legal departments. All these organizations are right holders and stakeholders in the preparation and regulation of legislation. The Social Security Institution is a state institution that informs the people it serves about their rights and obligations and implements social security policies [7]. For this reason, it is an effective part in taking legal decisions concerning people in the industry and technology system. In addition, TOBB, which is a professional body, provides its views on laws and regulations to the management branches and facilitates its activities by protecting the rights of its members [8]. Unions are independent organizations established to protect the rights and interests of employees and to solve their problems [9]. For this reason, unions are an effective factor in order to protect employee rights in regulatory activities. In addition to all these, related ministries and legal departments are also stakeholders who have rights on regulations. In addition to these, the relevant units of the General Directorate of Security responsible for security and the Information Technologies and Communication Authority responsible for cyber security and infrastructure are also included in this sub-layer.

4.2 2B – Audit and Security

This layer is the sub-layer within the 2L layer where the audit and control studies are carried out. The number of employees in this tier is 198,437. Layers that Layer 2B is directly related to are 2A (regulation), Layer 1 (ministry), 3A and 3D layers, which are neighbors in the triangular model. This layer has a volume ratio of 1.562% within the triangular pattern.

In this layer, studies such as research, inspection, audit and control are carried out in order to understand whether the system elements carry out their duties and responsibilities properly. The rules, authorities, rights, responsibilities and duties that the system members must comply with are included in the legislation prepared in the regulation layer. Whether the units comply with these regulations or not is determined through this layer. There are public and state institutions and organizations in the audit branches. DDK, Competition Authority and Capital Markets Board are institutions that carry out research, inspection and examinations among state institutions. These institutions carry out all kinds of audits related to industry and technology within the framework of their powers and responsibilities. In addition, the BDDK, TSE, TPMK institutions have auditing and inspection duties within the framework of their authorizations for the personnel within the industry and technology system. All these institutions and organizations examine the people, units and institutions in both the upper and lower layers and prevent deviations in the functioning of the system. In addition, there is a security center that ensures the security and protection of the administrative units in the system. The security center is also linked to the regulation unit and contributes to the creation of instructions to the units and personnel in the lower layers in order to ensure system security. The security center is the unit responsible for the cyber security of the system and the protection of the data of the parts that make up the system. In addition, activities in favor of the system such as standardization, certification, quality and international competition are also carried out in this layer.

4.3 2C – Improvement

This layer is the sub-layer where the improvement studies of the system are made. The number of employees in this tier is 198,437. The layers that Layer 2C is directly related to are 2A (regulation), Layer 1 (ministry), 3A and 3C layers, which are neighbors in the triangular model. This layer has a volume ratio of 1.562% within the triangular pattern. It is the layer where studies are carried out on how the system can be run more efficiently.

This layer is the layer where studies that contribute to the development of the system by adapting to new technology trends and the development of the elements that make up the industry and technology system are carried out. Financial institutions operating to financially support the companies in the system are in this layer. In the improvement layer, in addition to supporting activities such as grants and incentives, studies such as strengthening the relations between the stakeholders in the system and making the operation better and more efficient are also carried out. Studies are carried out with institutions such as TÜBA and TÜBİTAK to develop R&D activities and to have a say in the global market by catching new technology trends. Institutions such as TÜSİAD and MUSIAD work to ensure that companies' opinions are given importance in legislative arrangements by ensuring that the requests and suggestions of the companies are conveyed to the senior management.

5 Layer 3L

R&D studies and the level of education in the country are important factors for the development and growth of the country's activities in the fields of industry and technology. Knowledge and science form the basis of R&D, which is defined as producing any new product or making changes on an existing product. Education should be given importance in order to use knowledge and science. Education increases the knowledge and skills of the society.

This layer, which is the third layer of the system, includes the Education and R&D activities of the Industry and Technology System. Education activities aim to train personnel, which is the most important part of the system studied. Universities, institutes, vocational high schools and vocational trainings within institutions in the country regulate the educational activities of the system. R&D activities, which are important for the development of the system, are carried out under the leadership of institutions such as TÜBİTAK and TÜBA. R&D centers established for different sectors in the country and R&D units of companies carry out R&D activities in this layer.

The third layer has the workforce of 18.75% of the entire system. The number of personnel in this layer is 2,381,250. The force multipler of the layer is 12. The effect of a development in this layer on the second layer is 1/4 times. The effect on the first layer is 1/12 times. The effect on the fourth layer, which is the production layer, is 4 times.

The Education and R&D layer is divided into three sub-layers. In the sub-layers, there are education and R&D activities of the sectors within the system. Some of the sectors included here are not directly part of the Industry and Technology System. However, the development of technologies to be used in these sectors and personnel training activities are part of the system. Therefore, it is included in the third layer. Thanks to the relationship matrix created, the relations of the sectors with each other were examined and placed in the sub-layers according to the relationship levels. The sub-layers are 3A, 3B, 3C (R&D and Education).

5.1   3A

The sectors with the highest scores in the Relationship Matrix are included in this layer. The sectors located here act as suppliers to other sectors. In addition, some sectors here also meet vital needs for the system. The sectors included in Layer 3A are:

Security Sector, Health Sector, Electronic and Communications Sector, Manufacturing Sector, Logistics-Transportation Sector, Plastic Sector, Recycle Sector, Chemical Sector, Energy Sector.

5.2   3B

When sorting according to the relationship matrix, the sectors that have more relationships within themselves are divided into two groups. One of these groups constitutes Layer 3B. Here are the sectors:

IT Sector, Defense Sector, Automotive Sector, Glass and Ceramics Sector, Mining Sector, Maritime Sector, Construction Sector, Aerospace Sector.

5.3   3C

Other sectors in the relationship matrix form Layer 3C. These sectors are:

Agriculture, Animal Husbandry, Forestry Sector, Food & Beverage Sector, Furniture Sector, Textile Sector, Medical Sector, Service Sector, Tourism Sector.

6 Layer 4L

Production contributes to meeting the economic needs of the society and its social and cultural development with the economic needs met. As production increases, the country's self-sufficiency level also increases. Production, which is directly related to the welfare level of the society, plays an important role in the development of the country. For this reason, investments made in this layer are important for society.

The fourth layer, which is the production layer, has the workforce of 75% of the entire system. In this layer, which forms the lowest part of the model, the production of the sectors directly involved in the Industry and Technology System and the production of necessary machinery and equipment for the sectors in the third layer but not directly related to the system are also included. The number of personnel in this layer is 9,525,000. The force multiplier of the layer is 48. The effect of a development in this layer on the first layer is 1/48 fold. The effect on the second layer is 1/16 fold. The effect on the third layer is 1/4 fold.

Thanks to the relationship matrix created, the relations of the sectors with each other were examined and placed in the sub-layers according to the relationship levels. Within each sub-layer, there are production and service areas belonging to that sector. The lower layers are 4A, 4B, 4C (Production).

6.1 4A

In the 4A sub-layer of the model, there is the production of indispensable sectors for production sectors such as raw materials and by-products for production. The basic sub-layer of production is layer 4A, as it is a substrate containing the building block for the production of other sectors to take place. The sectors in this layer are:

Manufacturing Sector, Chemical Sector, Electronic and Communications Sector, Plastic Sector.

6.2 4B

The 4B sub-layer of the model includes defense, IT and technological sectors. This lower layer, fed from the 4A layer, has an important factor in increasing the welfare of the society and increasing the export size. The sectors in this layer are:

Maritime Sector, Aerospace Sector, Defense Sector, Glass and Ceramics Sector, Automotive Sector, IT Sector.

6.3 4C

In the 4C sub-layer of the model, there are sectors that produce the basic needs of the society. The increase in production in this layer directly increases the welfare of the society and contributes to the brand competition within the country or between the countries. The sectors in this layer are:

Food & Beverage Sector, Furniture Sector, Medical Sector, Textile Sector, Service Sector.

7 Matrix Interpretation

Matrix diagram is a planning and management tool used to analyze the relationship between two or more variables [10]. A matrix diagram is created with these dependent or independent relationships. This relationship matrix, which is created with the matrix diagram, is prepared with the values of "0" and "1". 0 means no or very weakly correlated between sectors, 1 means there is a relationship between sectors.

In this study, the purpose of using the relationship matrix is to determine the layout of the sectors in the third and fourth layers in the model. In this direction, two relationship matrices were prepared. The first matrix, which is given in Fig. 8, is prepared for the third layer. In this layer, there are sectors that are directly related to the Industry and Technology system and sectors that are indirectly related. After examining the relations of the sectors with each other with the dual system, the score received by each sector was calculated. In the next step, the sectors are ranked according to their scores. The highest scoring sectors are closely related to other sectors in the system and act as suppliers to many of them. In addition, these sectors are vital for the system. These highest scoring sectors are placed in Layer 3A, which is located in the center of the third layer.

Two sub-layers should be created among the remaining sectors. Therefore, these sectors were examined according to both the relation score and the sectors with which they have a more intense relation. In this direction, it is placed in Layer 3B and Layer 3C. For example, Mining Sector and Textile Sector got the same correlation score. However, the Textile sector has a weaker relationship with the sectors such as Defense and Automotive, which are taken into Layer 3B. It also has a stronger relationship with sectors such as Agriculture, which have a lower relationship score. So, it is built into Layer 3C.

After the sub-layers of the third layer were classified, the layout plan within the lower layer was constructed. Sectors with a higher correlation score are located in the center of the sub-layers or at their neighboring points with other layers, as they are more important for the system. The Second Matrix, which is given in Fig. 9, is prepared for the fourth layer. In this layer, there are sectors that are directly related to the Industry and Technology system, that is, the production activities are within the system.

After examining the relations of the sectors with each other with the dual system, the score received by each sector was calculated. In the next step, the sectors are ranked according to their scores. The highest scoring sectors are closely related to other sectors in the system or are in the role of suppliers to many of them. In addition, these sectors are vital for the system. These highest scoring sectors are placed in Layer 4A, which is located in the center of the third layer.

Two sub-layers should be created among the remaining sectors. Therefore, these sectors were examined according to both the relation score and the sectors with which they have a more intense relation. In this direction, it is placed in Layer 4B and Layer 4C. For example, the Medical sector and the Aerospace sector received the same correlation score. However, the Medical sector has a weaker relationship with the sectors included in Layer 4B. In addition, it has a stronger relationship with the Service sector, which has a lower relationship score. So, it is placed in Layer 4C.

After the sub-layers of the third layer were classified, the layout plan within the lower layer was constructed. Sectors with a higher correlation score are located in the center of the sub-layers or at their neighboring points with other layers, as they are more important for the system.

Layer 3	Security Sector	Health Sector	Logistics - Transportation Sector	Tourism Sector	Agriculture, Animal Husbandry, Forestry Sector	Construction Sector	Energy Sector	Mining Sector	Recycle Sector	Manufacturing Sector	Maritime Sector	Service Sector	Glass and Ceramics Sector	Food & Beverage Sector	Chemical Sector	Aerospace Sector	Defense Sector	IT Sector	Furniture Sector	Electronic and Communications Sector	Plastic Sector	Textile Sector	Medical Sector	Automotive Sector
Automotive Sector	1	1	1	0	0	0	1	1	1	1	0	1	1	0	1	0	1	1	0	1	1	0	0	x
Medical Sector	1	1	1	0	0	0	1	1	1	1	0	0	0	1	1	0	1	1	0	1	1	1	x	0
Textile Sector	1	1	1	0	1	0	1	0	1	1	0	1	0	0	0	0	1	0	1	1	1	x	1	0
Plastic Sector	1	1	1	0	0	1	1	1	1	1	1	0	0	1	1	1	1	0	1	1	x	1	1	1
Electronic and Communications Sector	1	1	1	0	0	1	1	1	1	1	1	0	0	0	1	1	1	1	0	x	1	1	1	1
Furniture Sector	0	1	1	0	0	0	1	0	1	1	0	1	1	0	1	0	0	0	x	0	1	1	0	0
IT Sector	1	0	0	0	0	1	1	0	0	0	1	1	0	0	1	1	1	x	0	1	0	0	1	1
Defense Sector	1	0	1	0	0	1	1	1	1	1	1	0	1	0	1	1	x	1	0	1	1	1	1	1
Aerospace Sector	1	1	1	0	0	0	1	1	1	1	0	0	1	0	1	x	1	1	0	1	1	0	0	0
Chemical Sector	1	1	0	0	1	1	1	1	1	1	1	0	1	0	x	1	1	1	1	1	1	1	1	1
Food & Beverage Sector	1	1	1	0	1	0	0	0	1	1	0	1	1	x	1	0	0	0	0	0	1	0	1	0
Glass and Ceramics Sector	1	1	1	0	0	1	1	1	1	1	0	0	x	1	1	1	1	0	1	0	0	0	0	1
Service Sector	0	1	1	1	0	1	0	0	0	1	0	x	0	1	0	0	0	1	0	0	1	0	1	1
Maritime Sector	1	0	1	0	0	1	1	0	1	1	x	0	0	0	1	0	1	1	0	1	1	0	0	0
Manufacturing Sector	1	1	1	0	1	1	1	1	1	x	1	1	1	1	1	1	1	0	1	1	1	1	1	1
Recycle Sector	1	1	1	0	1	1	1	0	x	1	1	0	1	1	1	1	1	0	1	1	1	1	1	1
Mining Sector	1	1	1	0	0	1	1	x	0	1	0	0	1	0	1	1	1	0	0	1	1	0	1	1
Energy Sector	1	0	1	0	1	1	x	1	1	1	1	0	1	0	1	1	1	1	1	1	1	0	0	1
Construction Sector	1	1	1	0	0	x	1	1	1	1	1	1	1	0	1	0	1	1	0	1	1	0	0	0
Agriculture, Animal Husbandry, Forestry Sector	1	1	1	0	x	0	1	0	1	1	0	0	0	1	1	0	0	0	1	0	0	1	0	0
Tourism Sector	1	1	1	x	0	0	0	0	0	0	0	1	0	0	0	0	0	0	0	0	0	0	0	0
Logistics - Transportation Sector	1	0	x	1	1	1	1	1	1	1	1	1	1	0	1	1	0	1	1	1	1	1	1	1
Health Sector	1	x	0	1	1	1	0	1	1	1	0	1	1	1	1	0	0	1	1	1	1	1	1	1
Security Sector	x	1	1	1	1	1	1	1	1	1	0	1	1	1	1	1	1	0	1	1	1	1	1	1
total	21	18	20	4	10	15	19	14	19	21	11	10	14	11	20	13	17	11	11	17	18	14	14	14

Fig. 8. Relationship Matrix of Layer 3 Sectors

Layer 4	Manufacturing Sector	Maritime Sector	Service Sector	Glass and Ceramics Sector	Food & Beverage Sector	Chemical Sector	Aerospace Sector	Defense Sector	IT Sector	Furniture Sector	Electronic and Communications Sector	Plastic Sector	Textile Sector	Medical Sector	Automotive Sector
Automotive Sector	1	0	1	1	0	1	0	1	1	0	1	1	0	0	X
Medical Sector	1	0	0	0	1	1	0	1	1	0	1	1	1	X	0
Textile Sector	1	0	1	0	0	1	0	1	0	1	1	1	X	1	0
Plastic Sector	1	1	0	0	1	1	1	1	0	1	1	X	1	1	1
Electronic and Communications Sector	1	1	0	0	0	1	1	1	1	0	X	1	1	1	1
Furniture Sector	1	0	1	1	0	1	0	0	0	X	0	1	1	0	0
IT Sector	0	1	1	0	0	1	1	1	X	0	1	0	0	1	1
Defense Sector	1	1	0	1	0	1	1	X	1	0	1	1	1	1	1
Aerospace Sector	1	0	0	1	0	1	X	1	1	0	1	1	0	0	0
Chemical Sector	1	1	0	1	1	X	1	1	1	1	1	1	1	1	1
Food & Beverage Sector	1	0	1	1	X	1	0	0	0	0	0	1	0	1	0
Glass and Ceramics Sector	1	0	0	X	1	1	1	1	0	1	0	0	0	0	1
Service Sector	1	0	X	0	1	0	0	0	1	1	0	0	1	0	1
Maritime Sector	1	X	0	0	0	1	0	1	1	0	1	1	0	0	0
Manufacturing Sector	X	1	1	1	1	1	1	1	0	1	1	1	1	1	1
total	13	6	6	7	6	13	7	11	8	6	10	11	8	8	8

Fig. 9. Relationship Matrix of Layer 4 Sectors

When the relationship matrices are created and analyzed, the relationship levels between the sectors and other sectors have been determined. As a result, the most related sectors were included in sublayers 3A and 4A, which are sublayers of the third and fourth layers. The sectors fed by the most related sectors are included in the 3B, 3C, 4B and 4C sublayers within their respective relationships.

The 4A sub-layer, which consists of the most basic sectors that provide raw material, parts, by-products, information and equipment flow to the sectors in the fields of industry and technology, constitutes the building block of the basic activities in the industry. All sectors and industries need these substrate outputs directly or indirectly. This sub-management covers the activities of manufacturing, chemical, electronics & communication and plastics sectors in general. In the 3A sub-layer, besides all these sectors, there are also logistics and recycling sectors that undertake the transportation and recycling of the products produced in the sector. In addition to these, energy, health and security sectors that directly affect all sectors are also in the 3A layer. R&D and training activities on the sectors in the 3A sub-layer can positively affect the sectors in the 4A sub-layer, products and production, personnel, added value, information processes and the economy.

In the industry, there are sectors where technology is used more and where it is needed. At the beginning of these sectors are sectors such as defense, information technologies, aviation, automotive, maritime, glass & ceramics. These sectors frequently use industry 4.0 elements such as cyber-physical systems and the internet of things. These sectors, which are within the scope of the 4B sublayer, produce products with high added value. Since the products in the 4B sublayer contain high technology, these sectors and products are affected by new trends that may occur. These trends should be followed, continuous research and development should be done about technology. For this reason, research, development and training activities about these sectors are carried out in the 3B sublayer. In addition to these sectors, it also carries out R&D and training activities on the 3B substrate, mining and construction sectors.

There are also products with lower added value and more used in the industry compared to technological products and services. These products and services are products and services that have a high usage rate in daily life. These products and services, which people acquire in return for their different needs, are frequently used continuously or periodically. The 4C substratum covers the food & beverage, furniture, medical, textile and service industries responsible for producing these products and services. Research and development, as well as training activities are carried out in order to improve the activities carried out in these sectors, the products and services produced. The 3C sector is the sub-layer where these activities are carried out. In addition to these sectors, the 3C sub-layer carries out R&D studies covering the tourism, agriculture, livestock and forestry sectors, and trains qualified personnel with training studies.

8 Shrinking

Some situations cause systems to be downsized. Downsizing of systems may be due to economic, environmental and political reasons. In case of possible system downsizing, the people responsible for the system want to eliminate the most insignificant elements of the system. However, this can lead to bottlenecks in the system. For this reason, systems can provide a healthier shrinkage by reducing the elements they have in certain proportions. This also applies to the expansion of the system. Shrinking of the model is given in Fig. 10.

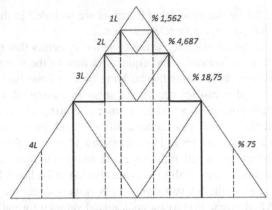

Fig. 10. Shrinking

The figure given above shows the scenario of a possible system shrinkage in the triangular model using the geometric ratio technique. The 2L, 3L and 4L layers of the industry and technology system on the triangular model have been shrunk at the same rate from their outer parts.The most important elements of the system, which form the middle part of the layers, are least affected in case of shrinkage. The volumetric sizes of the core elements in these 2L, 3L, and 4L layers are 1, 4, and 16, respectively. In addition, these central elements constitute 2/3 of the horizontal layers in which they are located. Shrinked situation of pyramid model is given in Fig. 11.

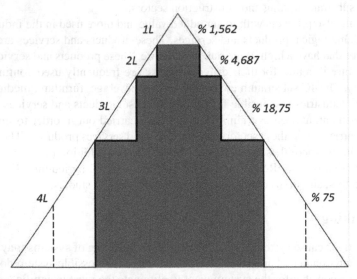

Fig. 11. Shrinked Situation of Pyramid Model

In the figure given above, the minimum level of shrinkage of the industry and technology system is shown. The dark area represents the state of the system after shrinkage.

In this case, the system decreases by 35% in general [2]. In the pyramid structure in which the industry and technology system is modeled, the operation to reduce the system should start from the lowest layer, 4L, to the upper layer. The shrinkage starting from the edges of the 4L layer continues with the 3L layer edges and the 2L layer edges, respectively. The limit of shrinkage in the system is up to the 2L layer. Further downsizing could pose a great danger to the entire system of industry and technology. System expansion is the opposite of shrinking. It should be performed from the top layer to the bottom layer.

9 Vertical Layers

9.1 Top Layer

In the Top Layer, there are Layer 1, which constitutes the management layer, Layer 2, which covers the Regulation / Audit and Security / Improvement activities, and 3A, which covers the education and R&D activities of the sectors that have the most relationship with the sectors within the Industry and Technology system. In this layer, there are the institutions that are in a decision-making position for the survival of the system and the main sectors that have an important position for the system by feeding all business lines within the system. When the stakeholders in the layer are examined, it is seen that the top layer is the most basic structure of the system and the other layers are built around this layer. Developments in these layers affect R&D, education, production and service activities in other sectors and contribute to the country's economy. In case of possible system shrinkage, the top layer is the layer that should be least affected among the vertical layers. Top Layer is given in Fig. 12.

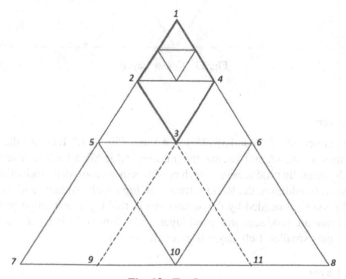

Fig. 12. Top Layer

9.2 Center Layer

In the center layer, there is the 4A layer, which covers the business sectors that are the feeder sector in the production layer, in addition to the 1 (management), Layer 2 (Regulation / Audit / Development) and Education and R&D layers. This layer is of great importance for the country's economy, as it includes all management and R&D activities, as well as the sectors that feed the production activities of other sectors. The sectors in the 4A layer provide the basic by-product and raw material supply in the product trees of other sectors. Therefore, the management, control and development of the 4A layer is of great importance. This layer can also be described as the core of the system. Therefore, it is one of the layers that should be least affected in case of shrinkage. Center Layer is given in Fig. 13.

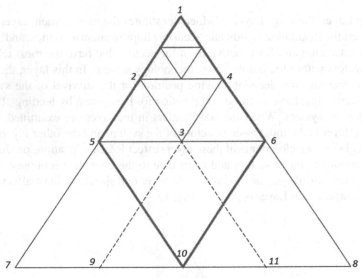

Fig. 13. Center Layer

9.3 Left Layer

The left layer covers all of 3A and 3B, 25% of 4A and 75% of 4B. It covers the production of some sectors within 4A and 4B, and the training and R&D activities of sectors within 3A and 3B. It generally produces high-tech products in sectors with production activities in the left layer. In addition, the R&D activities of high-tech products and the education of qualified personnel needed by the sectors are in this layer. Although products with high added value are produced in the left layer, the volume of this layer can be reduced if the system gets smaller. Left Layer is given in Fig. 14.

9.4 Right Layer

Right Layer covers all of 3A and 3C, 25% of 4A and 75% of 4C. It covers the production of some sectors in 4A and 4C, training and R&D activities of sectors within 3A and 3C.

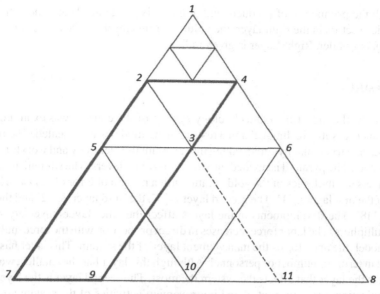

Fig. 14. Left Layer

In the right layer, there are the activities of the production activities and the service sectors of the products that have lower added value than the products in the left layer, but have a higher daily use need. In addition, the R&D activities of these products and services and the education of qualified personnel needed by the sectors are in this layer.

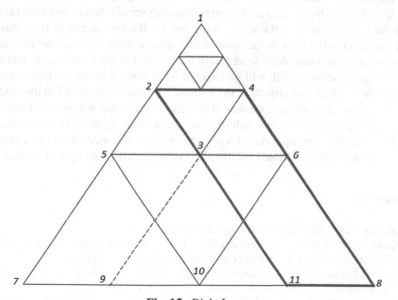

Fig. 15. Right Layer

Although the production of products with high daily usage needs and the activities of the service sectors in the right layer, the volume of this layer can be reduced in case the system gets smaller. Right Layer is given in Fig. 15.

10 Result

In this study, the industrial and technology system of the country was examined using the 'Geometric Ratio Technique' and a restructuring model was presented. The model is visualized as a triangular pyramid, taking into account the hierarchy and workforce ratios in the system. The pyramid is divided into four horizontal layers. The strength multipliers of the layers are multiples of the golden ratio with a margin of error of 3.39%. The force factor of the first layer is '1'. The second layer is '3', the third layer is '12' and the fourth layer is '48'. The developments in the layers affect the other layers inversely with the force multipliers. The labor force increases in direct proportion with the force multipliers. In the model, the apex forms the management layer of the system. This layer has a share of 1,562 in terms of number of personnel. Although this layer has the smallest workforce share, it is the layer that affects the system the most. The second layer is the layer where the organization, security, control and improvement activities of the system are carried out. This layer helps the management layer in the strategies determined for the future of the system. It also plays an important role in the supervision and support of companies in the system. The third layer in the model includes training and R&D activities. According to the relationship diagram, the relationships of the sectors were examined and divided into sub-layers. The fourth layer is the production layer of the system. As in the third layer, the layout of the sectors was made using the relationship diagram. The horizontal layers created also show the relations between the system stakeholders in the secondary dimension. These relationships are shown by creating vertical layers. With the presented GRT model, how important the stakeholders are for the system can also be classified. Thanks to this classification, in the event of a shrinkage in the system, vital stakeholders for the industry and technology system will be affected in the least way. In addition to the shrinkage, healthy growth will be ensured by maintaining the workforce ratios of all stakeholders in case of growth of the system. The model presented in the study was taken as a reference from open sources. It presents a study that will be beneficial for the general structuring of the Model Industry and Technology System. However, thanks to the more comprehensive opportunities and information resources that can be provided, healthier results will be obtained for the industry and technology system studied.

References

1. Bakanlığı, S.T.: https://www.sanayi.gov.tr/anasayfa
2. Gündoğan, M., Yıldırım, R.: Restructuring governments using a geometric ratio technique and its multiple effects. J. Turkish Oper. Manage. **2**(2), 125–154 (2018)
3. West, D.M., Lansang, C.: Brookings. 10 July 2018. https://www.brookings.edu/research/global-manufacturing-scorecard-how-the-us-compares-to-18-other-nations/
4. indexmundi. 28 December 2019. https://www.indexmundi.com/facts/indicators/NV.IND.TOTL.CD/rankings

5. TradingEconomics. https://tradingeconomics.com
6. TÜİK: TÜİK. 04 Şubat 2022. https://data.tuik.gov.tr/Bulten/Index?p=Adrese-Dayali-Nufus-Kayit-Sistemi-Sonuclari-2021-45500#:~:text=TÜİK%20Kurumsal&text=Türkiye%27de%20ikamet%20eden%20nüfus,252%20bin%20172%20kişi%20oldu
7. Wikipedia: SGK. https://tr.wikipedia.org/wiki/Türkiye_Cumhuriyeti_Sosyal_Güvenlik_Kurumu#Görevleri
8. Wikipedia: TOBB (2022). https://tr.wikipedia.org/wiki/Türkiye_Odalar_ve_Borsalar_Birliği
9. Wikipedia: Sendika. https://tr.wikipedia.org/wiki/Sendika. [Erişildi: 2022]
10. Wikipedia: Matrix Diagram. https://tr.wikipedia.org/wiki/Matris_diyagramı. [Erişildi: 2022]
11. TURKSTAT: www.tuik.gov.tr (2021). https://data.tuik.gov.tr/Bulten/Index?p=Adrese-Dayali-Nufus-Kayit-Sistemi-Sonuclari-2021-45500

Author Index

A. Mirzazadeh et al. (Eds.): SEMIT 2022, CCIS 1809, pp. 177–178, 2023.
https://doi.org/10.1007/978-3-031-40398-9